T0381167

Jesus Christ and His
REVELATION
Revised and Updated

COMMENTARY AND BIBLE STUDY ON
THE BOOK OF REVELATION

Ronald A. Clower

WESTBOW
PRESS®
A DIVISION OF THOMAS NELSON
& ZONDERVAN

WestBow Press books may be ordered through booksellers or by contacting:

WestBow Press
A Division of Thomas Nelson & Zondervan
1663 Liberty Drive
Bloomington, IN 47403
www.westbowpress.com
844-714-3454

Literary/Contributing Editor: Cheryl S. Clower
Literary/Contributing Editor: Michael H. Ellison
Artwork and Illustrations: Ronald A. Clower
A Publication of CenterpieceMinistries.com

ISBN: 978-1-6642-7586-7 (sc)
ISBN: 978-1-6642-7585-0 (e)

Print information available on the last page.

WestBow Press rev. date: 09/02/2022

Dedication

This book is dedicated to the glory and honor of

Our Lord & Savior Jesus Christ

The Messiah ...

The Alpha and the Omega ...

The Bright and Morning Star ...

If there is any glory in the work we do in this ministry, then
my family and I give it all to the Lord.

———————————

Proceeds from the sale of this book go to charity.

In the words of our Lord Jesus Christ:

"Behold, I am coming soon!
Blessed is he who keeps the words of the
prophecy in this book."
(Revelation 22:7)

Table of Contents

Abbreviations:
    NIV – New International Version
    NKJV – New King James Version
    KJV – King James Version
    OT – Old Testament
    NT – New Testament
    cf. – Compare to

Foreword

"In the beginning was the Word, and the Word was with God, and the Word was God. He was with God in the beginning ... The Word became flesh and made his dwelling among us. We have seen his glory, the glory of the One and Only, who came from the Father, full of grace and truth" (John 1:1, 2, 14).

God's original desire was to live in perfect communion with mankind, the glory of His creation. In response, mankind was to worship and praise the Creator and live in such a manner that glorified God's greatness. However, mankind was disobedient and that perfect communion was lost, for a time. God, gracious and loving as He is, provided another way. Now, perfect communion with the Father is possible again through a personal relationship with the Son, God's only begotten Son, Jesus Christ. Thus, Jesus comforted His disciples with these simple words: *"I am the way and the truth and the life. No one comes to the Father except through me"* (John 14:6).

The word "revelation" is translated from the Greek word *apokalupsis*, which means "manifestation" or "appearing." When used as a verb, the Greek word is *apokalupto*, which means "to uncover or unveil." This word describes the progressive and immediate unveiling of the otherwise unknown and unknowable God to His Church. Here, in the last book of the Word of God, is the unveiling of God's Son, Jesus Christ, in all His glory and majesty. Jesus Christ is the centerpiece of God's universe. He is the plumb line God uses to reconcile all things to Him. Jesus is our Lord and our Redeemer; He is our King and our Brother. The book of Revelation is God's message to the world and His children (the Church) revealing how He intends to finish out the history of mankind, as well as the fate of those who have trusted in His Son, and those who have not.

Eschatology is defined as theological doctrines associated with death, judgment, and immortality. To the layman, it is simply the study of end-time prophecies. Many fiction and non-fiction books have been written that use end-time prophecies as a basis for their narratives. Accordingly, a number of these books became the inspiration for me to begin my own practice of reading and studying the Scriptures in order to better understand the prophetic and apocalyptic message found in the book of Revelation.

God is omniscient. Simply stated, this means that God is all-knowing (Proverbs 15:3). God is omnipotent, meaning He is all-powerful (Romans 11:36). God is also omnipresent, which simply means that God is present everywhere (Psalm 139:7 – 12). Lastly, God is sovereign. The sovereignty of God is a phrase used to express the absolute, irresistible, infinite, and unconditional exercise of God's self-will over every aspect of His creation, including the eternal destiny of mankind; therefore, nothing can disrupt it. The book of Revelation reveals in detail the awesome prophecies describing the events leading up to and following the glorious return to earth of God's Son, the Lord Jesus Christ, when all things in heaven, on earth, and beneath are brought under Christ's complete dominion and authority.

Our study begins with a stern but wonderful message of encouragement from Christ to His Church through the apocalyptic visions given to the Apostle John (chapters 2 and 3). As we move further into John's *Revelation*, we will take a thorough look at the Rapture of the Church (chapter 4), when Christ descends to the clouds to call all His children home to be with Him in heaven and the Apostle Paul's detailed description of this wondrous event. In addition, we will study the dreadful Tribulation Period, the Antichrist, and the judgments imposed on a rebellious and unrepentant world (chapters 6 – 19). Afterward, Christ will return again to earth, not as Savior, but as Judge and Warrior-King. Consequently, we will discuss His final judgment of the nations, His Millennial Kingdom, the demise of Satan, and the fate of unbelievers from all ages (chapters 20). Lastly, we will look at what is in store for the redeemed people of God and His marvelous plan for eternity (chapters 21 and 22).

My first printing of *Jesus Christ and His REVELATION* (2017) was the result of almost a decade of disciplined study and multiple drafts which ultimately evolved into a concise verse-by-verse study of the *Revelation* of Jesus Christ. My goal was to make the study of the book of Revelation comprehensive but not complex, thorough yet easy to follow. Bible commentary, related subject lessons, charts and illustrations, and frequently asked questions (FAQ) taken from years of teaching Bible study classes on the subject all combined to add redundancy and visual appeal to the study.

This revised and updated edition is written to appeal to all age groups, young adults through seniors. Throughout the chapters references are made to supporting verses located elsewhere in Scripture. Some of these passages are quoted in their entirety, while others are simply noted in parentheses. Those references are left unquoted for the purpose of encouraging the reader to dive deeper into his/her Bible. This is why I have chosen not to include the complete Revelation Bible text in this book. Scripture segments are taken from the New International Version (NIV), unless otherwise noted. The unquoted passages can also be used in a classroom setting to facilitate oral class reading and participation. At the end of each chapter are *Review Questions* meant to highlight and emphasize key elements in order to build upon the reader's knowledge of the message. The *Up For Discussion* sections are optional and can be used for personal reflection or to facilitate additional classroom discussion on a deeper level. This may include relating the subject matter to current events or encouraging class members to share some of their own personal experiences.

Ever since I was given a Bible Reading Calendar by a wise reverend in 2004 at a weekend spiritual retreat called *The Walk to Emmaus*, it has been a disciplined practice of mine to read the Bible cover-to-cover every year. This year, 2022, marks my eighteenth reading of the Word of God. I am so thankful for the reverend's gift and inspiration; thus, there is nothing greater that I could recommend to anyone than to spend time every day reading and dwelling on God's Word. I have included a copy of our Bible Reading Calendar at the end of chapter 10 to encourage you to start your own tradition of reading God's Word daily, if you have not done so already. I promise you God will honor that commitment in your life. You will come to realize that the Holy Scriptures and the prophecies included, from the early chapters of Genesis to the last chapter of Revelation, all point to our Messiah and Lord Jesus Christ.

Introduction

The subject of this book is very important to recognize, and it is emphasized in the very first sentence of chapter one, *"The revelation of Jesus Christ ..."* (Revelation 1:1). The Lamb is the center around which everything in this book revolves. The Lamb is the Lord Jesus Christ, and our generation has more reason to believe Jesus could return for His children (the Church) during our lifetime than any generation in the almost 2,000 years of Church history. This removal of the Church from the earth, often referred to as the Rapture, puts into motion a string of prophetic events that are foretold in this book. The Lord Jesus Christ directs all these events from heaven while using various figures, both good and evil, to accomplish His plan and purpose on earth. There are a number of exciting and unique reasons for studying the book of Revelation:

1) Though some prophecy is mentioned in the gospels and epistles, Revelation is the only complete book of prophecy, containing both prophetic and apocalyptic (end-times) writings, to be found in the NT. In contrast, there are twenty-four books in the OT (including the Psalms) that contain some measure of prophecy.

2) A special blessing is promised to those who read this book. This book opens and closes with a blessing for those who read it and keep the message dear to their hearts.

3) Revelation is not a sealed book of prophecy. The Prophet Daniel was told to seal his book until the time of the end (Daniel 12:9) because it concerned a distant future time. We will consider Daniel's prophecy later in chapter 5. John, on the other hand, is told: *"Do not seal up the words of the prophecy of this book, because the time is near"* (Revelation 22:10). The book of Revelation reveals God's ultimate and wonderful plan for the future.

4) Revelation gives clearer detail concerning biblical prophecy than any other book in the Bible. All prophecies originating elsewhere in the Scriptures find their conclusion in the book of Revelation. For example, John describes the dreadful events of the Tribulation Period, the rise and fall of Antichrist, the glorious return of our Lord and Savior Jesus Christ, the establishment of His earthly kingdom, the demise of Satan, and the Holy City that Christ is preparing for His saints, to name just a few.

5) The book of Revelation completes the cycle of biblical truths – Genesis gives us the beginning and Revelation gives us the end.

Contrast between the Books of Genesis and Revelation

In Genesis, we see mankind's beginning and how he communed with God in a paradise called Eden (Genesis 2:8; 3:8). Revelation details the beautiful paradise yet to come where mankind will again commune intimately with God (Revelation 21:10 – 22:5).

In Genesis, the darkness was called night and the waters called seas (Genesis 1:4; 1:10). Revelation describes the new heaven and the new earth as having no more night and no longer any sea (Revelation 21:1, 25).

Genesis shows how mankind lost a chance to eat from the tree of life (Genesis 3:22, 23). Revelation tells us that God's people will one day eat fruit from that tree (Revelation 22:1, 2).

Genesis introduces the serpent (Satan) as the deceiver of mankind and pronounces his fate (Genesis 3:1 – 15). Revelation details Satan's last rebellion and his final judgment (Revelation 20:10).

Genesis tells of mankind's first rebellion against God (Genesis 3 – 4). Revelation promises an end to all rebellion against God (Revelation 20:10; 21:8).

In Genesis, we see mankind's first temptation from Satan in his attempt to discredit the Word of God (Genesis 3:1 – 5). In Revelation, God gives a dire warning to all who deliberately seek to manipulate His written Word (Revelation 22: 18, 19).

In Genesis, man's sin resulted in the curse (Genesis 3:15 – 18). Revelation promises an end to the curse (Revelation 22:3).

Genesis chronicles the first death (Genesis 4:8). Revelation also promises an end to death (Revelation 21:4).

Suggestions for Studying this Book

1) Follow the golden rule of interpretation of Bible prophecy: When the plain sense of Scripture makes common sense, then seek no other sense. Let us take every word at its usual and literal meaning unless the facts of the immediate text clearly indicate otherwise.

2) Locate the scene of activity. Keep in mind whether the scene under discussion takes place in heaven or on earth.

3) For the most part, Revelation unfolds chronologically. But rather than looking at it chronologically, let us approach this study in a logical order because some chapters represent an interlude in the chronology. These chapters will introduce elements or events that further on in the book will be recounted with added detail. The Holy Spirit has used this method throughout the Scriptures to convey God's truths. For example, we have the giving of the Mosaic Law in Exodus and then in Deuteronomy the interpretation of the Law with greater detail added. Also, in the NT, we find not only one but four Gospel records because it takes four to give the many sides of the glorious Person of Jesus Christ.

Author and Date of Revelation

All indications point to the writing of the book of Revelation by the Apostle John, the writer of the Gospel of John and the Epistles of John, while imprisoned on the Isle of Patmos during the reign of the Roman Emperor Domitian (A.D. 81 – 96). Historian and Christian theologian, Eusebius, confirmed that while in Ephesus, John was exiled by Emperor Domitian to the Isle of Patmos, a penal colony off the coast of present-day Turkey. That would place the writing of Revelation in and around the traditionally accepted date of A.D. 95, near the end of John's life.

It was at Patmos, according to tradition, that the sacred text of the book of Revelation was given to John and recorded while he was in a cave now known as the *cave of the Apocalypse.* This cave is now hidden inside and beneath the buildings of the Monastery of the Apocalypse, built in the seventeenth century to house a theological school called the Patmias. Its structure has been altered very little since then. The holy cave, or grotto, has long since been transformed into a small church dedicated to John. Inside remain signs of long tradition that bear witness to the apostle's presence. In one corner of the stone floor is the place where he laid his head to rest. Close by was the place where he spread his parchments. In the roof of the cave was the triple crevice in the rock through which he heard the great voice of the Lord. Eusebius wrote: "The cave is small, and the light is dim; it is a place that draws one to meditation, prayer, worship, contemplation … a place of which a man might say, 'How fearful is this place! This is none other than the house of God, and this is the gate of Heaven.'"

As a result of his excessive cruelty, the Emperor Domitian was assassinated in A.D. 96 by a conspiracy led by his own wife. Subsequently, the senate later annulled his acts and this allowed John to return to Ephesus under Emperor Nerva. Tradition has it that John lived until the time of Emperor Trajan, whose reign began in A.D. 98, sixty-eight years after the resurrection of Jesus.

John founded and built churches throughout Asia Minor. During his last days John appointed bishops in the new Christian community. John died a natural death and was buried in Ephesus. Polycarp and Papias were his disciples. Eusebius confirmed the location of the tomb of John by his quotation from the *Epistle of Polycarp* (the Bishop of the Church of Ephesus) which read: "John that rested on the bosom of our Lord … he also rests at Ephesus."

A story was told and handed down that John, as an old man in Ephesus, had to be carried to the church in the arms of his disciples. At these meetings, he was accustomed to say no more than, "Little children, love one another!" After a time his disciples, wearied at always hearing the same words, asked their leader, "Master, why do you always say this?" John replied, "It is the Lord's command. And if this alone be done, it is enough!"

John outlived all the other apostles; thereby making this unique revelation of Jesus Christ and the wonderful prophetic plan God has for all of His children a fitting closure for the entire volume of the sixty-six books of God's revelation to mankind.

Israel Becomes a Nation

Throughout the OT there are prophecies of a final return of the Jewish exiles to the Promised Land in the latter days. The Prophet Ezekiel, like Daniel, was carried off to Babylon as a captive. Also, like Daniel, he was aware from the prophecies of Jeremiah that the captivity in Babylon would last seventy years. When the Lord appeared to Ezekiel in a vision, he gave him the following prophecy:

"Then lie on your left side and put the sins of the house of Israel upon yourself. You are to bear their sins for the number of days you lie on your side. I have assigned you the same number of days as the years of their sins. So for 390 days you will bear the sin of the house of Israel. After you have finished this, lie down again, this time on your right side, and bear the sin of the house of Judah. I have assigned you 40 days, a day for each year" (Ezekiel 4: 4 – 6).

This prophecy makes it clear that each day represents one biblical year. Ezekiel was told Israel would be punished for 390 plus 40 years. Additionally, the Prophet Jeremiah wrote: *"This whole country will become a desolate wasteland, and these nations will serve the king of Babylon seventy years"* (Jeremiah 25:11). At the end of seventy years of captivity in Babylon, as prophesied, during the spring of 536 B.C. and under the decree of King Cyrus of Persia, less than 43,000 Jews, a small remnant of the house of Judah returned to Jerusalem to begin the rebuilding of the temple. However, the vast majority of Jews (an estimated 15 million) were content to remain in the pagan Persian Empire as colonists. From the total prophesied punishment of 430 years for Israel and Judah's sin (390 years + 40 years = 430 years), deducting the seventy years of Babylonian captivity which ended in 536 B.C., there yet remains a total of 360 years of further punishment beyond the year 536 B.C.

The Lord warned Israel regarding disobedience with these words: *"If after all this you will not listen to me, I will punish you for your sins seven times over"* (Leviticus 26:18). Remember that only a remnant returned to Jerusalem while the majority of the Jews remained in Persia. In other words, if Israel did not repent (which the majority did not), then the punishment already promised would be prolonged or multiplied seven times:

360 years × 7 = 2,520 biblical years. Next, we convert the years to days.

God's Word is consistent; thus our prophetical chronology should use a thirty-day month:

30 days × 12 months = 360 days

2,520 biblical years × 360 days = 907,200 days of further punishment.

Next, we must convert this figure to our present day calendar by dividing 365.25 into 907,200 days. We reach a total of 2,483.8 calendar years of further punishment remaining for Israel. We can now start our calculation from 536 B.C., keeping in mind there is only one year between 1 B.C. and A.D. 1 (because there is no year zero). This puts the end of Israel's worldwide captivity at 1948!

On May 15, 1948, the Jews proclaimed Israel as an independent state. As an old Jewish rabbi blew on the traditional shofar, the Jewish people celebrated the end of their worldwide dispersion and captivity at the exact time prophesied over twenty-five hundred years earlier by the Prophet Ezekiel.

This means that despite the apparent anarchy of the events of our time, God is still in full control of worldwide events and the universe is unfolding precisely as our Lord ordained millennia ago. This revelation regarding Israel's rebirth in 1948 renews our interest in the words of our Lord Jesus Christ taken from His Olivet Discourse:

"Now learn this lesson from the fig tree: As soon as its twigs get tender and its leaves come out, you know that summer is near. Even so, when you see all these things, you know that it is near, right at the door. I tell you the truth; this generation will certainly not pass away until all these things have happened" (Matthew 24:32 – 34).

The fig tree (Israel) has put forth its leaves (been reborn). It is our generation that has witnessed the miracle of Israel's rebirth from the valley which was full of dry bones as described by the prophet (Ezekiel 37:1). The Bible defines a generation as a hundred years (Genesis 15:13 – 16). A generation was also defined as the age of a man when his first son was born, and in the case of Abraham, the father of the nation of Israel, that also was a hundred years. Thus, we have more reason then any generation before to believe we are living in the last days – that is, the end-times.

With that in mind, what did our Lord Jesus Christ preach in his last sermon to his disciples? It was not love, or family, or the importance of the Church. Jesus made "preparedness" the theme of that last sermon. His message spoke of the wise and foolish servant. The wise one was ready for the return of the master where the foolish one was not. His message spoke about the ten virgins. Five were wise and ready when the groom came, and the other five were foolish and at the market looking to buy more oil. Lastly, His message spoke of the three servants and the bags of gold. Two of the servants put the money to work and made more money for their master while the third hid his money in a hole. The first two were ready and rewarded when the master returned. The third servant was unprepared and punished.

Be prepared and ready was the theme of Jesus' last sermon, and so in the words of our Lord:

"Therefore keep watch, because you do not know on what day your Lord will come" (Matthew 24:42).

Therefore, let us join with the Apostle John in his closing prayer: *"He who testifies to these things says, 'Yes, I am coming soon.' Amen. Come, Lord Jesus"* (Revelation 22:20).

One Day is with the Lord as a Thousand Years

Our Lord Jesus Christ taught the apostles for three years before His crucifixion and forty days following His resurrection. During this time, He opened the Scriptures to His disciples concerning prophecies about Himself (Luke 24:25 – 27, 45). As a result of this time of training, the Apostle Peter discussed the Lord's Second Coming. Knowing that this event was far into the future, he wrote the following:

"First of all, you must understand that in the last days scoffers will come, scoffing and following their own evil desires. They will say, 'Where is this 'coming' he promised? Ever since our fathers died, everything goes on as it has since the beginning of creation'" (2 Peter 3:3, 4).

Peter then explained to the Church that there was one particular fact regarding this apparent delay of the last days of which we should be aware:

"But do not forget this one thing, dear friends: With the Lord a day is like a thousand years, and a thousand years are like a day. The Lord is not slow in keeping His promise, as some understand slowness. He is patient with you, not wanting anyone to perish, but everyone to come to repentance" (2 Peter 3:8, 9).

The day the apostle spoke of referred to the days of the creation week, as a microcosm of the seven days of the great Sabbath Week of God's historic dealing with His creation – mankind. Just as the creation and replenishing of the earth took six days and then God rested on the seventh day; accordingly, there would be 6,000 years and then the great Sabbath rest of 1,000 years. This is the *Millennium* as described in Hebrews (4:4, 7 – 9) and Revelation (chapter 20).

The psalmist referred to the same symbolic time scale when he wrote: *"For a thousand years in your sight are like a day that has just gone by, or like a watch in the night"* (Psalm 90:4).

The Scriptures do not give any date for determining when the universe was originally created. However, the chronology of the OT suggests that the time of the creation of man, Adam and Eve, occurred approximately 4,000 B.C. In 1650, Archbishop Ussher wrote a volume titled *The Chronology on the Old and New Testament*, wherein he calculated back from the birth of Christ, based on the dates and chronological data given in Scriptures, and arrived at the date of 4,004 B.C. as the year of Adam's creation. I have done the same calculation and arrived at a date of around 4,100 B.C.

Early church commentators, including Methodius, Bishop of Tyre, point out that the reason Adam died at the age of 930 years (Genesis 5:5) and did not live past 1,000 years was because God had prophesied so: *"But you must not eat from the tree of the knowledge of good and evil, for when you eat of it you will surely die"* (Genesis 2:17). Therefore, since a day equals 1,000 years in God's sight, Adam had to die before the day (1,000 years) was completed.

Other ancient writings include those by Rabbi Elias, who lived 200 years before Christ. He wrote, "The world endures 6,000 years: 2,000 before the law, 2,000 under the law, and 2,000 under Messiah." The Christian scholar Lartantius (A.D. 300) held a similar view. In the seventh volume of his *Book of Divine Institutions*, he wrote the following: "Because all the works of God were finished in six days, it is necessary that the world should remain in this state six ages – that is, 6,000 years.

Because having finished the works He rested on the seventh day and blessed it; it is necessary that at the end of the 6,000th year all unrighteousness should be abolished out of the earth and justice should reign for a 1,000 years."

Considering all of the above, we might look for the beginning of the seventh day (the Millennium – the 1,000 years of peace described in Revelation 20:2 – 6) to commence at some point in our generation – 2,000 years following the death and resurrection of Christ. It is unfortunate, but perhaps providential, that changes in the calendar make it impossible to calculate with precision when the 2,000-year period will end, except to note that it could likely occur during our generation.

In regard to the above interpretation, it is important to remember that this is only interpretation and time will prove whether or not it is accurate. In addition, if this interpretation of the beginning of the Millennium is correct, then the time of the Rapture of the Church and the Second Coming of Christ still cannot be determined. The timing of these two events is known only to God. Let us be mindful of the words of our Lord Jesus Christ:

"No one knows about that day or hour, not even the angels in heaven, nor the Son, but only the Father. As it was in the days of Noah, so it will be at the coming of the Son of Man. For in the days before the flood, people were eating and drinking, marrying and giving in marriage, up to the day Noah entered the ark; and they knew nothing about what would happen until the flood came and took them all away. That is how it will be at the coming of the Son of Man … So you also must be ready, because the Son of Man will come at an hour when you do not expect him" (Matthew 24:36 – 39, 44).

Chapter 1

Please follow along in your Bible.

1:1: *"The revelation of Jesus Christ, which God gave him to show his servants what must soon take place ...."* The word "revelation" is translated from the Greek word *apokalupsis*, which means "appearing." When used as a verb, the Greek word is *apokalupto*, which means "to uncover or unveil," such as the unveiling of a piece of artwork for example. In this case, the revelation is the unveiling of Jesus Christ in all His glory and majesty. The phrase, "what must soon take place," or "shortly take place" (NKJV), emphasizes the imminent return of Christ.

In this opening verse of the first chapter, we also see the first of many angels portrayed throughout the book of Revelation. Angels are servants sent by God to accomplish His purpose on earth. The writer of Hebrews wrote: *"Are not all angels ministering spirits sent to serve those who will inherit salvation?"* (Hebrews 1:14)

1:2: The Apostle John is the eyewitness to the visions of the Revelation, and he will testify to them. The Word of God refers to the fact that the revelations shown to John are indeed divinely inspired. The expression, "the testimony of Jesus Christ," refers to the eternal Gospel. We will see this phrase used later in this book.

1:3: *"Blessed is the one who reads the words of this prophecy ...."* The word "blessed" means to declare or wish God's favor and goodness upon others. Translated from the Greek word *makarios* and used throughout Scripture, the word blessed or blessing is similar in meaning to the word happy. As you know, true happiness is not found in the things of this world but in the things that come from God. Therefore, this book is a source of happiness (or blessing) to who hear it and take to heart its message. The expression, "the time is near," again emphasizes the imminent return of Christ.

1:4: John addresses his Revelation to the seven churches in the province of Asia, a Roman province located in modern-day western Turkey, thereby intending it as a circular letter.

Grace and peace are both generated from God, not mankind. A person's relationship to God determines their possession of grace and peace. This verse and the next indicate that the Trinity shares in the administration of grace and peace: God the Father, God the Son, and God the Spirit.

The number seven denotes perfection or completeness. The expression, "seven spirits," does not mean seven Holy Spirits but the sevenfold ministry of the Holy Spirit as expressed by the Prophet Isaiah (Isaiah 11:2). They are as follows: 1) The Spirit of the Lord, 2) the Spirit of wisdom, 3) the Spirit of understanding, 4) the Spirit of counsel, 5) the Spirit of power, 6) the Spirit of knowledge, and 7) the Spirit of the fear of the Lord, which, according to Proverbs 1:7, is the beginning of knowledge.

There is another interpretation of the seven spirits which is illustrated by the solid gold lampstand (menorah) in Zechariah's vision (4:1 – 14). The lampstand is symbolic of Christ abiding in the Millennial Temple. The two olive trees in Zechariah's vision are representative of the source from which the oil flows into the bowl, through the pipes, and into the seven lamps. The oil is symbolic of the Holy Spirit. The resulting light which is given out represents Christ, because He is the *Light* of the world (John 8:12). Zerubbabel and Joshua represent the two olive trees that provide the oil to the lampstand. They are the two instruments that God uses in Zechariah's day to bring light back to the nation of Israel. Together, they foreshadow the Messiah, the Lord Jesus Christ, as the ultimate Priest/King and who is the true source of blessing during the Millennium.

1:5 – 6: These verses describe six subtitles given to the Lord Jesus Christ describing His works – past, present, and future:

1) Verse 5: The faithful witness: We cannot always trust in man, but the witness of Jesus Christ for the Word of God is trustworthy and true.
2) The firstborn from the dead: Jesus is the first and only one to return from the dead in a glorified body. All believers will likewise follow Him in resurrection one day.
3) The ruler of the kings of the earth: This refers to His ultimate kingship and rule during the Millennium (Revelation 20).
4) Him who loves us: This refers to Jesus' present works and should calm our fears about the book of Revelation. His love for us endures forever! (cf. Psalm 136)
5) Him who has freed us from our sins by His blood: The blood is important. The writer of Hebrews wrote: "*… without the shedding of blood there is no forgiveness*" (Hebrews 9:22). Christ shed His blood and died for the sins of all mankind, once and for all.
6) Verse 6: He has made us to be a kingdom and priests to serve His God and Father: The Apostle Peter wrote confirming this promise: "*But you are a chosen people, a royal priesthood, a holy nation, a people belonging to God, that you may declare the praises of him who called you out of darkness into his wonderful light*" (1 Peter 2:9). This refers to the believer's future position to rule alongside the Lord Jesus Christ during the Millennium.

1:7: "*Look, he is coming with the clouds, and every eye will see him ….*" Here we see the first of many descriptions of Jesus Christ in the glory and majesty that is appropriate to His person and nature. In His First Coming, Jesus was despised and rejected by men. In His Second Coming, our Lord will be worshiped by those who have trusted in Him and feared by those who have rejected Him, for He will come with power and great glory (Luke 21:27). Recall the angelic messengers' prophetic declaration: "*This same Jesus, who has been taken from you into heaven, will come back in the same way you have seen him go into heaven*" (Acts 1:11). This can only mean that Jesus will return visibly to the earth. Jesus Himself told His disciples: "*They will see the Son of Man coming on the clouds of the sky, with power and great glory*" (Matthew 24:30). The Prophet Daniel was given a similar vision of the Messiah (Daniel 7:13, 14). To Him is all glory and dominion forever!

1:8: *"I am the Alpha and the Omega … who is, and who was, and who is to come, the Almighty."* These are all messianic titles that describe the Lord Jesus in His deity as the beginning and the end and the sovereign ruler over the universe and all human history.

> **Do not lose sight of the fact that Revelation presents**
> **the Lord Jesus Christ in His glory as Judge of all the earth.**

The subject of this book is the Person of Jesus Christ. If the book of Revelation teaches us nothing else, it teaches us that Jesus Christ is coming again, not as Savior but as Judge, and the basis of His judgment will be whether or not people have placed their faith and trust in Him as Lord and Savior. For a list of scriptural references for Christ's return, see the illustration entitled, *Two Phases of the Second Coming of Christ,* at the end of chapter 5.

1:9: John is going through suffering as a member of the early church that was persecuted miserably by the emperors of Rome, who had already claimed the lives of James, Peter, and Paul and probably most of the other apostles. The kingdom mentioned here is the spiritual kingdom that Jesus set up on the Day of Pentecost. It is still relevant today and can be entered into only by being born again (John 3:3 – 7). The expression, "patient endurance," is a reference to faithfully enduring the trials of this fallen world until Christ returns. There are at least seven reasons why early Christians were persecuted by Rome:

1) They were revolutionary in their faith; their focus was evangelical and mission-based.
2) They required complete obedience to the Son of God, Jesus Christ, as their Lord and King; not to Caesar.
3) They refused to bow down before idols.
4) They were sometimes looked upon as cannibals because they met in secret, and it was overheard that they ate flesh and drank blood during their worship service (referring to the sacrament of Communion – the Lord's Supper).
5) They offended those who made their living fabricating and selling idols.
6) They usually recruited from the poor and slaves of society and were therefore looked down upon.
7) They refused emperor worship. Domitian, for example, would sign his decree as "Lord and God."

1:10: *"On the Lord's Day I was in the Spirit …."* The Holy Spirit was moving upon John and giving him a vivid vision. The Lord's Day is a reference to Sunday, the day the Lord Jesus Christ rose from the grave. This is the reason Christians traditionally worship on Sunday. The phrase, "a loud voice like a trumpet," is a reference similar to the mighty voice described in verse 15 and in 4:1 (cf. 1 Corinthians 15:52; 1 Thessalonians 4:16).

1:11: *"Write on a scroll what you see and send it to the seven churches …,"* was the Lord's command. Obviously, these were literal churches with which the apostle was familiar. However, some prophecy scholars suggest that, according to history, these seven churches also parallel seven periods or stages of evolution of the Church during the dispensation of grace, i.e., the Church Age. We will expound further on this theory in chapters 2 and 3.

1:12: Seven golden lampstands are a fitting symbol. While in this world, Jesus said, *"I am the light of the world"* (John 8:12); however, He told His disciples that you are the light of the world (Matthew 5:14) speaking forward to the age of the Church. The lampstands are defined in verse 20 as seven churches. Jesus is the Head of the Church made up of individual believers. He is walking in the midst of the churches, both then and now. He is also judging the churches – He pours His Holy Spirit (oil) into them and He wants them to give out the Word of God (light) to the world.

Ten Characteristics of the Glorified Christ

1) Verse 13: **Like a son of man**. This expression indicates that Christ was human in appearance – God manifest in the flesh.

2) **Dressed in a robe reaching down to his feet**. This was typical of the robe of the high priests as they ministered in the Holy Place in the temple. Two of the duties of the high priest were to tend to the lampstand in the temple and to intercede for the people before God. Today, Jesus Christ is in heaven serving as our great High Priest (Hebrews 4:14).

3) **A golden sash around his chest**. This is a symbol of strength and authority in the ancient world and is again reminiscent of the garment of the high priest.

4) Verse 14: **Head and hair were white**. The Lord's head and hair are described as white as sheep's wool or freshly fallen snow. The whiteness mentioned here, and elsewhere in Scripture, speaks of the righteousness of God.

5) **Eyes of blazing fire**. These eyes speak of judgment and Christ's perfect knowledge of the deceitful doctrine of apostate (false) teachers/churches.

6) Verse 15: **Feet of blazing bronze**. Bronze speaks of judgment as well in that it reminds us of the bronze altar of the tabernacle where sin was judged.

7) **A voice like the sound of rushing waters**. Like mighty waterfalls, in that day all other voices will be stilled by the deafening and overpowering voice of the Son of God. This is the voice that called the universe into existence, the voice that will call His Church up and out of this world to be with Him at the Rapture, and the same voice that will one day speak destruction upon all wickedness and rebellion. In chapter 4, we will see another reference to Christ's voice as the trumpet.

8) Verse 16: **Holding seven stars in His right hand**. As before, the Lord gives us the meaning of the seven stars in verse 20. They are defined as the seven angels of the seven churches. The word "angel" is translated from the Greek word *aggello*, which means "a messenger." It is believed that the term here refers, not to angelic beings, but to the messengers divinely appointed by God to lead the local congregations – that is, the spiritual leader or pastor of those churches.

9) **From out of His mouth came a sharp double-edged sword**. This is a symbolic reference to the spoken word of Christ, which will go forth as a sharp sword against which there will be no defense on the Day of Judgment – the day Christ returns to earth as Judge and Warrior-King (cf. Ephesians 6:17 and Hebrews 4:12).

10) **His face shone bright as the sun**. This speaks of the divine nature of Christ and reminds us of the event that took place on the Mount of Transfiguration (cf. Matthew 17:2 and Luke 9:29).

1:17: *"When I saw him, I fell at his feet as though dead ...."* John does what everyone will do someday when brought into the presence of the glorified Christ. The effect of the vision upon John was paralyzing. Since the apostle reacted like that, we can be sure that when we come into the presence of the Lord Jesus Christ, we are going to approach Him in similar manner.

Notice what the Lord Jesus does here. This is one of the most tender and precious scenes in the entire Bible. Jesus reaches down and touches John and says, *"Do not be afraid."* In the wonderful words of the late pastor and author, J. Vernon McGee, "This is a beautiful picture of Deity reaching down to humanity."

1:17 – 18: The greatest cure for one's natural fear is the personal presence of Jesus Christ. Our Lord gives us four reasons why we should not fear:

1) Verse 17: *"I am the First and the Last."* This speaks of Christ as the Creator coming out of eternity's past and the eternal King of eternity's future.
2) Verse 18: *"I am the Living One: I was dead …"* speaks of Christ's sacrificial death for our sins and His resurrection.
3) *"… I am alive for ever and ever!"* The apostle wrote: *"Christ died for sins once and for all"* (1 Peter 3:18). This assures us that Christ will not die again.
4) *"And I hold the keys of death and Hades."* These keys were purchased with His precious blood, for according to the writer of Hebrews, *"… by his death he might destroy him who holds the power of death – that is, the devil – and free those who all their lives were held in slavery by their fear of death"* (Hebrews 2:14, 15).

The writer of Hebrews further tells us: *"Jesus Christ is the same yesterday and today and forever"* (Hebrews 13:8).

John saw Jesus as no one else has ever seen Him before – unveiled in all His power and glory and majesty. This is how we will all see Him one day. As the song, by contemporary Christian artist, MercyMe, goes, "I can only imagine …."

1:19: Christ is giving John a basic three-part outline for the revelation. The vision of Christ and His introduction recorded in verses 12 – 20 make up the expression, "what you have seen." The phrase, "what is now," is represented by Christ's specific address to each of the seven churches chronicled in chapters 2 and 3, which we will look at next. The balance of the book of Revelation will cover the expression, "what will take place later."

1:20: *"… The seven stars are the angels of the seven churches, and the seven lampstands are the seven churches."* Here is our first example of rule number three for studying the book of Revelation as we recall earlier from the introduction. In verse 12, we have the mention of the seven lampstands and in verse 16, the mention of the seven stars. In this final verse, the Lord is giving John the meaning of the two symbols in order to assist us, as we look more closely at the churches in the following two chapters. This method will be used elsewhere in this remarkable revelation of the Lord Jesus Christ.

Review Questions

1) The word revelation means _____ or _____.

2) The number seven denotes _____.

3) The subject of the book of Revelation is _____.

4) The seven golden lampstands are representative of _____.

5) The seven stars represent _____.

6) What did John do when he was brought before the glorified Christ? _____

_____.

7) Give the four reasons why Jesus said we should not be afraid in His presence. _____

_____

_____.

Up For Discussion

"I was in the Spirit on the Lord's day,
and heard behind me a great voice, as of a trumpet."
(Revelation 1:10 KJV)

We have just looked at the ten characteristics of the glorified Christ. What John saw was a vision of Christ as He appears today after His resurrection and ascension to heaven in all His majesty. In contrast to the meek and humble Servant that we see depicted in the Gospel accounts, what is your initial reaction or impression?

Chapter 2

Please follow along in your Bible.

The Church is the body of Christ, Jesus Christ is its head, and it is of divine origin (cf. Ephesians 1:22, 23). The word "church" is translated from the Greek word *ekklesia*, which means "a calling out." The term stresses a group of people called out by God for a special purpose. Its purpose is to worship God, to pray, and to edify fellow believers. The mission of the Church is to evangelize the world. Unfortunately, there are things in this fallen world that divide the Church, such as heresy, false doctrine, and discord. So why did the Lord choose these specific seven churches and not the ones at Rome, Antioch, or Jerusalem? Seven is God's number for completeness, and these seven churches represent the complete message Jesus wants to give to the Church. Although these were seven literal churches at the time of John's writing, some contemporary scholars have theorized that they may also represent seven periods or stages of church evolution throughout the current Church Age. Regardless, Jesus is saying something to them and certainly to us today as well, and that is why He ends each message with, *"He who has an ear, let him hear …"* (Revelation 2:7, 11,17, 29; 3:6, 13, 22).

The speaker in this vision, as indicated by the red print in many Bibles, is Jesus Christ, described by John as walking in the midst of the seven golden lampstands. This indicates that Christ and His power have always been available to the Church. He is therefore fulfilling His promise to the apostles: *"Therefore, go and make disciples of all nations, baptizing them in the name of the Father and of the Son and of the Holy Spirit, and teaching them to obey everything I have commanded you. And surely I am with you always, to the very end of the age"* (Matthew 28:19).

For a summary chart of Christ's complete message to the church, see illustration entitled, *The Seven Churches of the Revelation,* at the end of chapter 3.

Church of Ephesus – the Apostolic Church, c. A.D. 30 – 100

2:1 – 3: The Lord Jesus Christ has seven expressions of commendation:

1) Verse 2: Their deeds. Recall from the epistle of James: *"As the body without the spirit is dead, so faith without deeds is dead"* (James 2:26). Calvin said, "Faith alone saves, but the faith that

saves is not alone." Christians are called to serve others through their good works – out of their love for the Savior.

2) Their hard work refers to physical labor and is often related to their deeds.

3) Their perseverance, or patience, is representative of the fruit of the Spirit (Galatians 5:22). They relied on the power and guidance of the indwelling Holy Spirit.

4) They did not put up with wicked men.

5) They tested those who claim to be apostles – that is, whether or not they were an eyewitness to the resurrected Christ.

6) Verse 3: They persevered and endured hardships for the name of Jesus Christ – that is, they preached Christ and defended the Gospel during a time of relentless persecution by Rome. Patient perseverance (#3) during times of trials and suffering is possible only through leaning on the awesome power of the indwelling Spirit of Christ.

7) They had not grown weary. A believer may get weary *in* the work of Christ, but it is tragic if he/she gets weary *of* the work of Christ.

2:4: *"… You have forsaken your first love."* Even though the Ephesians received much commendation from the Lord, they had somehow let go of the most important thing of all – their sacred romance with Jesus Christ. That romance was kindled over the years of close and intimate fellowship while the apostles were present with them. As these apostles, one by one, suffered and died as martyrs, that romance with Christ, subsequently, began to diminish.

2:5: *"… Repent and do the things you did at first …"* This was Christ's counsel. Some believers do not view an absence of intimate love for Jesus Christ as a sin, but simply something they lack. If God's absolute priority for all followers of Christ is love – for Him first and others second – then the absence of such love is sinful. All believers are called to love Christ above all others. The expression, "remove your lampstand," does not mean they would lose their place in heaven – that is, their salvation, but rather they would lose their godly position of influence on earth. In other words, they would lose their light in the world.

2:6: *"… You hate the practices of the Nicolaitans, which I also hate."* Nicolaitans is a compound word. *Nikao* means "to conquer," and *laos* means "the people." We get our word laity from it. In the early days of the Church, the followers of the Nicolaitans held two serious heretical views: 1) They practiced sensuality by completely separating one's spiritual and physical natures, thus giving them license to sin, and 2) they tried to establish an ecclesiastical order. Laypeople were given no voice in church affairs but were required to obey blindly the decrees of the church leaders.

2:7: *"… To him who overcomes, I will give the right to eat from the tree of life."* The tree of life was called such because the eating of its fruit resulted in eternal life (Genesis 3:22). It is now reserved for the righteous in heaven, as we will see later in chapter 22.

Church of Smyrna – the Persecuted Church, c. 100 – 312

It is interesting to note here that there was not one word of condemnation from the Lord to this church.

2:8: *"… These are the words of him who is the First and the Last, who died and came to life again."* Jesus identifies Himself to the church with the same divine characteristics He gave earlier to John (Revelation 1:17, 18).

2:9: *"I know your afflictions and your poverty …"* This was a severely persecuted and impoverished church. Because of the intense hatred of Christians, when a man took a stand for Jesus Christ, not only did his life become in danger of persecution, but his employment suffered economically as well.

"… yet you are rich!" This illustrates a divine principle: Regardless of one's economic state, knowing Jesus Christ brings spiritual wealth into this life and into the life to come.

As a warning to the local church, Jesus mentioned those who are a *synagogue of Satan*. The remnant of Israel, which was being saved, had left the synagogue by this time. They had given up the Law as a means of salvation and sanctification, and began the early Church. Those who continued in the synagogue rejected and ridiculed Jewish converts to Christianity. In fact, some may have even identified Christians to the government and greatly heightened the persecution against them. Jesus referred to the Scribes and Pharisees as hypocrites seven times and promised them the greater damnation (Matthew 23:14 KJV). The Lord even called them snakes and a brood of vipers (Matthew 23:33), which reminds us of mankind's first encounter with Satan in the Garden of Eden – as a serpent (Genesis 3:1 – 4). The Apostle Paul made it clear when he wrote: *"For not all who are descended from Israel are Israel"* (Romans 9:6). In other words, they were no longer true Jews. Paul considered the true Israelite to be one who turned to Christ.

2:10: *"Do not be afraid of what you are about to suffer. I tell you, the devil will put some of you in prison to test you …."* This was Christ's counsel. The word "devil" is translated from the Greek word *diabolos*, which means "false accuser." Commentators are not in agreement as to what Christ meant when He said they would suffer persecution for ten days. It might mean that their imprisonment would be brief, ending quickly in their execution. Others suggest that it may be a reference to the ten emperors of Rome that persecuted Christians. They included Nero, Domitian, Trajan, Marcus Aurelius, Severus, Maximinius, Decius, Valerian, Aurelian, and Diocletian. Each of these Roman emperors put Christians at the top of their hate list.

Christ further counseled them: *"Be faithful, even to the point of death and I will give you the crown of life."* They were martyrs for Christ. Crowns are a heavenly reward and the Lord Jesus Christ has a special crown for those who suffer. We will discuss heavenly rewards later in chapter 19.

How were the believers in Smyrna, or believers today, in light of increasing ridicule and persecution of Christians worldwide, able to be faithful through such terrible suffering? Those who are faithful in the midst of intense suffering learn to lean on the awesome power and grace of the indwelling Holy Spirit to allow their fiery trials to purify rather than destroy them. The Apostle Peter wrote: *"These have come so that your faith – of greater worth than gold, which perishes even though refined by fire – may be proved genuine and may result in praise, glory, and honor when Jesus Christ is revealed"* (1 Peter 1:7).

Christ wanted the believers in Smyrna to be aware, but He did not want them to be afraid. I believe that much of the book of Revelation was written to believers for the same reason.

2:11: *"... He who overcomes will not be hurt at all by the second death."* The first death is physical death. The second death is spiritual death and results in eternal punishment and separation from God. Hades is the present abode of the unbelieving dead. The lake of fire is their eventual fate. We will discuss this in greater detail in chapter 20.

Church of Pergamum – the Indulged Church, c. 312 – 606 (Liberty of the Flesh)

Christianity began to transition into the dominant religion of the Roman Empire under the reign of Constantine the Great (A.D. 306 – 337). His formal conversion in 312 to his mother's (Helena) Christianity is almost universally acknowledged among historians, despite the claim he was only baptized on his deathbed by the bishop Eusebius of Nicomedia in 337. Constantine's decision to cease the persecution of Christians in the Roman Empire was a turning point for early Christianity, sometimes referred to as the *Triumph of the Church*. In 313, Constantine issued the *Edict of Milan* decriminalizing Christian worship. The emperor became a great patron of the Church and set a precedent for the position of the Christian emperor within the Church and raised the notions of orthodoxy, Christendom, ecumenical councils which the state church of the Roman Empire declared by edict in 380. He is revered as a saint and equal to an apostle in the Eastern Orthodox Church, Oriental Orthodox Church, and various Eastern Catholic Churches for his example as a Christian monarch.

2:12: *"These are the words of him who has the sharp, double-edged sword."* Here, Jesus identifies Himself to the church with another divine characteristic, that which John earlier witnessed in his vision of the glorified Christ (Revelation 1:16).

2:13: *"I know where you live – where Satan has his throne ...."* Satan has a kingdom, and from ancient times, Babylon has been viewed as the capital of his kingdom. Idolatry and sexual immorality had its beginning in Babylon through Nimrod, grandson of Ham (Genesis 10) and his mother, both inspired by Satan. However, when Babylon's glory began to decline and it was left desolate, Satan looked for another location. He apparently selected Pergamum because of the many idolatrous religions instituted by the local Roman government found there. Pergamum was the recognized center of pagan worship in Asia Minor. Keep in mind that Satan's primary goal is to keep people blinded to truth while providing something that momentarily seems to satisfy their spiritual hunger. Pergamum delivered.

The reason our Lord said that Satan's throne was in Pergamum was likely because of the many heathen temples located there. They included the temple of Athena, the great temples of Caesar Augustus and Hadrian, the great altar to Zeus, the temple of Dionysius, and the temple of Asklepios. Some scholars believe that the great altar of Zeus represented Satan's throne, where others strongly feel it was the combination of all of these heathen temples that made up Satan's throne.

"... Yet you remain true to my name. You did not renounce your faith in me ...." This was Christ's commendation. Since the organized church in Pergamum held fast to Christ's name, it did not teach anything but the personal deity of Jesus Christ for over 1,000 years.

2:14: *"… You have people there who hold to the teaching of Balaam …."* This was Christ's condemnation. In chapter 22 of Numbers, we read an account of Balak, the king of Moab. He was afraid of the children of Israel as they were coming through his land. He hired Balaam to use his gift of prophecy against Israel, and Balaam sought every means at his disposal to do so. However, all his efforts failed when he encountered Israel's God. In desperation, he gave Balak the suggestion of enticing the Israelites into making an unholy alliance with the Moabites through intermarriage with them (Numbers 25:1 – 9; 31:16). Therefore, we might say that the basic concept of Balaam's teaching is as follows: If you can't curse them, try to seduce them. In other words, some in the church of Pergamum were being enticed into sin by others among them. It is unclear as to whether or not the seducers were truly saved. I suspect not.

2:15: Refer back to verse 6 for an explanation on the teaching of the Nicolaitans.

2:16: Christ's counsel to them was simply to repent. Recall from chapter 1 that we defined the expression, "the sword of my mouth," as the spoken Word of Christ for which there is no defense on the Day of Judgment. Keep in mind that Jesus Christ, the Son of God, has only to speak and His will is accomplished.

2:17: To those who overcome, Christ promised to give some of the hidden manna. Manna was the heavenly food sent by God to the children of Israel in the desert. It also represents the spiritual food provided by God in His Word. The words of our Lord Jesus tell us, *"I am the bread of life. He who comes to me will never go hungry, and he who believes in me will never be thirsty"* (John 6:35). No matter what life's dilemmas pose, if God's children will only look to Him, their needs will be supplied. Jesus Christ came to earth as the manna provided by the Father to bring salvation and eternal life.

Today, the Spirit of Christ, or Holy Spirit, falls like manna from heaven to all who hunger, all who believe, and all who overcome the world. It is hidden only to those who choose not to believe, thereby rejecting the precious gift of salvation offered by the Father. In recalling the Lord's reaction and words upon His triumphal entry into Jerusalem beginning the final week before His death, the Gospel writer wrote: *"As He approached Jerusalem and saw the city, He wept over it and said, 'If you, even you, had only known on this day what would bring you peace – but now it is hidden from your eyes'"* (Luke 19:41 – 42).

Because of Israel's rejection of Jesus as her Messiah, God has, for a time, spiritually blinded the eyes of the Jewish people and thus hidden from them the true Prince of Peace. Recall Saul's experience on the Damascus Road with the risen Lord that resulted in him being blinded and not wanting to eat or drink anything. After three days, the Lord sent Ananias to him to complete his conversion. Once Ananias laid hands on Saul, *"… something like scales fell from Saul's eyes, and he could see again"* (Acts 9:18). Afterward, *"… he got up and was baptized"* (Acts 9:18). Saul later became Paul, the father of our NT and God's messenger to the Gentiles.

The Lord also promised those who overcome a white stone with a new name written on it. In ancient times a white stone meant acquittal when used by jurors publishing their vote in a court case. Hence, the white stone stands as a beautiful symbol of the eternal acquittal we gain through faith in Jesus Christ, not because we are innocent, but because our Lord and Savior Jesus Christ paid our sin debt with His blood which was shed on a Roman cross. As for the new name on the stone, it could be Christ's name; or as some suggest, we may all be given a new name, just as Abram was given the name Abraham, Simon was called Peter, and Saul became Paul. Considering the multiple duplications of names used in this world today, Christ may likely desire that each of His children have their own special and unique name going into eternity.

Church of Thyatira – the Pagan Church, c. 606 – 1520 (The Dark Ages)

2:18: Recall from chapter 1 the ten characteristics of Christ which John revealed. We said that eyes like blazing fire and feet like burnished bronze represent judgment and are likened to the bronze altar of the tabernacle where sin was judged (Revelation 1:14, 15).

2:19: The Lord's commendations to this church were as follows:

1) Their deeds remind us that good works are proof of genuine salvation.
2) Their love for one another is also proof of genuine salvation and is representative of the fruit of the Spirit (Galatians 5:22) – that is, the indwelling Holy Spirit.
3) Their faith is what motivates the two.
4) Their ministry of service to others outside the church.
5) Their perseverance or patience is also representative of the fruit of the Spirit.
6) They were doing more than they did at first. In this church, works and service increased rather than diminished.

2:20: *"You tolerate that woman Jezebel, who calls herself a prophetess ...."* This was the Lord's condemnation. Thyatira was one of the most thriving commercial centers in all Asia. Her city boasted of the finest wool and linen workers, dyers, leather workers, potters, tanners, bakers, slave traders, and bronze smiths. Almost every commentary you read speaks about the powerful trade guilds that ran the city like the modern day mob. They were morally corrupt because they involved their members in all sorts of idolatrous practices. Not only did unethical deals and practices prevail, but sexual immorality was rampant. Jezebel could have been an actual woman, but perhaps Christ was more likely drawing a parallel between women of Thyatira who were successful and held positions of authority in the Church and the wicked, pagan wife of King Ahab.

Whenever a woman is used symbolically to convey a religious teaching, she always represents a false religion. The worship of Baal reached its heights during the days of King Ahab and Jezebel (1 Kings 16:31 – 33; 21:25). Ahab imported the Phoenician Baal worship of his wife Jezebel into the northern kingdom of Israel by building a temple of Baal in Samaria. The practice of sacrificing Israel's sons and daughters in the fire began with the pagan princess Jezebel, thereby pushing Israel into crossing a new line in regards to wickedness by her extreme, liberal form of Baal worship. The Jezebel mentioned here was obviously a wicked and powerful woman (or influence) that did everything she could to infiltrate the church. Christ says that the teaching of the false prophetess Jezebel took two forms, both of which are in stark opposition to the Word of God:

1) *"By her teaching she misleads my servants into sexual immorality ..."* This false teaching emphasized sensual self-indulgence, a practice common with all forms of pagan, idolatrous worship.
2) *"... the eating of food sacrificed to idols."* This was a practice which demonstrated union of the Church (its members) with the world (unbelievers).

2:21 – 23: *"I have given her time to repent of her immorality, but she is unwilling …."* The Lord has patiently dealt with this false system of religion, but there has been no real change; therefore, she and all who commit adultery with her will suffer judgment. The children mentioned here are those who were brought up under this system. The meaning of the word "dead" (v.23) refers to the second death (2:11), a reference to eternal punishment and separation from God. This is the intense suffering that Christ promises to those who do not repent, for the Lord searches hearts and minds and will repay everyone according to what they have done. The writer of Hebrews likewise wrote: *"Nothing in all creation is hidden from God's sight. Everything is uncovered and laid bare before the eyes of him to whom we must give account"* (Hebrews 4:13).

2:24: The expression, "Satan's so-called deep secrets," likely refers to a Gnostic sect at the time known as the Ophites who worshiped the serpent, who we know from the Garden of Eden as the devil. They also practiced libertinism, which is defined as a life devoid of moral authority in regards to sexual or religious matters. These Gnostics mocked the writings of the Apostle Paul, challenged his apostolic authority, and boasted of a higher spiritual perception.

2:25: *"Only hold on to what you have until I come."* This counsel from the Lord is a reference to the Rapture of the Church. We will discuss this in detail in chapter 4. Christ is telling the Church, both then and today, that He is coming back for her; thus, the Church should stand firm in their faith in the Lord Jesus Christ.

2:26: *"I will give authority over the nations …."* This is Christ's promise to those who overcome. The Apostle Paul wrote likewise: *"Do you not know that the saints will judge the world?"* (1 Corinthians 6:2). This is a reference to the millennial reign of Christ in which believers will participate. We will look at this in greater detail in our study of chapter 20.

2:27: *"He will rule them with an iron scepter; he will dash them to pieces like pottery …."* The word "them" is a reference to the nations of the world. This speaks of Christ's strength and the absolute sovereignty of His rule during the Millennium.

2:28: *"I will also give him the morning star."* The expression, "morning star," is a beautiful messianic title as understood in light of the Lord's final words, wherein Christ explains that He is the *"Bright and Morning Star"* (Revelation 22:16 NKJV). The children of Jezebel will not listen, but the true child of God will listen and respond in faith. This promise is clearly the promise of Christ to come and abide with all those who overcome the world.

2:29: *"He who has an ear, let him hear what the Spirit says to the churches."* As we suggested in our chapter introduction, these words from the Lord Jesus apply, not only to the churches of John's day, but also to the universal Church of Christ today.

Chapters 2 and 3 combined make up Christ's complete message to the churches of all ages.
Review Questions for this section are included at the end of chapter 3.

FAQ: Women and False Religion

In chapter 2 (vv.20 – 22), the Lord Jesus Christ, in His discourse concerning the church at Thyatira, compares the successful women of high position in that city with Jezebel, the wife and driving force behind the wicked rule of King Ahab of Israel during the time of the divided kingdom. These women infiltrated the church and, according to the Lord, *"… mislead my servants into sexual immorality and the eating of food sacrificed to idols"* (Revelation 2:20). In other words, they corrupted the church!

In my exposition, I mentioned that whenever a woman is used symbolically in Scripture to convey a religious teaching, she always represents a false teaching. The absoluteness of that statement would naturally raise questions, and in classroom discussion, I have found it oftentimes does.

There is a simple answer, but let's first take a quick look at some background:

1) In chapter 14, I give a brief history of Babylon, the place where idolatry began. It was here that Semiramis, wife (some scholars say mother) of Nimrod was queen of Babel, which later became Babylon. She devised a story (a lie) in which she stepped fully grown out of an egg in the Euphrates River, thus beginning a whole system of idolatry. The worship of Semiramis introduced the female deity of false religion and identifies Babylon as the birthplace of all false religion.

2) The goddess Asherah was believed to be the wife of Baal, the chief male deity of the Canaanites. The Lord commanded the Israelites through Moses to drive out the Canaanites and cut down their Asherah poles, and *"Do not worship any other god, for the Lord, whose name is Jealous, is a jealous God"* (Exodus 34:10 – 14).

3) Throughout the time of the divided kingdom, the wicked kings would allow the worship of Asherah and the erecting of Asherah poles. In turn, when a righteous king came into power, he would command that these poles be cut down as he sought to bring the people back to the Lord. Even the Prophet Elijah challenged the four hundred prophets of Asherah on Mount Carmel (1 Kings 18:19).

4) As with Ahab and Jezebel, other wicked kings had women as the driving force behind their reign. One such example was Ahaziah, King of Judah. After his death, his mother, Athaliah, proceeded to destroy the whole royal family of the house of Judah. She went on to assume power and ruled the land for six years. She was killed in a coup led by Jehoiada the priest and Joash, the only remaining son of Ahaziah, was crowned king (2 Kings 11).

Throughout the Bible we are commanded to worship the one true, living God. The NT introduces and teaches the concept of the Trinity – that is, God in three persons – God the Father, God the Son, and God the Spirit. Later in our study of the book of Revelation, we will witness as the Apostle John bows twice at the feet of an angel sent by Christ, and is twice told, "Do not do it!" (Revelation 19:10; 22:9) The consistent pattern in the Word of God is that we worship God only, and to worship anyone or anything else is a false religion.

Chapter 3

Please follow along in your Bible.

Church of Sardis – the Dead Church, c. 1520 – 1790 (The Protestant Reformation)

The Protestant Reformation developed as the result of continued emphasis by the Church of Rome on pagan doctrines rather than adherence to scriptural principles. A key element of the early Reformation Church was Martin Luther's position statement, taken from Paul's Epistle to the Romans: *"The righteous will live by faith"* (Romans 1:17).

3:1: *"These are the words of him who holds the seven spirits of God and the seven stars ...."* Here again, Christ identifies Himself to the church using divine characteristics, that which John earlier witnessed in his vision of the glorified Christ (Revelation 1:4, 16).

"I know your deeds; you have a reputation of being alive ...." This was Christ's commendation. If we look at the church of Sardis as a historical stage of the Church, this may well refer to the early stages of the Reformation when Martin Luther and others chose to defy Roman authority, even at the risk of their own lives. The Reformation recovered the doctrine of justification by faith, and this faith produced good works.

"... but you are dead," is Christ's condemnation. The tragedy of the Reformation churches that earned them condemnation by the Lord for being dead was formalism – they appeared alive on the outside but were spiritually dead on the inside. The result was twofold. First, they became state churches. The danger was that the church included the entire population, thus eliminating the need for personal acceptance of Jesus Christ and an emphasis on the individual's relationship to God. Secondly, there was the tendency to please the government rather than God.

As for the church of Sardis at the time of John's writing, how can anything that carries the name of Jesus Christ be dead? Above all things, Christ is life! The city of Sardis was best known for a necropolis called the *Cemetery of the Thousand Hills* about seven miles from town. Sardis was built on a small, elevated plateau that looked out onto a distant horizon of burial mounds. The people of Sardis became obsessed with death and thoughts of death over-shadowed thoughts of life. Sardis also tried to rely on their past achievements and fame. Sadly, these same factors contributed to the dead nature that characterized the church in Sardis. The church was dead in that it had lost its authority and stopped proclaiming the Word of God; consequently, the church was full of unredeemed, unregenerate people.

3:2 – 3: *"Wake up! Strengthen what remains and is about to die, for I have not found your deeds complete in the sight of my God ...."* This was Christ's condemnation. Twice in its history the enemies of Sardis invaded them because they felt secure. Christ's warning was to wake up, repent, and strengthen what little faith remained. Today, just as in Sardis, Christ's imminent return is what believers should anticipate. Sardis did not know when the enemy was coming, and we do not know when Christ is coming. Considering that the Rapture, the next event on God's prophetic calendar, could take place at any moment, the Church is to be alert and ready. Remember that preparedness was the theme of Christ's last sermon.

3:4: *"Yet you have a few people in Sardis who have not soiled their clothes. They will walk with me, dressed in white, for they are worthy ...."* This was Christ's commendation. As in all church ages, the Reformation had individuals who were faithful to the Lord and had not conformed to the attitude and conduct of the world around them. They chose to live separate and godly lives.

3:5: *"He who overcomes will, like them, be dressed in white ...."* The fact that the overcomers were dressed in white reinforces what we said earlier, that white represents the righteousness of God (1:14), and here, the righteousness of Christ with which believers are clothed when reconciled to God through faith in His Son, Jesus Christ (cf. 2 Corinthians 5:21).

"... I will never blot out his name from the book of life, but will acknowledge his name before my Father and his angels." This is another promise from Christ. It indicates the security with which a believer is held against the Day of Judgment in contrast to nonbelievers as we will study later in chapter 20. The book of life is not a record of those who are saved, but rather a list of those for whom Christ died – all mankind. The only way to guarantee that your name will never be blotted out of the book of life is to accept Jesus Christ as your Lord and Savior. The adverb "never" suggests that once a person is truly saved through faith in Jesus Christ, then their salvation is secured for eternity. The following words of Jesus ought to comfort every believer: *"I give them eternal life, and they shall never perish; no one can snatch them out of my hand"* (John 10:28). Pastor and best-selling author, Dr. Charles Stanley, stated: "If God is big enough to save you, then He is big enough to keep you." I strongly believe that once saved (genuinely), always saved.

3:6: *"He who has an ear, let him hear what the Spirit says to the churches."* Christ is speaking this same message to all of mankind today.

Church of Philadelphia – the Missionary Church, c. 1750 up to the Rapture (The Church Christ Loved)

The word Philadelphia literally means "brotherly love." Philadelphia was marked by vitality of life. In this church age – that is, the age in which we are living, God began to work in a thrilling manner that produced revivals in Europe and the British Isles, spreading even to America. These revivals in turn produced what is known today as the modern missionary movement. Just as with the church in Smyrna, our Lord did not have a single word of condemnation for this church. It is interesting to note that these are the only two cities of the seven that have had a continuous existence. Their lampstands have been moved, but there are a few Christians still remaining there. They do not come out in the open because Christians are persecuted even today in modern Turkey.

3:7: *"These are the words of him who is …."* Christ reveals His divine nature to the Church:

1) **He is holy**, which means "sacred or consecrated," set apart solely for the use of God. Jesus Christ was holy at His birth, He lived a sinless life, He was holy at His death, and He is holy today.
2) **He is true**, which means "genuine." Jesus told His disciples: *"I am the way, the truth, and the life. No one comes to the Father except through me."* (John 14:6).
3) **He holds the key of David**. Here and in number 4, the Lord Jesus is quoting the Prophet Isaiah (22:22). These are the keys to the kingdom over which He will reign from the throne of David during the Millennium.
4) **The doors that Christ opens no one can shut**. Likewise, **the doors He shuts no one can open**. The Lord Jesus Christ controls the doors of opportunity for preaching the Gospel and no one can close them unless Christ so wills it. In the next verse this point is emphasized by their deeds.

3:8: Christ has four commendations for this church:

1) The word "deeds" is a reference to the churches' missionary works.
2) The expression, "little strength," is a reference to churches, then and today, that are characterized by small congregations.
3) They kept God's Word. As with the church of Philadelphia in John's day, these churches obey the Word of God and faithfully continue to sow seeds even though the harvest, at times, seems disappointingly small.
4) They did not deny the Lord. These churches refuse to deny the name of the Lord Jesus Christ despite existing during a time of the greatest increase in the number of false messiahs and false religions.

3:9 – 10: Christ promises the church in Philadelphia two things:

1) Verse 9: Vindication: Christ promised that all false religions (including the synagogue of Satan we examined in chapter 2) would someday fall down before them, and that the very people who mocked and ridiculed them would one day acknowledge how much Christ loved the Church.
2) Verse 10: Preservation: *"I will also keep you from the hour of trial that is going to come upon the whole world to test those who live on the earth."* The world has never known a universal period of tribulation. This is an obvious reference to the 7-year Tribulation Period that we will cover in our study of chapters 6 through 18. Christ's promise to the church in Philadelphia is a promise to all who make up the body of Christ by their trust and faith in our Lord and Savior – the Church will be removed before the Tribulation Period begins. These words from the Lord represent one of several passages in Scripture that support our belief in a pre-tribulation Rapture (cf. 1 Thessalonians 1:10; 5:9).

3:11: *"I am coming soon …."* This is the Lord's promise. It is made on the basis that the church of Philadelphia will be in existence at His return. The church of Philadelphia is characterized by a spirit of revival that promotes evangelism, a return to the Word of God, and a great emphasis on the Second Coming (Advent) of Christ.

3:12: Christ makes three promises to those who overcome:

1) *"I will make a pillar in the temple of my God …."* A pillar is symbolic of strength and stability; thus, Christians have stability in this life and a hope for eternity to come.

2) *"I will write on him the name of my God and the name of the city of my God, the New Jerusalem …."* True believers are identified with Christ by the seal of the name of God (Ephesians 1:13), which entitles them entrance into the Holy City of the New Jerusalem described in awesome detail later in chapters 21 and 22.

3) *"… I will also write on him my new name."* Believers of the church of Philadelphia will also have the name of Christ, which will be on their foreheads and entitle them to be His servants and to see His face (Revelation 22:3, 4).

3:13: *"He who has an ear, let him hear what the Spirit says to the churches."* Again, the Lord uses this repeated command to the church to listen and faithfully act upon His words.

Church of Laodicea – the Apostate (False) Church, c. 1900 – The Midpoint of The Tribulation Period

3:14: Christ describes Himself with the following messianic titles:

1) **The Amen.** Amen is a Hebrew word that means "true" and carries with it the meaning of finality, i.e., "so be it." In this sense, Christ is the final truth. The Apostle Paul wrote concerning this truth: *"For no matter how many promises God has made, they are "Yes" in Christ. And so through him the "Amen" is spoken by us to the glory of God"* (2 Corinthians 1:20).

2) **The faithful and true witness.** The Lord Jesus is Truth (John 14:6) and the faithful witness of truth. His Word is infallible and inerrant because He is God.

3) **The ruler of God's creation.** All things were created through Christ's power as the apostle confirmed: *"Through him all things were made; without him nothing was made that has been made"* (John 1:3).

This is the only church whose conduct was so reprehensible that even Christ, who knew all about her, could not find one thing on which to commend her.

3:15 – 16: *"I know your deeds, that you are neither cold nor hot … you are lukewarm …."* This was Christ's condemnation. The word "lukewarm" carries a twofold meaning:

1) Lukewarm means dishonest or deceptive. This church claimed to represent Jesus Christ, but instead deceived many because they never acknowledged the power of the Gospel of Christ. Consequently, only a few ever experienced genuine spiritual regeneration.

2) Lukewarm is indicative of indifference. Genuine believers are called to faith-centered works, but the church in Laodicea was more focused on work-centered faith. They were more

into social functions than they were studying the Word of God. This church attempted to maintain a middle-of-the-road position. They were not against God, but they were certainly not excited about God either. Consequently, they were sickening to the Lord.

My brethren, there is nothing lukewarm about Christ!
All believers need to get excited and be committed to Jesus.

3:17: *"You say, 'I am rich; I have acquired wealth and do not need a thing ....'"* Laodicea was a rich city; however, wealth by itself is not the issue. We serve a God of infinite wealth who can distribute the riches of this world any way He sees fit. The problem is the deceitfulness of wealth and unfortunately, as was the case here, material abundance was not conducive to spiritual vitality. From a spiritual standpoint, this church was the worst of the seven. In it was no study of God's Word, no love of Christ, and no witnessing of His saving grace; yet it is blind to its own true condition. This church, with its vast material wealth, did not grasp the principle Jesus taught us: *"From everyone who has been given much, much will be demanded"* (Luke 12:48).

Recall how Christ's address to the church at Smyrna stands in stark contrast to Laodicea: *"I know your afflictions and your poverty – yet you are rich!"* (Revelation 2:9)

A true test of any works claiming to be performed in the name of Jesus Christ is: Does it glorify Jesus Christ or does it glorify mankind?

3:18 – 19: Christ's counsel to the church in Laodicea:

1) Verse 18: *"Buy from me gold refined in the fire, so you can become rich ..."* The spiritual counterpart to gold, something of great worth or value is salvation and eternal life. Salvation is not purchased through human efforts, but has been purchased for us by the precious blood of Christ. Salvation is the gift of God through faith in Christ.
2) *"... and white clothes to wear, so you can cover your shameful nakedness ...."* As we have already said, white clothes denote the righteousness required to come into God's presence. Believers possess that righteousness because of their faith in Christ's sacrificial death. Ironically, Laodicea was famous world over for its black wool fabric. Christ suggested they trade their fashions for holiness.
3) *"... and salve to put on your eyes, so you can see."* This is an indication of a person's need for spiritual enlightenment. We must be indwelled by the Holy Spirit in order to understand the ways of God.
4) Verse 19: *"So be earnest, and repent."* This lukewarm, indifferent, and materialistic church was challenged by our Lord, on the basis of His love for them (even in their lost state), to repent and turn to Him.

3:20: *"Here I am! I stand at the door and knock. If anyone hears my voice and opens the door, I will come in and eat with him, and he with me."* The door is one's heart. This verse refers to fellowship and a personal relationship with the Savior, Jesus Christ. You are incomplete until you have fellowship with God through His Son Jesus Christ (1 John 1:3), which is only possible by inviting Him into your heart.

3:21: *"To him who overcomes, I will give the right to sit with me on my throne, just as I overcame and sat down with my Father on his throne."* Here is a divine promise that all believers will one day rule and reign alongside Christ when He returns to earth to establish His Millennial Kingdom. This ultimate victory for all Christians, not seen in this life but in the life to come, is a challenge to faithfulness.

3:22: *"He who has an ear, let him hear what the Spirit says to the churches."* As we stated in our introduction to this section (chapter 2), the seven churches represent the complete message Jesus wants to give to the Church. Although Jesus was speaking to each of these early Christian churches with a specific message, His total message is certainly relevant today and should serve as a soul-stirring warning to all of us, and that is why He ended each message with the same exhortation.

The overcomers are those who have placed their faith, trust, and hope in the Lord Jesus Christ. Jesus is the Head of the Church and He never takes His eyes off of her.

Review Questions

1) Define the church. _____

_____

_____

2) The purpose of the church is _____.

3) The mission of the church is _____.

4) The speaker in the vision is _____.

5) Which churches did Christ have no rebuke for? _____

_____.

6) Which church did Christ have no praise for? _____.

7) The overcomers are those who _____.

Up For Discussion

"He that hath an ear, let him hear what the Spirit saith unto the churches."
(Revelation 2:7, 11, 17, 29, 3:6, 13, 22 KJV)

Today, Jesus Christ is walking amongst the churches of the world, including your own. His power is always available to inspire and motivate the ministry of His church. Using the chart entitled, *The Seven Churches of the Revelation*, compare and contrast your home church with those of the seven churches of Asia Minor that John described. Discuss how your church might stand up under the all-knowing witness of the Lord Jesus Christ.

What would Christ's praise be for your church? Would He commend your ministry to the local community, to charities throughout our country, or to the needy worldwide? Would He witness your love for one another? Would He praise your love for His Word and the teaching of it?

What would Christ's rebuke be? Are there divisions in your church? Is there gossip? Is blatant sin such as adultery, substance addiction, or abuse being addressed, or worse, overlooked? Is the Word of God being taught, or worse, compromised? Do your pastor and church leaders believe the entire Bible to be the inspired and infallible Word of God?

What would Christ's counsel to your church be? Would it be to simply continue in the good work that you are doing? Or is your church able to do more?

The Seven Churches of the Revelation
Christ's Complete Message to the Church Then & to Us Today

	Ephesus Apostolic Church Rev. 2:1-7	Smyrna Persecuted Church Rev. 2:8-11	Pergamum Indulged Church Rev. 2:12-17	Thyatira The Pagan Church Rev. 2:18-29	Sardis The Dead Church Rev. 3:1-6	Philadelphia Missionary Church Rev. 3:7-13	Laodicea Lukewarm Church Rev. 3:14-22
	A.D. 30-100	A.D. 100-312	A.D. 312-606	A.D. 606-1520 Dark Ages	A.D. 1520-1790 Reformation	A.D. 1750- The Rapture	A.D. 1900- Tribulation Midpoint
Christ's Praise	Good deeds, hard works, perseverance, and hated the Nicolaitans.	Poverty, but rich in faith, endure persecution.	Remained true to my name, did not deny your faith.	Good deeds, love, faith, service, and perseverance.	Good deeds and a reputation for being alive.	Mission deeds, little strength, kept my word, have not denied my name.	None
Christ's Rebuke	You have forsaken your first love.	None	You have false teachers of Balaam, and Nicolaitans.	You allow Jezebel to teach sexual immorality and idolatry.	You are dead, and your deeds are incomplete.	None	You are lukewarm, wretched, pitiful, poor, blind, & naked.
Christ's Counsel	Remember from where you have fallen and repent.	Do not be afraid, and be faithful.	Repent	Hold on to what you have until I come.	Wake up! Strengthen what remains. Remember, obey and repent.	Hold on to what you have.	Buy gold tried by fire, white clothes, anoint your eyes, and repent.
Christ's Challenge	Will give to eat from the tree of life.	Will not be hurt by the second death.	Will give hidden manna, and a white stone with a new name.	Will give authority over the nations and the morning star.	Will walk with me dressed in white, names remain in the book of life.	Will make them pillars, will write on them name of God & My new name.	Will give right to sit with me on my throne.

22

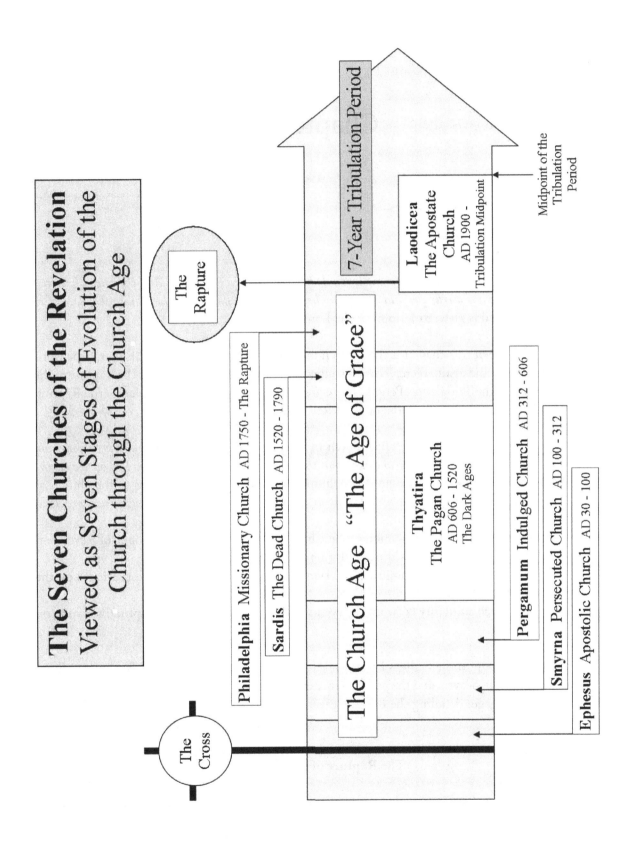

The Seven Churches of the Revelation
Viewed as Seven Stages of Evolution of the
Church through the Church Age

The Rapture

7-Year Tribulation Period

Laodicea
The Apostate Church
AD 1900 -
Tribulation Midpoint

Midpoint of the Tribulation Period

The Church Age "The Age of Grace"

Philadelphia Missionary Church AD 1750 - The Rapture

Sardis The Dead Church AD 1520 - 1790

Thyatira
The Pagan Church
AD 606 - 1520
The Dark Ages

Pergamum Indulged Church AD 312 - 606

Smyrna Persecuted Church AD 100 - 312

Ephesus Apostolic Church AD 30 - 100

The Cross

Chapter 4

Please follow along in your Bible.

4:1: *"After this I looked, and there before me was a door standing open in heaven. And the voice I had first heard speaking to me like a trumpet said, 'Come up here, and I will show you what must take place after this.'"* This command is given to John from the Lord Jesus.

The assumed theme of this chapter is the Church in heaven with Christ. Up to this point, the word church occurs again and again. Here, John's invitation to heaven is representative of the Rapture of the Church just before the Tribulation Period. There are at least four reasons why we locate the Rapture at this spot in the flow of events in the book of Revelation:

1) Our Lord promised this to His Church in the previous chapter: *"I will also keep you from the hour of trial that is going to come upon the whole world to test those who live on the earth"* (Revelation 3:10). The Apostle Paul reinforced this promise in his letter to the church at Thessalonica: *"For God did not appoint us to wrath but to salvation through our Lord Jesus Christ"* (1 Thessalonians 5:9).
2) The absence of any other mention of the Church in the remainder of the book of Revelation indicates it is no longer on the earth during the Tribulation Period.
3) The extensive use of OT language and symbols in chapters 4 – 18 suggests a focus on the nation of Israel, not the Church.
4) There is much similarity between the events of this passage and other scriptural teaching on the Rapture.

The calling of John up to the Father's house in heaven represents the Church. This, along with the door standing open in heaven, and the personal invitation of Christ Himself to come up here, parallels other prophetic passages detailing the Rapture of the Church.

The Rapture of the Church

The Apostle Paul was God's uniquely chosen writer to reveal to His Church the wonderful details of the Rapture, when all Christians, both dead and living, will be caught up to heaven to be with Christ. The expression, "caught up," is translated from the Greek word *harpazo*, which means "to snatch up or catch away." Our English word "rapture" is derived from the Latin word *rapio*, which means to seize or snatch in relation to a state of spirit or the actual removal from one place to another. In other words, it means to be carried away in spirit or in body. The Rapture of the Church means the carrying away of all Christians from earth to heaven. The apostle wrote: *"For the Lord himself will come down from heaven, with a loud command, with the voice of the archangel and with the trumpet call of God, and the dead in Christ will rise first. After that, we who are still alive and are left will be caught up together with them in the clouds to meet the Lord in the air"* (1 Thessalonians 4:16, 17).

After the dead are raised, the spirit of each, which is already with the Lord in heaven (2 Corinthians 5:8; Philippians 1:23), will be reunited with their body in permanent resurrection. The apostle tells us that when the Rapture occurs, *"… God will bring with Jesus those who have fallen asleep in Him"* (1 Thessalonians 4:14), meaning those who have died in Christ. Paul explains that Christians living at the time of the Rapture will be instantly changed: *"Listen, I tell you a mystery: We will not all sleep, but we will all be changed – in a flash, in the twinkling of an eye, at the last trumpet. For the trumpet will sound, the dead will be raised imperishable, and we will be changed. For the perishable must clothe itself with the imperishable and the mortal with immortality"* (1 Corinthians 15:51 – 53). The KJV is translated: *"For this corruptible must put on incorruption, and this mortal must put on immortality."* In other words, all believers will receive a new, glorified body, such as that of our Risen Lord. We need a new body, thus imperishable and incorruptible means holy or pure, without and never again to have a sinful nature. This will enable the child of God to stand and bow our knees in the presence of the Lord Jesus Christ; that we may rejoice in Him throughout eternity to come. Furthermore, with new, glorified bodies, our sanctification becomes complete; and we are, in the words of the writer of Hebrews, *"… made perfect"* (Hebrews 12:23).

There is only one Second Coming of Christ, but it occurs in two phases. The first phase is called the *Rapture* and occurs prior to the Tribulation Period when Christ comes down to the clouds to remove His Church (all believers) from the world before the judgments of the Tribulation Period begin. The second phase is called the *Revelation* and occurs at the end of the Tribulation Period when Christ returns to earth to put an end to all wickedness and rebellion and establishes His Millennial Kingdom. This fact cannot be questioned as Jesus Himself foretold that His return would come, *"Immediately after the distress of those days …"* (Matthew 24:29).

Seven Characteristics of the Throne of God

The remainder of chapter 4 gives us seven distinct characteristics of the throne of God:

1) 4:2 – 3: **The Trinity**: We know that God the Father is there and, as taught in Scripture, God the Son is seated at the right hand of God (Colossians 3:1). Verse 2 indicates that the Holy Spirit is present as well; and as in chapter 1, is still moving upon John and guiding him into new truths. We also know from several passages of Scripture that God the Father cannot be seen (John 1:18; 6:46; 1 Timothy 6:16). John could distinguish no form of a person so he simply describes the splendor of the One seated on the throne like brilliant gems, *"appearance of jasper and carnelian"* (v.3). Jasper is later described as clear crystal (21:11) and is likened to the most brilliant of all precious jewels, the diamond. The other stone, carnelian, is blood red and may well be likened to the ruby. Thus, the two together might symbolically represent the

idea of glory and sacrifice. John's next description is that, *"a rainbow, resembling an emerald, encircled the throne"* (v.3). John's vision is consistent with that of the Prophet Ezekiel (1:26 – 28). The throne of God is beyond anything we can imagine, yet the writer of Hebrews tells us that because of our great High Priest Jesus, we can approach it with confidence (Hebrews 4:14 – 16).

2) 4:4: Around the throne were **twenty-four elders**: Elders are representatives. We know that Israel had elders and that elders were appointed in the early church to help govern and represent the entire church (Titus 1:5). These twenty-four elders likely represent the Church in its totality in heaven. The fact that they are dressed in white and had crowns of gold on their heads further reinforces what we have already read, that white represents the righteousness of God through faith and that crowns are a heavenly reward for the believer. It is my opinion that all twelve apostles (including Paul) are here, as well as those representing the redeemed from the nation of Israel. Our Lord told His disciples at the Last Supper that they would, *"… sit on thrones, judging the twelve tribes of Israel"* (Luke 22:30).

3) 4:5a: The signs of judgment: Three things are mentioned here: **Lightning, rumblings, and peals of thunder**, all proceeding from the throne of God. These cosmic signs have long been associated with the concept of judgment; thus, we might conclude that they are a prelude to the judgment about to fall upon the earth as described in chapters 6 – 19.

4) 4:5b: Before the throne **seven lamps were blazing**. They are defined as **the seven spirits of God**. These were described in chapter 1 (v.4) as the sevenfold ministry of the Holy Spirit: 1) the Spirit of the Lord, 2) the Spirit of wisdom, 3) the Spirit of understanding, 4) the Spirit of counsel, 5) the Spirit of power, 6) the Spirit of knowledge, and 7) the Spirit of the fear of the Lord (Isaiah 11:2) and represented by a blazing menorah.

5) 4:6a: Also before the throne was **a sea of glass**: Its meaning is uncertain. It may represent stability because a glassy sea is a calm sea, untroubled by winds and storms. Two interpretations have been suggested for this calm and stable sea: 1) the Church at rest and in heaven, no longer a victim of the storms of life, and 2) the Word of God symbolized by the Lord's holiness and purity. This imagery is also similar to that found in Ezekiel (1:22, 25 – 28).

6) 4:6b – 8a: Around the throne were **four living creatures**: These four living creatures are the seraphim described by the Prophet Isaiah in his vision of the throne of God (Isaiah 6:1 – 3). The fact that they are covered with eyes, in front and in back speaks of knowledge or awareness. Because of their nature, they may well be leaders of the realm they depict – that is, of the heavenly hosts. Some commentators identify each with one of the four Gospels, while others see each as representing specific characteristics of God. Let's look briefly at each representation:

A lion is the leader of the kingdom of wild animals. The Gospel of Matthew presents the Lord Jesus as the King. The lion represents majesty and omnipotence – God is all-powerful.

A calf or ox is the leader of the domestic animals. The Gospel of Mark presents Christ as the Servant. The ox speaks of strength and might.

Man is the leader of the angelic host responsible for the human race. The Gospel of Luke presents the Lord Jesus as the Son of Man, and emphasizes His humanity. Man characterizes knowledge.

A flying eagle is the leader of the kingdom of fowls of the air. The Gospel of John communicates the deity of Christ. The eagle represents the sovereignty and supremacy of God.

7) 4:8b – 11: **The heavenly worship of Christ**: As mighty as these celestial beings of the heavenly order are, none of them could have qualified to redeem mankind from their sins. They are unworthy and that is why they fall down and lay their crowns before the throne. However, the blood of God's own Son could – and did! This act of worship seems to be their expression of devotion and adoration to the Lord Jesus Christ for redeeming from the earth what they could not redeem. The song they sing is also a song of glory and honor to God because He is the Creator of all things. The apostle tells us: *"Through Him all things were made; without Him nothing was made that has been made"* (John 1:3). This is another acknowledgement that the Lord Jesus Christ is the one being worshiped.

How much more should our hearts rejoice as we worship Him?
We are the recipients of His redemption!

Review Questions

1) The theme of this chapter is _____.

2) The Rapture of the Church occurs before _____.

3) The two phases of the Second Coming are _____

   _____.

4) We can approach the throne of God because of _____.

5) The twenty-four elders are representatives of _____.

6) The four living creatures are _____.

7) To whom is the heavenly worship directed? _____.

Up For Discussion

"After this I looked, and behold, a door was opened in heaven:
and the first voice which I heard was as it were of a trumpet talking with me;
which said, 'Come up hither ....'"
(Revelation 4:1 KJV)

Skip to the end of chapter 5 and to the illustration entitled, *Two Phases of the Second Coming of Christ.* Using the illustration, review on your own or, as a class, take turns reading aloud the Scripture verses, alternating between Rapture passages and Revelation passages. Compare them in class discussion as you go. Note, below, any newfound revelations from your readings.

Sodom and Gomorrah:
A Rapture Analogy

"Then the Lord said, 'The outcry against Sodom and Gomorrah is so great and their sin so grievous that I will go down and see if what they have done is as bad as the outcry that has reached me. If not, I will know'" (Genesis 18:20, 21).

Here is the account of the three visitors that came to see Abraham. The *Lord* referred to in these verses, as in other accounts throughout the OT, is believed to have been the pre-incarnate Christ, while the other two visitors with Him were angels. Before leaving, the Lord told Abraham He was going down to Sodom and Gomorrah to investigate the wickedness that had come to His attention. The first thing that came to Abraham's mind was his nephew Lot and his relationship with God. Abraham began to plead to the Lord for the righteous with the following question: *"Will you sweep away the righteous with the wicked?"* (Genesis 18:23) Abraham then asked: *"Will the Judge of all the earth do right?"* (Genesis 18:25) My brethren, the Word of God testifies to the fact that whatever God does is right! Abraham began to plead with the Lord. He started at fifty, then he went to forty-five, then to forty, then to thirty, then to twenty, and finally Abraham pleaded down to ten, and the Lord agreed that if even ten righteous were found there, then He would not destroy the cities and all their dwellings. As it turned out, there was only one righteous man there – Lot – and God told Lot (along with his family) to get out before He destroyed them.

The same is true today. The Tribulation Period, described in chapters 6 – 18 of the book of Revelation, cannot begin as long as the Church – that is, the righteous remain in the world. Why? The reason is that Jesus Christ died for the sins of all mankind and bore our judgment on Calvary's cross once and for all. All believers who place their faith in Christ's sacrificial death are, therefore, no longer destined to some future time of wrath. The Apostle Paul wrote: *"For God did not appoint us to wrath but to receive salvation through our Lord Jesus Christ"* (1 Thessalonians 5:9). The Tribulation Period is God's judgment that is coming upon the rest of the world – the unrighteous, wicked, rebellious, and unbelieving. This is the reason the Church cannot go through the Tribulation Period. Sodom and Gomorrah is an illustration of the world today. The Lord is returning soon, and that is in keeping with the story we have here in Genesis.

Words Not Found in the Bible

It is in chapter 4 of Revelation, when we discuss the Rapture of the Church before the Tribulation Period, that Bible skeptics question this teaching and point to the fact that the word *Rapture* is not found in the Bible. We do not have to see a specific word in the Bible in order for the concept it describes to be true. Let's take a look at just a few words, common to our faith, that do not appear in the Bible.

1) Rapture: This term defines the concept of a person or group of people caught up or taken to heaven to be with God without experiencing death. The Apostle Paul explained the wonderful details of the Rapture, when all Christians, both dead and living, will be caught up (raptured) to heaven to be with Christ. The apostle writes: *"For the Lord Himself will come down from heaven, with a loud command, with the voice of the archangel and with the trumpet call of God, and the dead in Christ will rise first. After that, we who are still alive and are left will be caught up together with them in the clouds to meet the Lord in the air"* (1 Thessalonians 4:16, 17). Moreover, this concept is not exclusive to the NT. In Genesis, we have the account of the patriarch Enoch: *"Enoch walked with God; then he was no more, because God took him away"* (Genesis 5:24). Secondly, there is the OT story concerning the Prophets Elijah and Elisha. It is written: *"As they were walking along and talking together, suddenly a chariot of fire and horses of fire appeared and separated the two of them, and Elijah went up to heaven in a whirlwind"* (2 Kings 2:11). As you can see, the concept of rapture is not new, and definitely seems to be an important part of God's future plan for His children.

2) Trinity: Refers to the concept of God in three Persons – God the Father, God the Son, and God the Spirit. No true Christian disputes this doctrine.

3) Divinity: Means to have divine quality or God-like character.

4) Incarnate or incarnation: God manifest in the flesh. The Apostle John describes this concept: *"In the beginning was the Word, and the Word was with God, and the Word was God. The Word became flesh and made his dwelling among us. We have seen his glory, the glory of the One and only, who came from the Father, full of grace and truth"* (John 1:1, 14). Regrettably, this term has also come to be used by Bible commentators of the book of Revelation to describe the embodiment and deceitful resurrection of the end-time dictator of the world – Antichrist – by Satan at the mid-point of the 7-year Tribulation Period.

5) Monotheism: The teaching that there is only one God.

6) Sacrament: One of the ceremonial observances of the Christian church, e.g., Baptism and Communion (the Lord's Supper).

This is simply a list of the more obvious examples. In addition, the word *Bible* itself is only mentioned in the title of God's Word, and the word *Christian* is only mentioned twice throughout the entire NT. When people question or challenge these words, they are attempting to rob you of the hope and joy that is yours through faith in Jesus Christ. I call them *joy robbers*. Don't let a joy robber distract you from studying God's Word and from the faith we hold so dear.

Pre-Tribulation Rapture View

The Father's House (John 14:1-3)

Judgment Seat (1 Cor. 3:9-15)	Marriage of the Lamb

The Rapture

The Revelation

1 Thes. 4:13-17
1 Cor. 15:51-58

Matthew 24:30
Rev. 19:11-16

The Cross

Past Ages

The Church Age "Age of Grace"

7-Year Tribulation

The Millennium
The Wedding Supper of the Lamb

Eternity

The Church does not go through the Tribulation
(1 Thessalonians 1:10, 5:9; Revelation 3:10)

Chapter 5

Please follow along in your Bible.

Whenever a chapter in the Bible opens with the word "and" or "then," we know it should be joined to the proceeding chapter. Therefore, we continue the scene of the Church in heaven with Christ. The throne was the center of chapter 4. The Lion and the Lamb, both of which represent Christ, are the center of chapter 5. John has seen the throne of God, and now his attention focuses on an object in the hand of God.

5:1 – 4: *"Then I saw in the right hand of him who sat on the throne a scroll with writing on both sides and sealed with seven seals. And I saw a mighty angel proclaiming in a loud voice, 'Who is worthy to break the seals and open the scroll?' … I wept and wept because no one was found who was worthy to open the scroll and look inside."*

Here is the first of three mighty angels as witnessed by John in his apocalyptic visions of the Revelation (10:1; 18:21). Although they are members of God's heavenly host, they are apparently diverse from the four seraphim that surround the throne of God (4:6). Because they are described as mighty, perhaps they are archangels similar to Michael, whom we will see later in our study of chapter 12.

John weeps because he knows that this scroll contains God's final plan for the redemption of the earth, and as long as the scroll is left sealed, Satan will continue his destructive influence in the world. Jesus Himself referred to Satan as, *the prince of this world* (John 12:31; 16:11). The scroll is being handed to the Lord Jesus because this earth belongs to Him. He created it, and He redeemed it. Therefore, only He is worthy to break the seals and open the scroll. As a student of prophecy in the Word of God, I personally identify this scroll as the Book of Judgment and believe it to be the same scroll as the one from Daniel's vision, whereby the prophet was commanded to, *"seal the words of the scroll until the time of the end"* (Daniel 12:4). This scroll could also be likened to the flying scroll from the vision given to the Prophet Zechariah (5:1 – 3). The Prophet Isaiah, as well, had a vision of judgment which came to him as, *"… nothing but words sealed in a scroll"* (Isaiah 29:11). Nevertheless, as we will see, the opening of this scroll and its seals will bring a series of judgments upon the earth leading to its eventual redemption.

Who has the right to bring judgment upon a wicked and rebellious world and to establish eternal justice and righteousness? The words of our Lord Jesus Christ tell us: *"Moreover, the Father judges no one, but has entrusted all judgment to the Son"* (John 5:22).

Five Characteristics of the Lord Jesus Christ

5:5 – 6: *"Then one of the elders said to me, 'Do not weep!....'"* As John looks on, he sees a Lamb that appears as if it has already been sacrificed. This vision gives us five characteristics of the Lord Jesus Christ:

1) Verse 5: **The Lion of the tribe of Judah**: This identifies Christ with the tribe of Judah of the people of Israel. Before his death, Jacob blessed his sons, and to Judah he said, *"You are a lion's cub ... The scepter will not depart from Judah, nor the ruler's staff from between his feet, until he comes to whom it belongs and the obedience of the nations is his"* (Genesis 49:9 – 11).

2) **The Root of David**: This refers to Jesus' incarnation – His birth with His roots in the royal line of David. God told David: *"I will raise up your offspring to succeed you, who will come from your own body ... Your house and your kingdom will endure forever before me; your throne will be established forever"* (2 Samuel 7:12 – 16). This OT prophecy finds its ultimate fulfillment in the Messiah, the Lord Jesus Christ at His Second Coming.

3) Verse 6: **A Lamb**, looking as if it has been slain, standing in the center of the throne: Slain refers to the redemptive and substitutionary death of Christ, where standing speaks of His resurrection. In John's vision, Christ is no longer seated at the right hand of God. He is standing, and He is coming soon to judge this earth.

4) **Seven horns**: In Scripture, a horn refers to a power or authority, and the number seven represents completeness. The Lamb's power and authority to redeem on earth came through His willingness to be slain. When Christ came the first time as a Lamb, though He displayed certain powers, He did not manifest all of His power. When He comes the next time as a Lion, at the Revelation, it will be in the manifestation of His complete omnipotence – His all-consuming power.

5) **Seven eyes**: These eyes are defined as the seven spirits of God sent out into all the earth. These eyes speak of the knowledge and wisdom of our Lord. Here again, seven is God's number for completeness. For that reason, when Christ comes to judge the world at the end of the Tribulation Period, it will be as the perfect Judge, who has all power and complete knowledge about mankind.

The Lord Jesus Christ is a Lamb and a Lion:

1) The lamb referred to Jesus' First Coming. The lion refers to His Second Coming.
2) The lamb was symbolic of Jesus' meekness. The lion is symbolic of His majesty.
3) As a lamb, Jesus is our Savior. As a lion, He is our King.
4) As a lamb, Jesus was judged by the world. As a lion, He will return as Judge of the earth.
5) The lamb represents the grace of God. The lion represents the sovereignty of God.

5:7 – 8: *"He came and took the scroll from the right hand of him who sat on the throne...."* The moment Christ takes the seven-sealed scroll, the four living creatures and the twenty-four elders fall down before Him. They are described as having two things in their hands:

1) Verse 8: Harps: This instrument represents the music and praise of heaven.
2) Golden bowls filled with prayers of the saints: Who are the saints? All believers in the Lord Jesus Christ are saints. These golden bowls are filled with unanswered prayers that will be answered at the return and revelation of Jesus Christ. All Christians have prayed as our Lord taught us: *"Your kingdom come, your will be done on earth as it is in heaven"* (Matthew 6:10). This will not be accomplished until Christ returns to earth to set up His Millennial Kingdom

and righteous rule. This is another indication that all prayer is answered, though we may not receive the answer in our lifetime.

5:9 – 10: This is a song of praise. It indicates that the Lord Jesus Christ is worthy, not only to take the scroll and to open its seals, but more importantly, Jesus is worthy of our praise and worship. Three reasons are given:

1) Verses 9: "*… because you were slain …*" This refers to Christ's sacrificial death on Calvary's cross to pay our sin debt.
2) "*… with your blood you purchased men for God from every tribe and language and people and nation.*" The precious blood of Jesus was shed for all mankind. This assures us that millions of people in the world who have never heard the Gospel will one day hear about our Lord and Savior Jesus Christ (as we will see in chapter 7).
3) Verse 10: "*You have made them to be a kingdom and priests to serve our God, and they will reign on the earth.*" This is the Church in heaven. This is a reference to the millennial reign of Christ in which believers will participate (cf. 2:26).

5:11: "*Then I looked and heard the voice of many angels, numbering thousands upon thousands, and ten thousand times ten thousand ….*" This verse gives us a rare glimpse of the enormity of the number of those in heaven, both angelic and human. The Church is now in heaven and joining in the singing of praise. When questioned by the Sadducees, our Lord replied: "*At the resurrection people will neither marry nor be given in marriage; they will be like the angels*" (Matthew 22:30).

5:12: The angels in heaven, who know Christ best, proclaim Him worthy to receive seven things: 1) power, 2) wealth, 3) wisdom, 4) strength, 5) honor, 6) glory, and 7) blessing. We should accept the angels' description of these qualities inherent to God and to the Lamb, Jesus Christ that, in return, demand our praise.

5:13 – 14: The remainder of God's creation joins in the glorious song of praise to our Lord. This passage of Scripture should be viewed alongside that which the Apostle Paul wrote: "*Therefore God exalted him to the highest place and gave him the name that is above every name, that at the name of Jesus every knee should bow, in heaven and on earth and under the earth, and every tongue confess that Jesus Christ is Lord, to the glory of God the Father*" (Philippians 2:9 – 11). As we see, all the animals on earth and fish in the sea are going to join in this singing of praise to our Lord. The phrase, "under the earth," refers to the underworld – hell – even those in hell awaiting their final judgment will sing praises to the Lord Jesus Christ.

What John saw was heaven in complete joyful jubilation and celebration of the Lord Jesus Christ, the Son of God. All of heaven breaks loose in praise. Jesus is the one who paid the price for man's redemption. He is the only one worthy to break the seals and judge mankind. Jesus, and only Jesus, is worthy of our praise and worship.

Worthy is the Lamb.

Review Questions

1) The Lion and the Lamb both represent _____.

2) We suggest in our study that the scroll is the _____.

3) A horn in Scripture is symbolic of _____.

4) Eyes in Scripture are symbolic of _____.

5) Harps in Scripture are symbolic of _____.

6) Incense in Scripture is symbolic of _____.

7) Name the seven things Jesus is worthy to receive. _____

_____.

Up For Discussion

"And every creature which is in heaven, and on the earth, and under the earth,
and such as are in the sea, and all that are in them, heard I saying,
Blessing, and honour, and glory, and power, be unto Him
That sitteth upon the throne, and unto
the Lamb for ever and ever."
(Revelation 5:13 KJV)

Does it seem odd that all creation would sing out praises to our Lord?

Recall the story of Jesus' triumphal entry into Jerusalem the Sunday before His death, and how the crowd was joyfully singing praises to God in loud voices for all the miracles they had witnessed. The multitude sang, *"Hosanna to the Son of David! Blessed is he who comes in the name of the Lord! Hosanna in the highest!"* (Matthew 21:9). Recall also that some of the Pharisees told Jesus to rebuke his disciples. But Jesus' reply was, *"If they keep quiet, the stones will cry out,"* (Luke 19:40).

Discuss how nature reveals the majesty of God.

Discuss how nature reveals the curse of mankind.

Two Phases of the Second Coming of Christ

| The Rapture | The Seven-Year Tribulation Period | The Revelation |

Rapture Passages

Matthew 24:36-41, John 14:1-3
1 Corinthians 1:7-8, 15:51-53
Philippians 3:20-21, 4:5
Colossians 3:4
1 Thessalonians 1:10, 2:19
4:13-18, 5:9, 5:23
2 Thessalonians 2:1
1 Timothy 6:14
2 Timothy 4:1, 4:8
Hebrews 9:28,   James 5:7-9
1 Peter 1:7, 1:13, 4:12-13, 5:4
1 John 2:28-3:2,   Jude 21
Revelation 2:25, 3:10

Titus 2:13

Revelation Passages

Isaiah 9:6-7, 66:15-16
Daniel 2:44-45, 7:13-14, 12:1-3
Zechariah 12:10, 14:1-9
Matthew 13:41, 24:27-31
Matthew 26:64
Mark 13:24-27, 14:62
Luke 21:25-28
Acts 1:9-11, 3:19-21
1 Thessalonians 3:13
2 Thessalonians 1:6-10, 2:8
2 Peter 3:3-14,   Jude 14-15
Revelation 1:7, 19:11-16
Revelation 22:7, 22:12, 22:20

Contrasting Events of the Second Coming

The Rapture

1– Christ comes down to clouds to take all Christians to Heaven.
2– Judgment Seat in Heaven.
3– Rapture is imminent. It could happen at any moment.
4– For believers only.
5– Before the "Day of the Lord."
6– No mention of Satan.
7– Only Christians will see Him.
8– The Tribulation Period begins.

The Revelation

1– Christ returns to earth to judge & set up His earthly Kingdom.
2– Judgment of the nations on earth.
3– Christ's return cannot occur for at least 7 years.
4– Affects all of humanity.
5– After the Tribulation Period.
6– Satan bound for a 1,000 years.
7– Every eye on earth will see Him.
8– The Millennial Kingdom begins.

Chapter 6

Please follow along in your Bible.

The Tribulation Period

As we come to chapter 6, the scene shifts back to earth. Now that the Church is out of the world and in heaven, the question is: "What is to happen to the earth?"

The Tribulation Period is one of the most significant periods of God's dealing with mankind and certainly occupies a most prominent place in His prophetic plan. The actual event that triggers the Tribulation Period is found in the prophecy of Daniel: *"He will confirm a covenant with many for one 'seven'"* (Daniel 9:27). To further clarify, let's take a closer look at the elements in Daniel's prophecy:

1) The pronoun "he" refers to the end-times ruler of the world – Antichrist.
2) The word "covenant" is a reference to a covenant of peace, i.e., a peace treaty.
3) The word "many" refers to the nation of Israel and nine other nations.
4) The term "seven" refers to a period of seven years.

Chapter 6 introduces the seal judgments, which make up the first quarter of the 7-year Tribulation Period. As John beholds the Lord Jesus Christ, represented by a Lamb, breaking the first seal, we encounter the first of a long series of events that begin in heaven and are brought to completion on earth. God will use this time, through a progressive series of judgments, to force all people remaining on earth after the Rapture of the Church to make a choice:

1) Repent of their sinful lifestyle and be saved by receiving God's Son, Jesus Christ as their Lord and Savior; or
2) Continue to reject Him and suffer eternal punishment and separation from God.

Each of these judgments is a symbolic announcement in heaven of an event that actually takes place on earth. This 7-year period of future world history, graphically described in chapters 6 – 18, will be the darkest time the world has ever known. The good news is: If you have put your trust and faith in Jesus Christ as your Lord and Savior, then you are not destined to some future time of judgment.

Our sin debt was paid for eternity on the cross by the atoning death of Jesus Christ. The Apostle Paul tells us that the Lord Jesus rescues all believers from the coming wrath (1 Thessalonians 1:10).

The Four Horsemen of the Apocalypse

6:1: At first glance, this opening verse gives the impression that a command was given to John to "Come!" However, since the order is issued from heaven and carried out on earth, a more appropriate translation would be "Watch!" The KJV uses the phrase, "come and see." John heard and then he saw, and his vision began with that of four horsemen.

6:2: The first seal – the rider on the white horse: The rider on the white horse represents the end-times Antichrist and his kingdom. We will take a closer look at the Antichrist in chapter 13. His purpose is clearly stated: *"… he rode out as a conqueror bent on conquest."* One interesting characteristic of his coming is that he has a bow in his hand, which is symbolic of warfare, but there is no mention of arrows, indicating that he will conquer by diplomacy, rather than by war. Amidst widespread chaos throughout the world resulting from the Rapture, Antichrist will come onto the scene as a great diplomat and problem solver, ushering in a false peace. The crown on his head indicates his rise to a worldwide position of power and authority. Unfortunately, the peace that he brings is only temporary.

6:3 – 4: The second seal – the rider on the red horse: The red horse is symbolic of war; thus, this rider has the authority to, *"take peace from the earth and to make men slay each other"* (v.4). This is also evident by the fact that a great sword is given to him. As Antichrist rises politically to international acceptance, some disenchanted nations will choose to revolt, thus beginning a world war. Their attempt will ultimately be unsuccessful, evident from the opening of the third seal. This will be a widespread, bloody war.

6:5 – 6: The third seal – the rider on the black horse: The black horse is symbolic of famine. Black is used to depict famine in other passages of Scripture (cf. Lamentations 4:8, 9), and famine often follows war as it did after World War I. Inflation also tends to grip the world right after a world war. The pair of scales in the hands of this rider indicates the scarcity of food. *"A quart of wheat for a day's wages and three quarts of barley for a day's wages …"* (v.6), suggests that a person will have to work for a whole day just to earn enough money to survive. The rider is instructed not to damage the oil and the wine, which are traditionally foods of the rich. Thus, this famine will take its heaviest toll on the common people.

6:7 – 8: The fourth seal – the rider on the pale horse: The pale horse is literally corpse-like. His name is Death, and he represents plague and pestilence. The death rate of the first twenty-one months of the Tribulation Period will be tremendously high as a result of war, famine, and inflation. In fact, one-fourth of the entire world's population will die. The fact that Hades follows the pale horse and its rider indicates that these are unsaved dead. Hades is the place reserved for the wicked, rebellious, and unbelieving of all generations while they await their final judgment as we will study later in chapters 20.

6:9 – 11: The fifth seal – the OT saints and martyred Tribulation saints: These are individuals who had not received Christ during the dispensation of grace (the Church Age). These OT saints have the righteousness that comes through faith (Romans 4:13). The Tribulation saints will receive Christ as a result of the faithful servants depicted in chapter 7. These Tribulation saints died, *"because of the word of God and the testimony they had maintained"* (v.9). We know that they are believers because each one is clothed in a white robe. Recall from chapter 3 (v.5), the phrase, "dressed in white," is symbolic of the righteousness of Christ with which we are clothed when we accept God's Son, Jesus Christ, as our Lord and Savior. Without a doubt, the Tribulation Period will be the greatest period of Christian persecution the world has ever known.

6:12 – 14: The sixth seal – catastrophe on earth – *the wrath of the Lamb!* (v.16) When the sixth seal is opened, the entire earth is violently shaken by a giant earthquake, the likes of which the world has never seen. As persecution of God's people by Antichrist begins, the Lord shows His displeasure. This judgment describes a physical shaking of the whole earth caused by earthquakes and volcanic eruptions. Such things have happened before. As the result of a volcanic eruption, ash has often blotted out the sun for hundreds of miles and caused the moon to appear red.

John also says, *"... the stars in the sky fell to earth, as late figs drop from a fig tree when shaken by a strong wind"* (v.13). This suggests that meteors will shower down from the sky.

In addition, *"The sky receded like a scroll, rolling up, and every mountain and island was removed from its place"* (v.14). All we can conclude is that this catastrophe will bring about widespread changes to the physical earth and atmosphere. The earthquakes that we see today in Haiti and elsewhere throughout the world *are not* a fulfillment – they merely demonstrate that these things can happen just as God's Word says it will. On the other hand, the apparent increase in earthquakes, wildfires, hurricanes and tornadoes, floods, and other naturally occurring disasters *does* represent a fulfillment of the Word of God. Jesus warned His disciples: *"Nation will rise against nation, and kingdom against kingdom. There will be famines and earthquakes in various places. All these are the beginning of birth pains"* (Matthew 24:7). The phrase, "the beginning of birth pains," simply means that they will become more intense and closer together as the time draws near. The increase in natural disasters that we are seeing today is not the result of some ideological belief in climate change – it is the Word of God!

6:15 – 17: *"Then the kings of the earth, the princes, the generals, the rich, the mighty, and every slave and every free man hid in caves and among the rocks of the mountains ...."* Great fear will come upon the unredeemed. As the result of their stubborn and rebellious ways, instead of turning to God in their hour of peril, they will hide in the rocks and dens of the earth. Folks need to understand that when you live a lifestyle in rejection of God, your heart eventually becomes hardened and fixed against God, just as Pharaoh's did during the time of the Exodus.

It seems evident from these verses that the world will know this is a judgment from the Lord Jesus Christ, for they refer to Him as, *"... him who sits on the throne and ... the Lamb"* (v.16).

Let's take to heart the words of King David: *"Be wise now therefore, O ye kings, be instructed, ye judges of the earth. Serve the Lord with fear, and rejoice with trembling. Kiss the Son, lest he be angry, and ye perish from the way, when his wrath is kindled but a little. Blessed are all they that put their trust in him"* (Psalm 2:10 – 12 KJV).

Review Questions

1) The event that triggers the Tribulation Period is _____

_____.

2) The rider on the white horse symbolizes _____.

3) The rider on the red horse symbolizes _____.

4) The rider on the black horse symbolizes _____.

5) The judgment resulting from the rider on the pale horse is _____

_____.

6) White robes are symbolic of _____.

7) Another name for the catastrophe on earth caused by the opening of the sixth seal is _____

_____.

Up For Discussion

The late pastor and author, J. Vernon McGee, stated the following: "But what about 'the wrath of the Lamb?' Wrath is strange and foreign even to the person of God, is it not? You see God loves the good, but God hates the evil. God does not hate as you and I hate. He is not vindictive. God is righteous. God is holy. And He hates that which is contrary to Himself."

The Apostle Paul wrote: *"The wrath of God is being revealed from heaven against all the godlessness and wickedness of men who suppress the truth by their wickedness"* (Romans 1:18).

Today, Christians worldwide seem to be increasingly under attack and ridiculed by the mainstream secular press and societal elites. Does the world or our nation reveal the wrath of God, or the judgment of God, as the Apostle Paul suggests above? Give some examples. One example might be the continued loss of religious freedoms for Christians in order to accommodate the needs of nonbelievers in an ever-growing "politically correct" or "woke" society.

Using the illustration, *Daniel's Seventy Sevens*, review on your own or begin classroom discussion by reading the Daniel passage in the top title block. Continue reading and discussing each block of the chart moving from left to right. For a complete analysis, see chapter 9 of my book, *Captivity to Eternity, DANIEL, God's Faithful Servant.*

Do more: Compare and contrast the six seal judgments with Christ's Olivet Discourse found in chapter 24 of Matthew.

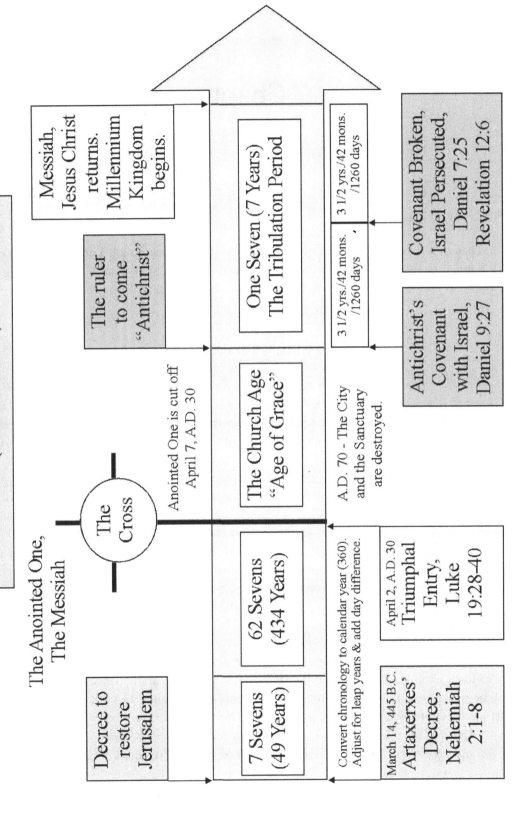

Daniel's "Seventy Sevens"
(Daniel 9:24-27)

The Anointed One, The Messiah

The Cross

Messiah, Jesus Christ returns. Millennium Kingdom begins.

The ruler to come "Antichrist"

One Seven (7 Years) The Tribulation Period

3 1/2 yrs./42 mons. /1260 days

3 1/2 yrs./42 mons. /1260 days

Covenant Broken, Israel Persecuted, Daniel 7:25 Revelation 12:6

Antichrist's Covenant with Israel, Daniel 9:27

Anointed One is cut off April 7, A.D. 30

The Church Age "Age of Grace"

A.D. 70 - The City and the Sanctuary are destroyed.

Decree to restore Jerusalem

62 Sevens (434 Years)

7 Sevens (49 Years)

Convert chronology to calendar year (360). Adjust for leap years & add day difference.

April 2, A.D. 30 Triumphal Entry, Luke 19:28-40

March 14, 445 B.C. Artaxerxes' Decree, Nehemiah 2:1-8

41

Chapter 7

Please follow along in your Bible.

This chapter represents an interlude between the sixth and seventh seal. The reason is to explain what will happen to those people who turn to God and receive Christ as their Savior during the 7-year Tribulation Period. We will refer to these newborn believers as Tribulation saints.

144,000 Sealed Servants

7:1 – 3: *"After this I saw four angels standing at the four corners of the earth, holding back the four winds of the earth to prevent any wind from blowing on the land or on the sea or on any tree. Then I saw another angel coming up from the east, having the seal of the living God …."* The work of angels in the book of Revelation reveals they are the special ministers of God. In this chapter we find that they supervise the administration of two things:

1) The angels control the winds of wrath (forces of nature) from the four corners of the earth. In other words, they halt God's judgment for a time. The expression, "the four corners of the earth," refers to the north, south, east, and west – meaning the entire earth.
2) Another angel (v.2) places a seal on the foreheads of the servants of our God (v.3) – the 144,000 Tribulation servants. This corresponds with the breaking of the fifth seal. Once the sealing angel finished his work, then the destroying angels were allowed to continue their execution of judgment, as we saw with the breaking of the sixth seal and the wrath of the Lamb.

7:4 – 8: The Bible is more easily understood if we simply accept God's Word at face value and do not try to force upon it any meaning other than that which it naturally conveys. Twelve thousand Jews will be sealed from twelve of the fourteen tribes of Israel, totaling 144,000. Recall, at the end of his life, Jacob adopted the two sons of Joseph: *"Now then, your two sons born to you in Egypt before I came to you here will be reckoned as mine; Ephraim and Manasseh will be mine, just as Reuben and Simeon are mine. Any children born to you after them will be yours …"* (Genesis 48:5, 6).

Verses 5 – 8 list the twelve tribes of Israel from which the Tribulation servants will be selected and sealed. It is believed that the tribes of Dan and Ephraim are omitted because of their worship of idols

(Judges 18:30 and Hosea 4:17). In some manner, these servants will have the seal of God on their forehead. It is not certain as to the composition of this seal, but the text suggests that it will be visible and for the purpose of protecting the 144,000 servants from any judgments as they evangelize the world during the Tribulation Period. The Holy Spirit will undoubtedly be present to empower the ministry of the 144,000. Concerning the day of the Lord and this time of tribulation, the Prophet Joel foretold that the outpouring of the Holy Spirit would be much the same as was experienced on the Day of Pentecost (Joel 2:28 – 32).

A Great Multitude in Heaven

7:9 – 10: *"After this I looked and there before me was a great multitude that no one could count, from every nation, tribe, people and language, standing before the throne and in front of the Lamb …."* The phrase, "after this" (after the sealing of the servants), simply means next chronologically as John's vision again shifts to heaven. Foremost in the mind of God is the salvation of souls. The Apostle Peter believed that when he wrote: *"He is patient with you, not wanting anyone to perish, but everyone to come to repentance"* (2 Peter 3:9). This great multitude that no one could count is a reference to those from every nation, language, and tribe of the world who will receive the Gospel of Jesus Christ as a result of the ministry of the 144,000 servants. In fact, it is believed by many NT scholars that more people will turn to Christ as Lord and Savior during the time of the Tribulation than have been saved during the entire Church Age. In other words, the 144,000 servants of the Tribulation Period will do in seven years what the Church has not done in nearly 2,000 years. The fact that this multitude stands before the throne and before the Lamb confirms they are redeemed from the earth, and their song indicates they are the recipients of personal salvation (v.10). The white robes, mentioned here again, represent the righteousness of Christ (Corinthians 5:21) and the palm branches (the Greek word *phoinix*, meaning palm trees) are signs of victory; both represent our victory in Christ.

7:11 – 12: We have heard time and again in church: *"I tell you that in the same way there will be more rejoicing in heaven over one sinner who repents than over ninety-nine righteous who do not need to repent"* (Luke 15:7). The angels continue their song of praise to God and the Lamb that they began back in chapter 5 while looking on and rejoicing over the multitudes who have been redeemed from the earth during this time of divine judgment.

7:13 – 14: The identity of this multitude is clearly spelled out; they are, *"… out of the great tribulation"* (v.14; cf. Matthew 24:21). That explains why John cannot identify any of them. The fact that these are believers is unquestionable because they have, *"… washed their robes and made them white in the blood of the Lamb"* (v.14).

The Prophet Isaiah wrote: *"How then can we be saved? All of us have become like one who is unclean, and all our righteous acts are like filthy rags …"* (Isaiah 64:5, 6). Here in verse 14, John gives us a beautiful picture of our personal acceptance of salvation. When a person is willing to come to God by the blood of His Son, acknowledging personal sin, then their filthy rags are cleansed by the blood of the Lamb, Jesus Christ, and that person is made righteous and white as snow.

7:15 – 17: Eternal rewards for this great multitude:

1) Verse 15: *"They are before the throne of God and serve him day and night in his temple ..."* This confirms what we already know – this multitude in John's vision is not the Church. The Church is never identified with the temple. As we will see later, the eternal home of the Church is the New Jerusalem, and there is no temple there. However, there will be a temple on the New Earth.

2) *"... he who sits on the throne will spread his tent over them."* This symbolizes God's eternal protection over this redeemed multitude.

3) Verse 16: Their every need will be supplied. They will evidently experience hunger and thirst during the Tribulation Period and will undergo extreme exposure to the elements, but their faith in the Savior will guarantee them entry into Christ's earthly kingdom where they will never suffer hardship again.

4) Verse 17: *"... God will wipe away every tear from their eyes."* It is possible to believe that this may also relate to God's omnipotent ability, for His children, to remove or clear our memories of unpleasant experiences in life, including loved-ones eternally lost (Psalm 34:16, Isaiah 65:17).

The most important decision a person will ever make in their life is whether he/she will accept God's wonderful gift of salvation and eternal life through faith in His Son, the Lord Jesus Christ. This multitude is permitted to stand before the throne of God, because by faith, they voluntarily washed their robes and made them white in the blood of the Lamb.

Review Questions

1) Those who turn to God and receive His Son Jesus Christ as Lord and Savior during the Tribulation Period are referred to as _____.

2) The angels holding back the four winds is a reference to the holding back of _____
_____.

3) The tribes of Dan and Ephraim were not included with the 144,000 servants because of _____
_____.

4) The purpose of sealing the 144,000 servants was to _____
_____.

5) The ministry of the 144,000 servants will be empowered by _____.

6) The great multitude in heaven is made up of _____
_____.

7) This multitude washed their robes and made them white in _____.

Up For Discussion

*"And I saw another angel ascending from the east, having the seal of the living God, and
he cried with a loud voice to the four angels … 'Hurt not the earth, neither the sea,
nor the trees, till we have sealed the servants of our God in their foreheads.'"*
(Revelation 7:2, 3 KJV)

The 144,000 Jewish servants are given the seal of God on their foreheads for the distinct purpose of protecting them from harm as they witness to the Gospel of Jesus Christ throughout the world and to all people during the 7-year Tribulation Period. They are protected against any harm resulting from the divine judgments that are coming upon the earth and from those on the earth who are in direct rebellion against God and His children.

The Apostle Paul wrote, *"Now it is God who makes both us and you stand firm in Christ. He anointed us, set his seal of ownership on us, and put his Spirit in our hearts as a deposit, guaranteeing what is to come"* (2 Corinthians 1:21, 22).

I strongly believe every Christian has a divine purpose in life. Could it be that once an individual turns their life over to Christ through faith, then God places this seal that the apostle mentioned on their forehead in order to protect them, physically and spiritually, until their divine purpose is fulfilled on earth? Discuss as a class.

Chapter 8

Please follow along in your Bible.

As we come to this section containing symbols, let us keep in mind that a symbol is a representation of a fact. When symbols are used in Scripture, the clues to their meaning are given as well. Scripture will supply the explanation. The Apostle Peter wrote: *"Knowing this first that no prophecy of the scripture is of any private interpretation"* (2 Peter 1:20). The book of Revelation is the last book in the Bible because a working knowledge of the sixty-five books preceding it is necessary for an understanding of its vivid language. The symbols are going to be given to us, but we need to understand the symbols stand for awesome realities to come.

8:1 – 2: *"When he opened the seventh seal, there was silence in heaven for about half an hour ...."* The pronoun "he" refers to the Lord Jesus Christ. The significance of the silence in heaven is twofold:

1) It is entirely opposite the usual sound patterns of heaven as seen in earlier chapters, sounds of great joy, praise, and worship.
2) It is a result of the revelation by Jesus Christ to the heavenly host concerning what is about to fall upon the earth. It is literally the calm before the storm.

The opening of the seventh seal introduces the seven trumpet judgments – judgments that are a direct action from the Lord Jesus Christ. The Lord directs all actions from heaven. Do not lose sight of the fact that the book of Revelation presents the Lord Jesus Christ in His glory as the Judge of all the earth. These judgments are so terrible the angels stand in awe. Each of the seven angels (v.2) is given a trumpet that will be blown in proper sequence, introducing a form of future judgment.

The late pastor and author, J. Vernon McGee, wrote: "As the trumpets of Israel were used at the battle of Jericho, so will the walls of this world's opposition to God crumble and fall during the Great Tribulation." What an insightful statement and an appropriate OT analogy for the condition of the world today.

8:3: The golden altar is the place where prayer is offered. Incense is likened to prayer and is a type of prayer. The psalmist wrote: *"May my prayer be set before you like incense; may the lifting up of my hands be like the evening sacrifice"* (Psalm 141:2).

8:4 – 6: *"The smoke of the incense, together with the prayers of the saints, went up before God from the angel's hands …."* This is a beautiful symbol which expresses the fact that God always hears our prayers and now those prayers are going to be answered by the Lord Jesus Christ. Recall from chapter 6, the OT saints and the martyred Tribulation saints under the altar sang, *"How long, Sovereign Lord, holy and true, until you judge the inhabitants of the earth and avenge our blood?"* (Revelation 6:10). Their prayerful song is symbolized here by the incense that ascends before God. The censer, filled with fire from the altar and hurled to earth (v.5) is also a symbol. It represents the answer to those prayers, and it comes in the form of the next set of judgments upon the earth – the trumpet judgments. The people on earth, who have rejected Christ's sacrificial death as payment for their sins, must now bear the judgments themselves.

In his vision, John saw peals of thunder and rumblings as the censer was hurled to the earth. These cosmic disturbances denote the approach of the coming storm of God's judgment. Additionally, John saw flashes of lightning which normally accompany thunder and an earthquake on the earth – all introducing the fact that the seven angels are about to sound their trumpets (v.6).

The Trumpet Judgments

One way to consider whether the trumpet judgments are literal or symbolic would be to study them in connection with the plagues of Egypt as described in chapters 7 – 11 of Exodus. There we see Moses performing the symbolic act of waving his staff over the waters of Egypt, which then literally turns the water into blood. Here we see an angel performing the symbolic act of blowing a trumpet thereby initiating a form of judgment upon the earth. It is interesting to note that five of the plagues of Egypt are repeated here in the book of Revelation.

8:7: The first trumpet: Hail and fire mixed with blood was hurled down upon the earth. Hail and fire are literal judgments that fall on one-third of the earth's surface, burning up all the trees and grass it rains down upon. The first worldwide judgment was the Flood; now it is going to be fire. This should not strike us as strange for such things have happened before: *"Then the Lord rained down burning sulfur on Sodom and Gomorrah – from the Lord out of heaven"* (Genesis 19:24). The hail and fire described here also parallel the seventh plague of Egypt (Exodus 9:18 – 26), and nearly every advocate of the Bible believes the plagues of Egypt to be true and literal. Nevertheless, this judgment will result in a third of the earth being burned up.

It is not certain what is meant by the phrase, "mixed with blood." However, the words of the prophet foretold of this horrific occurrence concerning the coming great and dreadful day of the Lord: *"I will show wonders in the heavens and on the earth, blood and fire and billows of smoke"* (Joel 2:30). At any given time, there could be hundreds of thousands of people traveling in planes and other aircraft around the globe. This blood may be the result of the hail and fire as it passes through our atmosphere destroying these aircraft and all aboard. Another suggestion might be ash and gases generated from the earthquake that contaminates the accompanying rain making it appear blood red. On the other hand, the blood may be symbolic and represent the immense suffering of mankind as a result of these judgments from God.

8:8 – 9: The second trumpet: John says that he saw, *"… something like a huge mountain, all ablaze thrown into the sea."* This may refer to a giant, burning meteorite; however, we do not know for certain. Whatever this mass is, its impact will result in turning one-third of the sea to blood, killing one-third of the creatures living in the sea, and destroying one-third of the ships (v.9) – that fact John makes very clear.

8:10 – 11: The third trumpet: A great, blazing star fell from the sky on a third of the rivers and springs of water. This great star is literal and may be another meteor or even a comet, since it is described as blazing like a torch. Perhaps it will disintegrate as it enters the earth's atmosphere, scattering poisonous matter over the globe contaminating one-third of the earth's fresh water supply. This divine judgment will embitter great rivers causing those dependent on them to die. Its name is *Wormwood* (v.11), for God created all the stars and named them (cf. Job 9:9). Wormwood is a name used as a metaphor in the OT in the following ways:

1) The idolatry of Israel (Deuteronomy 29:18 KJV).
2) As calamity and sorrow (Jeremiah 9:15, 23:15; Lamentations 3:15, 19 KJV).
3) As false judgment (Amos 5:7 KJV).

8:12: The fourth trumpet: *"… a third of the sun was struck, a third of the moon, and a third of the stars, so that a third of them turned dark …."* This judgment deals with the celestial bodies as they illuminate the earth. The same God that created the light in the first chapter of Genesis is also able to diminish it by one-third. This corresponds to the ninth plague of Egypt (Exodus 10:21 – 23). Again the prophet foretold this: *"The sun will be turned to darkness and the moon to blood before the coming of the great and dreadful day of the Lord"* (Joel 2:31). Jesus warned His disciples likewise concerning His coming and the end of the age: *"Immediately after the distress of those days, the sun will be darkened, and the moon will not give its light; the stars will fall from the sky, and the heavenly bodies will be shaken"* (Matthew 24:29). Jesus also foretold: *"There will be signs in the sun, moon, and stars. On the earth, nations will be in anguish and perplexity at the roaring and tossing of the sea. Men will faint from terror, apprehensive of what is coming on the earth, for the heavenly bodies will be shaken"* (Luke 21:25, 26).

8:13: As John continued to look on, he heard an eagle, *"… call out in a loud voice: 'Woe! Woe! Woe to the inhabitants of the earth ….'"* Is this literally an eagle (NIV) speaking, or is this an angelic being of the heavenly order, as translated by the KJV, making this loud proclamation? I suspect that it is more likely an angel; however, if God made the donkey of the Moabite prophet Balaam speak (Numbers 22:28 – 30), then I believe God would have no problem enabling an eagle to speak as well. This verse introduces the three woes of the book of Revelation. As horrific as the first four trumpet judgments were; they apparently will be surpassed in misery by the woe judgments to follow. The rebellion of human beings against God strangely gets progressively worse. The first and second woes of the Tribulation Period are actually the fifth and sixth trumpet judgments, beginning our study in the next chapter. The third woe coincides with the seventh trumpet judgment at the mid-point of the Tribulation Period.

It is interesting to note that the Lord used the eagle to speak of His Second Coming – referring to the carnage following the great battle of Armageddon (Matthew 24:27, 28 KJV).

Review Questions

1) All judgments are the direct action from _____.

2) The incense is symbolic of _____.

3) The censer filled with fire from the altar and hurled to earth is symbolic of _____

   _____.

4) The first trumpet judgment of hail, fire, and blood does what? _____

   _____.

5) The second trumpet judgment of a huge, blazing mass falling into the sea causes what? _____

   _____

   _____.

6) The third trumpet judgment of another giant, poisonous mass striking the earth results in what?

   _____.

7) The fourth trumpet judgment did what? _____

   _____.

Up For Discussion

"And I saw the seven angels which stood before God,
and to them were given seven trumpets."
(Revelation 8:2 KJV)

As John's vision of heaven continued from the previous chapter, we interpreted the different elements in verses 3 – 6 symbolically and pointed to the Psalms for reference. However, when John's vision shifted back to earth, we took a more literal interpretation of the judgments described in verses 7 – 13.

Recall the first rule of interpretation from our introduction: When the plain sense of Scripture makes common sense, seek no other sense; therefore, take every word at its usual and literal meaning unless the facts of the immediate text clearly indicate otherwise. Thus far in our study, do you think that our analysis is proper, and as such, giving you a clearer understanding of the book of Revelation? Can you point to anything specifically that stands out as a new-found revelation in this study of God's Word? How might our analysis contrast with other interpretations you may have read or studied previously?

Chapter 9

Please follow along in your Bible.

We are moving into a section of our study that is very strange and wild, and admittedly difficult to interpret. However, let us continue with our rule of following the literal line even though the figures presented are the most vivid and wild. If another interpretation is in order, then John will supply the explanation.

The Fifth and Sixth Trumpet Judgments

9:1: The fifth trumpet – the first woe: *"The fifth angel sounded his trumpet and I saw a star that had fallen from the sky to the earth. The star was given the key to the shaft of the Abyss."* The use of the word "star" in this verse is obviously intended figuratively rather than literally, for the star is referred to as "he" (v.2), hence clearly having personality. I have studied this passage extensively and still cannot be certain as to the identity of this being. There seems to be two possible explanations adopted by most commentators:

1) Some indicate that at this point in the tribulation, an angel is given this key. This would coincide with events we find at the end of the Tribulation Period, that of an angel coming down from heaven, *"... having the key to the Abyss and holding in his hand a great chain"* (Revelation 20:1). In other words, this angel retains the key during the Tribulation Period and is given the enormous responsibility of controlling the awful demonic forces to be released from the shaft of the Abyss. His location in heaven indicates that he is a good angel, for fallen angels do not reside in heaven.

2) Others identify this star as Satan because of the phrase, "star that had fallen from the sky." They see this as the fulfillment of the words of the Prophet Isaiah: *"How you have fallen from heaven, O morning star, son of the dawn! You have been cast down to earth, you who once laid low the nations!"* (Isaiah 14:12). In our NT, the Lord Jesus stated likewise: *"I saw Satan fall like lightning from heaven"* (Luke 10:18).

Although both explanations seem quite opposite of one another, I lean towards the first interpretation for the following three reasons:

1) The events of the book of Revelation are unfolding chronologically (for the most part). As such, Satan cannot be the star that falls from heaven at this point in the Tribulation Period because we will see shortly that it is at the mid-point of the Tribulation Period when Satan, the great dragon, is hurled to earth (12:9).

2) Recall from chapter 1 (v.18) that Jesus holds the keys to death and Hades and that they were purchased with His precious blood. Assuming Hades and the Abyss to be closely related, it is not my opinion that Christ would entrust the key to Satan.

3) In the above mentioned reference to Revelation 20:1, I must give emphasis to the word "having." This angel already has the key. If Satan had the key, then I do not believe he would voluntarily turn it over to a good angel so that the angel could, in turn, imprison him with it. Whoever this being is, he is given a key which denotes power and authority – and this is given from the Lord Jesus Christ.

The Abyss, or bottomless pit (KJV), represents the extreme, remote opposite of heaven. Originally, the term referred to a deep mass of water and was associated with the water in the creation story (Genesis 1:2). In the NT, its meaning has been broadened to refer to the literal place of confinement for evil spirits (fallen angels/demons) until their day of judgment (Luke 8:30 – 31, 2 Peter 2:4, and Jude 6). Furthermore, the term Abyss has become synonymous with hell or *Hades* (the Greek word translated from the OT Hebrew word *Sheol*) and defined as the present abode of all wicked/unsaved spirits. Our Lord taught that, in Hades, there exists a great chasm or gulf which separates the place of torment from the place of comfort (Luke 16:19 – 31). In His parable, Jesus explained, *"In hell, where he was in torment, he looked up and saw Abraham far away …"* (Luke 16:23). These words, again, illustrate the deep remoteness of the abyss of hell. Though its precise meaning is uncertain, there are other commentators that believe the Abyss to simply be the great chasm – that is, the deep shaft leading downwards to Hades as mentioned here in verse 1. (See, *Hades Illustration*, at the end of this chapter)

9:2 – 10: When the Abyss was opened, smoke rose from it until the air was filled with a smog-like condition worse than any metropolitan area today has ever experienced. Out of this smog came locust-like, scorpion creatures that have no counterpart in all history. They are called locusts but are in some way likened to a horse. They have faces like men, hair like women, teeth as lions, and breastplates of iron. Their wings are as, *"… the thundering of many horses and chariots rushing into battle"* (v.9) and they possess stingers in their tails as do scorpions. These locusts are to be interpreted spiritually, for they depict a demonic creature (from the spiritual realm) able to inflict physical torture on unrepentant mankind, though they are beyond our human comprehension.

Unlike any kind of locust that has existed before, they are not going to harm the vegetation. They wore crowns, which indicate a power or authority, and the power given to them is to harm unsaved human beings, *"… those people who do not have the seal of God on their forehead"* (v.4). They do not have the authority to kill; they will only torment them, and for only five months. This torment is described as, *"… the sting of a scorpion when it strikes a man"* (v.5). The pain will be so intense, producing unimaginable agony and suffering, that, *"… men will seek death, but will not find it; they will long to die, but death will elude them"* (v.6). The power of God over the spirit world will protect believers from these demonic creatures. Just as God protected the children of Israel in the land of Goshen from the plagues of Egypt, so He will also protect His children (the 144,000 Jewish servants and all believers) during the Tribulation Period. The Lord Jesus told His disciples: *"He who stands firm to the end will be saved"* (Matthew 24:13). So far, martyrdom (6:9) is the only means by which believers, i.e., Tribulation saints will die during this period.

9:11 – 12: The leading demonic angel of these evil spirits from out of the pit of the Abyss is, in the Hebrew *Abaddon* which means "destruction," and in the Greek *Apollyon* which means "the destroyer." He is a very powerful fallen angel – a demon that assists Satan in his evil spirit kingdom. He may well be comparable in Satan's kingdom to the archangel Michael in God's heavenly host.

9:13 – 15: The sixth trumpet – the second woe: The sixth trumpet judgment reveals another army of demonic creatures to be unleashed on unrepentant mankind. This time the judgment is far more severe because these demonic spirits are not only able to inflict pain on people, but also physical death.

At the blowing of the sixth trumpet, John heard the voice of the Lord, *"… coming from the horns of the golden altar before God"* (v.13) and He said, *"Release the four angels who are bound at the great river Euphrates"* (v.14). The fact these angels are bound indicates that they are evil; in other words, they are fallen angels – demons. Apparently, their purpose is to wreak havoc on mankind, but they have been bound by God until their specified time has arrived. Now, they will be, *"… released to kill a third of mankind"* (v.15). The very hour is even marked out.

No doubt the Euphrates River is the most prominent river referenced in the Bible, and the importance of its surrounding area in Scripture cannot be overlooked. This river formed one of the boundaries of the Garden of Eden, and was also a boundary for ancient Israel. The sin of man began here. The first murder was committed here. Here is where the Flood began and spread over the entire world. The tower of Babel was erected here. It was to this area that the Israelites were exiled during the Babylonian captivity. The Euphrates River and its surrounding area have been used throughout Scripture as a symbol of Israel's enemies. Lastly, it is here, according to chapter 18 of our study, that the ancient city of Babylon will be rebuilt and become headquarters of the commercial and governmental activities of the world under the rule of the end-times Antichrist. In Zechariah (5:5 – 11), the prophet describes Babylon as the last stand of false religion.

9:16 – 19: A demonic army of two hundred million would be a dreadful host to confront mankind. These four demonic angels seem to be the leaders of these evil spirits, riding on horse-like creatures, having heads of lions, and emitting fire, smoke, and sulfur. They have tails, *"… like snakes, having heads with which they inflict injury"* (v.19). Their power comes from their mouths and their tails. These horsemen are not to be taken as human, but literally as evil, demonic spirits. What John sees and is attempting to describe in these verses is an all out invasion of the earth by the demonic world, which is a further result of opening the door to the shaft of the Abyss (cf. Luke 8:30, 31). The underworld is now bringing war to mankind, and these creatures from the Abyss are unnatural, terrifying, and very real.

At this point, another one-third of the world's unrepentant population is killed. Remember that one-fourth of the world's population has already been slain as a result of the fourth seal judgment.

It seems as if the purpose of this judgment, like the preceding one, is to rid the earth of those who will never trust in the Lord Jesus Christ and receive God's gift of salvation through faith in His Son as their Savior. Over one-half of the population of the earth will be destroyed during the Tribulation Period. No wonder our Lord Jesus told His disciples: *"If those days had not been cut short, no one would survive …"* (Matthew 24:22).

9:20 – 21: *"The rest of mankind that were not killed by these plagues still did not repent of the work of their hands …."* Instead of turning to God during the Tribulation Period, mankind will turn in rebellion away from God to indulge the pleasures of the flesh, and in so doing, condemn their depraved and wicked souls for eternity. These are the same sins that keep people from coming to God today:

1) **Worshiping demons and idols**. Mankind will never be truly happy unless they have communion with God. Since the days of Nimrod, Satan has used idolatry to deceive and lead men away from a relationship with the one, true God in heaven.
2) **Committing murder**. Wherever the influence of the Gospel is unknown, human life is cheap; thus, violence and murder will become common practice during the Tribulation Period.
3) **Practicing magic arts**. The KJV uses the term "sorceries." The Greek word is *pharmakeia*, from which we get our English word pharmacy. Pharmacy means drugs, which suggests there will be widespread use of drugs for any and all purposes, most specifically evil. In fact, the use of drugs most likely will not be controlled and may even play a large role in the apostate religion of the times. As a result, drug addiction will flourish. Sorceries are also a linked reference to witchcraft and the occult, all of which are in opposition to the Word of God.
4) **Sexual immorality**. Even during the Tribulation Period, when the world is in a state of chaos, sexual promiscuity will continue to thrive worldwide as a destructive force spreading disease, corrupting souls, and destroying lives.
5) **Committing robbery**. This larceny substantiates the lawlessness that will abound during the Tribulation Period. Godless thugs at every level of society will openly rob, cheat, and steal monetary funds and other material possessions by any means possible.

The Tribulation Period will be a time when people give in to the fulfillment of the desires and lust of the flesh. Unrepentant mankind will turn further and further from God and will resort to anything and everything that will deaden the pain and lift them out of the trouble of that time. Please understand this: The moment you reject the Gospel and shut your heart to God, you make yourself wide open for the big lie when it comes. The Apostle Paul, when writing about the man of lawlessness (the end-times Antichrist), wrote: *"For this reason God sends them a powerful delusion so that they will believe the lie and so that all will be condemned who have not believed the truth but have delighted in wickedness"* (2 Thessalonians 2:11 – 12). Someone once said that those who stand for nothing will fall for anything. Anyone today who is not standing for the Word of God is easy prey to the dangerous deceptions of false teachers, false doctrines, and the occult.

Therefore, it will be during the Tribulation Period, just as it is today:
"Be not deceived; God is not mocked: for whatsoever a
man soweth, that shall he also reap."
(Galatians 6:7 KJV)

Review Questions

1) We reasoned that the star of verse 1 is _____

   _____.

2) In the NT, the term "Abyss" has become synonymous with _____ and is defined
   as _____.

3) The fifth trumpet (the first woe) consists of a swarm of locust-like scorpion creatures that have
   the power to _____.

4) The demonic leading angel of the Abyss is _____.

5) The four angels at the river Euphrates are bound because _____

   _____.

6) What prominent ancient city was located on the shores of this river? _____.

7) The sixth trumpet (the second woe) was made up of an army of evil-spirit horses and riders that
   did what? _____.

Up For Discussion

*"And they had hair as the hair of women, and their teeth were as the teeth of lions.
And they had breastplates, as it were breastplates of iron; and the sound of their
wings was as the sound of chariots of many horses running into battle."*
(Revelation 9:8, 9 KJV)

Many earnest Christians attempt to read the book of Revelation, but end up concluding that it is much too difficult to understand or impossible to interpret. One problem is that many of these well-intended Christians have not read or studied the entirety of God's Word and thereby do not have a working knowledge of the other sixty-five preceding books. Another problem may simply be that they do not believe what they are reading. If they would simply read it and accept it as God's Word, then it might become easier to understand.

Why is it that a number of us have no problem believing some visions found in Scripture, e.g., those that John and Isaiah had of God's throne in heaven (4:2 – 11; Isaiah 6:1 – 3), but here in this chapter of Revelation, have great difficulty believing visions and descriptions of demons? Isn't our entire Bible the infallible, inerrant Word of God? Of course, it is!

Review the *Hades Illustration*, either on your own or aloud in class. Discuss each block, going from left to right, and read the Scripture references associated with each.

Hades Illustration
Before and After the Cross

HEAVEN "Paradise"

"Today you will be with Me in Paradise." Luke 23:43

"We are confident, I say, and would prefer to be away from the body and at home with the Lord."
2 Corinthians 5:8

Ephesians 4:8-10

The Cross

Matthew 12:40

Empty

*Abyss [shaft of] or Bottomless Pit

Unrighteous
"Darkness"
"Weeping and Gnashing of Teeth"

Great Chasm or Gulf

Hades: In the New Testament, Christ emptied the "righteous" side. Today, only the "wicked" side remains and still receives the souls and spirits of the unrighteous.
Matthew 8:12, 25:30
*Luke 8:31; *Revelation 9:1, 20:1-3

Wicked Side
"Hell"
"Torment"
"Fire"

Great Chasm or Gulf

Righteous Side
"Comfort"
"Abraham's Bosom"

Sheol: In the Old Testament, this was the place made up of two compartments where the souls and spirits of the dead went before Christ's death.
Luke 16:22-26

55

Chapter 10

Please follow along in your Bible.

Chapter 10 and the first fourteen verses of chapter 11 represent another interlude in our study – that is, an intermission or pause in the Revelation chronology. This time it occurs between the sixth and seventh trumpets. Recall that chapter 7 was an interlude between the sixth and seventh seal judgments. In these verses, we will be introduced to three distinctively divine servants of the Tribulation.

The Mighty Angel

10:1: *"Then I saw another mighty angel coming down from heaven ...."* Who is this mighty angel? The identity of this mighty angel has been debated, and I have read of many who believe him to be the Lord Jesus Christ. It is true that in the OT, the pre-incarnate Christ, on occasions, was referred to as the *Angel of the Lord* (Genesis 22:11, 15 – 18 NKJV). However, the Lord Jesus Christ does not appear in the book of Revelation, or elsewhere in the NT, as an angel. An angel is a created being and our Lord Jesus Christ is the Creator (John 1:3). Ever since Jesus took on flesh, died for the sins of all mankind, was crucified, rose from the dead, and ascended into heaven, He has always appeared as the Son of God in all His deity. More importantly, in the book of Revelation, Jesus is revealed as the glorified Christ. Let's remember that this book is the unveiling of Jesus Christ (1:1). This is not the first time we have been introduced to a mighty angel, for in chapter 5 (v.2) we saw the same term used; in fact, John says he saw another mighty angel. Angels do, however, play a prominent role in the book of Revelation, always in a position of service. They do not create things but fulfill the administration of God in human affairs.

Do not be deceived by the glorious description of this angel. Although this angel possesses some God-like characteristics, he is not God. His description as being robed in a cloud suggests an attire characteristic of the glory associated with the Second Coming of Christ. A rainbow above his head would be his halo and is a reminder of God's covenant with man. The phrase, "his face was like the sun," reminds us of Moses' face, and how it shone after he had been in the presence of God (Exodus 34:29). This angel's face is shining because he has just come from the presence of Christ. Lastly, his legs, described as fiery pillars, indicate that he has come to make an awesome and grave announcement of coming judgment.

The Little Scroll

10:2 – 3: The angel was, *"… holding a little scroll, which lay open in his hands"* (v.2). In chapter 5 (v.1), I suggested that the seven-sealed scroll likely represents the Book of Judgment for the earth. Here, I believe that the little scroll in the hand of this mighty angel and the seven-seal scroll from chapter 5 are one and the same. Of course, the scroll appears little in the hands of this mighty angel. The scroll contains the judgments of the Tribulation Period through which the Lord Jesus is coming to power. The book is now open, and the judgments are in force. The scroll was originally in the hand of God the Father. He gave it to His Son, the Lord Jesus Christ who, as we saw, was the only one worthy to open it. John says that the scroll lay open in the angel's hand, thus reinforcing the fact that Jesus has removed the seals. The Lord then handed the opened scroll to the mighty angel, who brings it to earth to finally give to John.

The fact that this mighty angel stands with, *"… his right foot in the sea and his left foot on the land …"* (v.2), indicates that he has authority for claiming both the sea and the earth for Christ. Now, with the scroll opened in hand, the mighty angel in, *"… a loud shout like the roar of a lion …"* (v.3), claims all for Christ. The kingdom of this world will become the kingdom of the Lord Jesus Christ through judgment. As Creator and Redeemer, the world belongs to Him.

The seven thunders here are the voices of God. In Psalm 29, the voice of the Lord occurs seven times (vv.3 – 9). The psalmist spoke of thunder as being the voice of the Lord (Psalm 29:3), the God of glory. Here is God's acknowledgement of this mighty angel's claim.

10:4: John was preparing to write down what these thunderous voices said since apparently what he heard was literally spoken words. However, he was forbidden to do so. John then heard the voice of the Lord Jesus from heaven saying, *"Seal up what the seven thunders have said and do not write it down."* This is the only proclamation in the entire book of Revelation that is sealed up. Although Jesus Christ is being revealed in this book, there are still some things that God is waiting to tell us according to His timing.

10:5 – 6: *"Then the angel … raised his right hand to heaven. And he swore by Him who lives for ever and ever, who created the heavens and all that is in them, the earth and all that is in it, and the sea and all that is in it …."* These words are proof that this mighty angel is not the Lord Jesus Christ. He is making an oath by the only sure guarantee – that is, Christ Himself. Jesus Christ is the eternal God and the Creator. The apostle wrote: *"Through Him all things were made; without Him nothing was made that has been made"* (John 1:3). The Apostle Paul wrote in even greater detail about our Creator Jesus Christ (see, Colossians 1:16).

"There will be no more delay!" (v.6) Mankind has been living in the time of God's delay for centuries. This angel now warns those who have rejected Him that God is about to conclude His patience in the face of their rebellion. The angel is also informing God's saints on earth that it will not be long until Christ returns.

10:7: *"But in the days when the seventh angel is about to sound his trumpet, the mystery of God will be accomplished, just as he announced to his servants the prophets."* What is this mystery of God? The word "mystery" appears several times in the Bible, meaning that God is going to disclose a truth only possible to know through His Word. Human wisdom has never comprehended nor will ever be able to understand these truths apart from the Word of God. The mystery referenced here can only mean salvation through faith in God's Messiah, the Lord Jesus Christ. One of the characteristics of salvation involves the mystery of how a holy God could love sinful human beings so much as to send His only Son into the world to die for their sins. Paul wrote extensively about this same mystery in his letters to the early church. He revealed two truths. First, Paul proclaimed the Gospel, which was given directly to him by the Lord Jesus Christ (Galatians 1:11, 12). Secondly, Paul taught that the Gentiles, as well as the remnant of Israel, would share in the glorious riches and inheritance of the kingdom of God (cf. Romans 16:25, 26; Ephesians 3:6; Colossians 1:26 – 28; Colossians 2:2, 3). Though Paul was writing concerning the Church, these same truths will continue into and, as John says, will be accomplished during the Tribulation Period. God's gift of salvation will be available through and up to the last day of the dreadful Tribulation Period to all who turn to Christ in faith as their Lord and Savior.

10:8: Then the voice of the Lord Jesus Christ commands John to take the opened scroll from the hand of the mighty angel. Keep in mind that the scene is now on earth.

10:9 – 10: After asking for the scroll, the angel tells John: *"Take it and eat it …"* (v.9). The meaning of this expression is symbolic in that it refers to eating the Word of God. In other words, before someone can be a spokesman for God, he must first mentally feed on or digest the Word of God and receive it in faith. The Prophet Jeremiah used this analogy while speaking to the Lord: *"When your words came I ate them; they were my joy and my heart's delight, for I bear your name, O Lord God Almighty"* (Jeremiah 15:16). The Prophet Ezekiel used the same analogy of eating the scroll before speaking to the house of Israel (Ezekiel 3:1 – 4). In the wonderful Psalm 119, which glorifies the Word of God, the psalmist wrote: *"How sweet your words are to my taste, sweeter than honey to my mouth!"* (Psalm 119:103) The sweetness comes to John in the predictions concerning our blessed Lord's return – the future is sweet. The bitterness comes to John when confronted by the fact that judgment is pronounced and coming upon the wicked and rebellious world during this dreadful time of God's wrath.

10:11: After John had eaten the scroll, the mighty angel says to him: *"You must prophesy again about many peoples, nations, languages and kings."* Through the written Word of God, which includes John's Gospel, his three epistles, and his Revelation (of Jesus Christ), this command to the apostle is being fulfilled today. Many peoples, nations, languages and kings are indeed studying the Word of God. After all, the Bible is the number one best-selling book of all time! There is much prophecy to follow; and the entire world needs to be warned that judgment is coming.

The Gospel of Jesus Christ is much like the little scroll as follows:

1) It is sweet to those who hear it and respond, thus being guaranteed salvation and eternal life as the free gift of God.
2) It is bitter to those who reject it, for them it guarantees judgment and eternal separation from God.

Review Questions

1) In the OT, the pre-incarnate Christ was referred to as _____.

2) In the NT, Christ has always appeared as _____.

3) Angels always play a prominent role in the position of _____.

4) The seven thunders are symbolic of _____.

5) The mystery of God refers to _____

_____.

6) The meaning of the phrase, "take it and eat it," regarding the scroll, is symbolic of _____

_____.

7) How is the Gospel of Jesus Christ like the little scroll? _____

_____.

Up For Discussion

"Till I come, give attendance to reading, to exhortation, to doctrine."
"Meditate upon these things; give thyself wholly to them;
that thy profiting may appear to all."
(1 Timothy 4:13, 15 KJV)

A one-year Bible Reading Calendar, comprised of four quarter pages, is included as the remaining pages of this chapter. Are you currently engaged in a tradition of reading the Word of God daily? If so, how has it impacted your life and your daily Christian walk? Why is it important for all believers to read and study God's Word daily?

Do more: Make a commitment to read God's Word daily:

1) Purchase a Study Bible with commentary in a version you are comfortable reading.
2) Purchase a complete Bible commentary that is easy for you to read and understand.
3) Purchase a Bible Dictionary – some are even illustrated.
4) Purchase a complete Concordance – those in your Bible are usually not complete.
5) Lastly, copy and share our Bible Reading Calendar with others and make it a part of your ministry!

Bible Reading Calendar

JANUARY

Date	Morning	Evening	Date	Morning	Evening
1	Gen. 1, 2	Matt. 1	17	Gen. 41	Matt. 13:1-32
2	Gen. 3, 4, 5	Matt. 2	18	Gen. 42, 43	Matt. 13:33-58
3	Gen. 6, 7, 8	Matt. 3	19	Gen. 44, 45	Matt. 14:1-21
4	Gen. 9, 10, 11	Matt. 4	20	Gen. 46, 47, 48	Matt. 14:22-36
5	Gen. 12, 13, 14	Matt. 5:1-26	21	Gen. 49, 50	Matt. 15:1-20
6	Gen. 15, 16, 17	Matt. 5:27-48	22	Exod. 1, 2, 3	Matt. 15:21-39
7	Gen. 18, 19	Matt. 6	23	Exod. 4, 5, 6	Matt. 16
8	Gen. 20, 21, 22	Matt. 7	24	Exod. 7, 8	Matt. 17
9	Gen. 23, 24	Matt. 8	25	Exod. 9, 10	Matt. 18:1-20
10	Gen. 25, 26	Matt. 9:1-17	26	Exod. 11, 12	Matt. 18:21-35
11	Gen. 27, 28	Matt. 9:18-38	27	Exod. 13, 14, 15	Matt. 19:1-15
12	Gen. 29, 30	Matt. 10:1-23	28	Exod. 16, 17, 18	Matt. 19:16-30
13	Gen. 31, 32	Matt. 10:24-42	29	Exod. 19, 20, 21	Matt. 20:1-16
14	Gen. 33, 34, 35	Matt. 11	30	Exod. 22, 23, 24	Matt. 20:17-34
15	Gen. 36, 37	Matt. 12:1-21	31	Exod. 25, 26	Matt. 21:1-22
16	Gen. 38, 39, 40	Matt. 12:22-50			

FEBRUARY

Date	Morning	Evening	Date	Morning	Evening
1	Exod. 27, 28	Matt. 21:23-46	17	Lev. 24, 25	Mark 1:23-45
2	Exod. 29, 30	Matt. 22:1-22	18	Lev. 26, 27	Mark 2
3	Exod. 31, 32, 33	Matt. 22:23-46	19	Num. 1, 2	Mark 3:1-21
4	Exod. 34, 35, 36	Matt. 23:1-22	20	Num. 3, 4	Mark 3:22-35
5	Exod. 37, 38	Matt. 23:23-39	21	Num. 5, 6	Mark 4:1-20
6	Exod. 39, 40	Matt. 24:1-22	22	Num. 7	Mark 4:21-41
7	Lev. 1, 2, 3	Matt. 24:23-51	23	Num. 8, 9, 10	Mark 5:1-20
8	Lev. 4, 5, 6	Matt. 25:1-30	24	Num. 11, 12, 13	Mark 5:21-43
9	Lev. 7, 8, 9	Matt. 25:31-46	25	Num. 14, 15	Mark 6:1-32
10	Lev. 10, 11, 12	Matt. 26:1-19	26	Num. 16, 17	Mark 6:33-56
11	Lev. 13	Matt. 26:20-54	27	Num. 18, 19, 20	Mark 7:1-13
12	Lev. 14, 15	Matt. 26:55-75	28	Num. 21, 22	Mark 7:14-37
13	Lev. 16, 17	Matt. 27:1-31	29	Num. 23, 24, 25	Mark 8:1-21
14	Lev. 18, 19	Matt. 27:32-66	Divide chapters for February 29 and read them		
15	Lev. 20, 21	Matt. 28	February 28 and March 1		
16	Lev. 22, 23	Mark 1:1-22	when February has only 28 days.		

MARCH

Date	Morning	Evening	Date	Morning	Evening
1	Num. 26, 27	Mark 8:22-38	17	Deut. 29, 30	Mark 16
2	Num. 28, 29	Mark 9:1-29	18	Deut. 31, 32	Luke 1:1-23
3	Num. 30, 31	Mark 9:30-50	19	Deut. 33, 34	Luke 1:24-56
4	Num. 32, 33	Mark 10:1-31	20	Joshua 1, 2, 3	Luke 1:57-80
5	Num. 34, 35, 36	Mark 10:32-52	21	Joshua 4, 5, 6	Luke 2:1-24
6	Deut. 1, 2	Mark 11:1-19	22	Joshua 7, 8	Luke 2:25-52
7	Deut. 3, 4	Mark 11:20-33	23	Joshua 9, 10	Luke 3
8	Deut. 5, 6, 7	Mark 12:1-27	24	Joshua 11, 12, 13	Luke 4:1-32
9	Deut. 8, 9, 10	Mark 12:28-44	25	Joshua 14, 15	Luke 4:33-44
10	Deut. 11, 12, 13	Mark 13:1-13	26	Joshua 16, 17, 18	Luke 5:1-16
11	Deut. 14, 15, 16	Mark 13:14-37	27	Joshua 19, 20	Luke 5:17-39
12	Deut. 17, 18, 19	Mark 14:1-25	28	Joshua 21, 22	Luke 6:1-26
13	Deut. 20, 21, 22	Mark 14:26-50	29	Joshua 23, 24	Luke 6:27-49
14	Deut. 23, 24, 25	Mark 14:51-72	30	Judges 1, 2	Luke 7:1-30
15	Deut. 26, 27	Mark 15:1-26	31	Judges 3, 4, 5	Luke 7:31-50
16	Deut. 28	Mark 15:27-47			

"Till I come, give attendance to reading, to exhortation, to doctrine."
1 Timothy 4:13

APRIL

Date	Morning	Evening	Date	Morning	Evening
1	Judges 6, 7	Luke 8:1-21	17	I Sam. 22, 23, 24	Luke 16:1-18
2	Judges 8, 9	Luke 8:22-56	18	I Sam. 25, 26	Luke 16:19-31
3	Judges 10, 11	Luke 9:1-36	19	I Sam. 27, 28, 29	Luke 17:1-19
4	Judges 12, 13, 14	Luke 9:37-62	20	I Sam. 30, 31	Luke 17:20-37
5	Judges 15, 16, 17	Luke 10:1-24	21	II Sam. 1, 2, 3	Luke 18:1-17
6	Judges 18, 19	Luke 10:25-42	22	II Sam. 4, 5, 6	Luke 18:18-43
7	Judges 20, 21	Luke 11:1-28	23	II Sam. 7, 8, 9	Luke 19:1-28
8	Ruth 1, 2, 3, 4	Luke 11:29-54	24	II Sam. 10, 11, 12	Luke 19:29-48
9	I Sam. 1, 2, 3	Luke 12:1-34	25	II Sam. 13, 14	Luke 20:1-26
10	I Sam. 4, 5, 6	Luke 12:35-59	26	II Sam. 15, 16	Luke 20:27-47
11	I Sam. 7, 8, 9	Luke 13:1-21	27	II Sam. 17, 18	Luke 21:1-19
12	I Sam. 10, 11, 12	Luke 13:22-35	28	II Sam. 19, 20	Luke 21:20-38
13	I Sam. 13, 14	Luke 14:1-24	29	II Sam. 21, 22	Luke 22:1-30
14	I Sam. 15, 16	Luke 14:25-35	30	II Sam. 23, 24	Luke 22:31-53
15	I Sam. 17, 18	Luke 15:1-10			
16	I Sam. 19, 20, 21	Luke 15:11-32			

MAY

Date	Morning	Evening	Date	Morning	Evening
1	I Kings 1, 2	Luke 22:54-71	17	II Kings 18, 19	John 6:22-44
2	I Kings 3, 4, 5	Luke 23:1-26	18	II Kings 20, 21, 22	John 6:45-71
3	I Kings 6, 7	Luke 23:27-38	19	II Kings 23, 24, 25	John 7:1-31
4	I Kings 8, 9	Luke 23:39-56	20	I Chron. 1, 2	John 7:32-53
5	I Kings 10, 11	Luke 24:1-35	21	I Chron. 3, 4, 5	John 8:1-20
6	I Kings 12, 13	Luke 24:36-53	22	I Chron. 6, 7	John 8:21-36
7	I Kings 14, 15	John 1:1-28	23	I Chron. 8, 9, 10	John 8:37-59
8	I Kings 16, 17, 18	John 1:29-51	24	I Chron. 11, 12, 13	John 9:1-23
9	I Kings 19, 20	John 2	25	I Chron. 14, 15, 16	John 9:24-41
10	I Kings 21, 22	John 3:1-21	26	I Chron. 17, 18, 19	John 10:1-21
11	II Kings 1, 2, 3	John 3:22-36	27	I Chron. 20, 21, 22	John 10:22-42
12	II Kings 4, 5	John 4:1-30	28	I Chron. 23, 24, 25	John 11:1-17
13	II Kings 6, 7, 8	John 4:31-54	29	I Chron. 26, 27	John 11:18-46
14	II Kings 9, 10, 11	John 5:1-24	30	I Chron. 28, 29	John 11:47-57
15	II Kings 12, 13, 14	John 5:25-47	31	II Chr. 1, 2, 3	John 12:1-19
16	II Kings 15, 16, 17	John 6:1-21			

JUNE

Date	Morning	Evening	Date	Morning	Evening
1	II Chr. 4, 5, 6	John 12:20-50	17	Neh. 4, 5, 6	Acts 2:14-47
2	II Chr. 7, 8, 9	John 13:1-17	18	Neh. 7, 8	Acts 3
3	II Chr. 10, 11, 12	John 13:18-38	19	Neh. 9, 10, 11	Acts 4:1-22
4	II Chr. 13-16	John 14	20	Neh. 12, 13	Acts 4:23-37
5	II Chr. 17, 18, 19	John 15	21	Esther 1, 2, 3	Acts 5:1-16
6	II Chr. 20, 21, 22	John 16:1-15	22	Esther 4, 5, 6	Acts 5:17-42
7	II Chr. 23, 24, 25	John 16:16-33	23	Esther 7-10	Acts 6
8	II Chr. 26, 27, 28	John 17	24	Job 1, 2, 3	Acts 7:1-19
9	II Chr. 29, 30, 31	John 18:1-23	25	Job 4, 5, 6	Acts 7:20-43
10	II Chr. 32, 33, 34	John 18:24-40	26	Job 7, 8, 9	Acts 7:44-60
11	II Chr. 35, 36	John 19:1-22	27	Job 10, 11, 12	Acts 8:1-25
12	Ezra 1, 2	John 19:23-42	28	Job 13, 14, 15	Acts 8:26-40
13	Ezra 3, 4, 5	John 20	29	Job 16, 17, 18	Acts 9:1-22
14	Ezra 6, 7, 8	John 21	30	Job 19, 20	Acts 9:23-43
15	Ezra 9, 10	Acts 1			
16	Neh. 1, 2, 3	Acts 2:1-13			

JULY

Date	Morning	Evening	Date	Morning	Evening
1	Job 21, 22	Acts 10:1-23	17	Psalm 22, 23, 24	Acts 20:1-16
2	Job 23, 24, 25	Acts 10:24-48	18	Psalm 25, 26, 27	Acts 20:17-38
3	Job 26, 27, 28	Acts 11	19	Psalm 28, 29, 30	Acts 21:1-14
4	Job 29, 30	Acts 12	20	Psalm 31, 32, 33	Acts 21:15-40
5	Job 31, 32	Acts 13:1-23	21	Psalm 34, 35	Acts 22
6	Job 33, 34	Acts 13:24-52	22	Psalm 36, 37	Acts 23:1-11
7	Job 35, 36, 37	Acts 14	23	Psalm 38, 39, 40	Acts 23:12-35
8	Job 38, 39	Acts 15:1-21	24	Psalm 41, 42, 43	Acts 24
9	Job 40, 41, 42	Acts 15:22-41	25	Psalm 44, 45, 46	Acts 25
10	Psalm 1, 2, 3	Acts 16:1-15	26	Psalm 47, 48, 49	Acts 26
11	Psalm 4, 5, 6	Acts 16:16-40	27	Psalm 50, 51, 52	Acts 27:1-25
12	Psalm 7, 8, 9	Acts 17:1-15	28	Psalm 53, 54, 55	Acts 27:26-44
13	Psalm 10, 11, 12	Acts 17:16-34	29	Psalm 56, 57, 58	Acts 28:1-15
14	Psalm 13, 14, 15, 16	Acts 18	30	Psalm 59, 60, 61	Acts 28:16-31
15	Psalm 17, 18	Acts 19:1-20	31	Psalm 62, 63, 64	Rom. 1
16	Psalm 19, 20, 21	Acts 19:21-41			

AUGUST

Date	Morning	Evening	Date	Morning	Evening
1	Psalm 65, 66, 67	Rom. 2	17	Psalm 107, 108	Rom. 15:21-33
2	Psalm 68, 69	Rom. 3	18	Psalm 109, 110, 111	Rom. 16
3	Psalm 70, 71, 72	Rom. 4	19	Psalm 112-115	I Cor. 1
4	Psalm 73, 74	Rom. 5	20	Psalm 116-118	I Cor. 2
5	Psalm 75, 76, 77	Rom. 6	21	Psalm 119:1-48	I Cor. 3
6	Psalm 78	Rom. 7	22	Psalm 119:49-104	I Cor. 4
7	Psalm 79, 80, 81	Rom. 8:1-18	23	Psalm 119:105-176	I Cor. 5
8	Psalm 82, 83, 84	Rom. 8:19-39	24	Psalm 120-123	I Cor. 6
9	Psalm 85, 86, 87	Rom. 9	25	Psalm 124-127	I Cor. 7:1-24
10	Psalm 88, 89	Rom. 10	26	Psalm 128-131	I Cor. 7:25-40
11	Psalm 90, 91, 92	Rom. 11:1-21	27	Psalm 132-135	I Cor. 8
12	Psalm 93, 94, 95	Rom. 11:22-36	28	Psalm 136-138	I Cor. 9
13	Psalm 96, 97, 98	Rom. 12	29	Psalm 139-141	I Cor. 10:1-13
14	Psalm 99-102	Rom. 13	30	Psalm 142-144	I Cor. 10:14-33
15	Psalm 103, 104	Rom. 14	31	Psalm 145-147	I Cor. 11:1-15
16	Psalm 105, 106	Rom. 15:1-20			

SEPTEMBER

Date	Morning	Evening	Date	Morning	Evening
1	Psalm 148-150	I Cor. 11:16-34	17	Eccles. 1, 2, 3	II Cor. 9
2	Proverbs 1, 2	I Cor. 12	18	Eccles. 4, 5, 6	II Cor. 10
3	Proverbs 3, 4	I Cor. 13	19	Eccles. 7, 8, 9	II Cor. 11:1-15
4	Proverbs 5, 6	I Cor. 14:1-20	20	Eccles. 10, 11, 12	II Cor. 11:16-33
5	Proverbs 7, 8	I Cor. 14:21-40	21	Songs 1, 2, 3	II Cor. 12
6	Proverbs 9, 10	I Cor. 15:1-32	22	Songs 4, 5	II Cor. 13
7	Proverbs 11, 12	I Cor. 15:33-58	23	Songs 6, 7, 8	Gal. 1
8	Proverbs 13, 14	I Cor. 16	24	Isaiah 1, 2, 3	Gal. 2
9	Proverbs 15, 16	II Cor. 1	25	Isaiah 4, 5, 6	Gal. 3
10	Proverbs 17, 18	II Cor. 2	26	Isaiah 7, 8, 9	Gal. 4
11	Proverbs 19, 20	II Cor. 3	27	Isaiah 10, 11, 12	Gal. 5
12	Proverbs 21, 22	II Cor. 4	28	Isaiah 13, 14, 15	Gal. 6
13	Proverbs 23, 24	II Cor. 5	29	Isaiah 16, 17, 18	Eph. 1
14	Proverbs 25, 26, 27	II Cor. 6	30	Isaiah 19, 20, 21	Eph. 2
15	Proverbs 28, 29	II Cor. 7			
16	Proverbs 30, 31	II Cor. 8			

> **"Meditate upon these things, give thyself wholly to them..."**
> **1 Timothy 4:15**

OCTOBER

Date	Morning		Evening		Date	Morning		Evening	
1	Isaiah	22, 23	Eph.	3	17	Isaiah	62, 63, 64	I Thess.	5
2	Isaiah	24, 25, 26	Eph.	4	18	Isaiah	65, 66	II Thess.	1
3	Isaiah	27, 28	Eph.	5	19	Jer.	1, 2	II Thess.	2
4	Isaiah	29, 30	Eph.	6	20	Jer.	3, 4	II Thess.	3
5	Isaiah	31, 32, 33	Phil.	1	21	Jer.	5, 6	I Tim.	1
6	Isaiah	34, 35, 36	Phil.	2	22	Jer.	7, 8	I Tim.	2
7	Isaiah	37, 38	Phil.	3	23	Jer.	9, 10	I Tim.	3
8	Isaiah	39, 40	Phil.	4	24	Jer.	11, 12, 13	I Tim.	4
9	Isaiah	41, 42	Col.	1	25	Jer.	14, 15, 16	I Tim.	5
10	Isaiah	43, 44	Col.	2	26	Jer.	17, 18, 19	I Tim.	6
11	Isaiah	45, 46, 47	Col.	3	27	Jer.	20, 21, 22	II Tim.	1
12	Isaiah	48, 49	Col.	4	28	Jer.	23, 24	II Tim.	2
13	Isaiah	50, 51, 52	I Thess.	1	29	Jer.	25, 26	II Tim.	3
14	Isaiah	53, 54, 55	I Thess.	2	30	Jer.	27, 28	II Tim.	4
15	Isaiah	56, 57, 58	I Thess.	3	31	Jer.	29, 30	Titus	1
16	Isaiah	59, 60, 61	I Thess.	4					

NOVEMBER

Date	Morning		Evening		Date	Morning		Evening	
1	Jer.	31, 32	Titus	2	17	Ezek.	16	Hebrews	12
2	Jer.	33, 34, 35	Titus	3	18	Ezek.	17, 18, 19	Hebrews	13
3	Jer.	36, 37	Philemon		19	Ezek.	20, 21	James	1
4	Jer.	38, 39	Hebrews	1	20	Ezek.	22, 23	James	2
5	Jer.	40, 41, 42	Hebrews	2	21	Ezek.	24, 25, 26	James	3
6	Jer.	43, 44, 45	Hebrews	3	22	Ezek.	27, 28	James	4
7	Jer.	46, 47, 48	Hebrews	4	23	Ezek.	29, 30, 31	James	5
8	Jer.	49, 50	Hebrews	5	24	Ezek.	32, 33	I Peter	1
9	Jer.	51, 52	Hebrews	6	25	Ezek.	34, 35	I Peter	2
10	Lam.	1, 2	Hebrews	7	26	Ezek.	36, 37	I Peter	3
11	Lam.	3, 4, 5	Hebrews	8	27	Ezek.	38, 39	I Peter	4
12	Ezek.	1, 2, 3	Hebrews	9	28	Ezek.	40	I Peter	5
13	Ezek	4, 5, 6	Hebrews	10:1-23	29	Ezek.	41, 42	II Peter	1
14	Ezek.	7, 8, 9	Hebrews	10:24-39	30	Ezek.	43, 44	II Peter	2
15	Ezek.	10, 11, 12	Hebrews	11:1-19					
16	Ezek	13, 14, 15	Hebrews	11:20-40					

DECEMBER

Date	Morning		Evening		Date	Morning		Evening	
1	Ezek.	45, 46	II Peter	3	17	Obadiah		Rev.	8
2	Ezek.	47, 48	I John	1	18	Jonah		Rev.	9
3	Dan.	1, 2	I John	2	19	Micah	1, 2, 3	Rev.	10
4	Dan.	3, 4	I John	3	20	Micah	4, 5	Rev.	11
5	Dan.	5, 6	I John	4	21	Micah	6, 7	Rev.	12
6	Dan	7, 8	I John	5	22	Nahum		Rev.	13
7	Dan.	9, 10	II John		23	Habakkuk		Rev.	14
8	Dan.	11, 12	III John		24	Zephaniah		Rev.	15
9	Hosea	1-4	Jude		25	Haggai		Rev.	16
10	Hosea	5-8	Rev.	1	26	Zech.	1, 2, 3	Rev.	17
11	Hosea	9, 10, 11	Rev.	2	27	Zech.	4, 5, 6	Rev.	18
12	Hosea	12, 13, 14	Rev.	3	28	Zech.	7, 8, 9	Rev.	19
13	Joel		Rev.	4	29	Zech.	10, 11, 12	Rev.	20
14	Amos	1, 2, 3	Rev.	5	30	Zech.	13, 14	Rev.	21
15	Amos	4, 5, 6	Rev.	6	31	Malachi		Rev.	22
16	Amos	7, 8, 9	Rev.	7					

Chapter 11

Please follow along in your Bible.

The first fourteen verses of this chapter continue the interlude between the sixth and seventh trumpet. These verses reflect back to the beginning of the Tribulation Period in order to acquaint us with the Tribulation Temple and to introduce God's two witnesses.

Verses 1 – 14 have to do with the spiritual life of Israel as we witness the nation of Israel reverting back to the OT form of worship. They rebuild the temple, likely as a result of the covenant confirmed with Antichrist (Daniel 9:27) and apart from the Messiah, since they believe He has not yet come. Christians are not called to build a temple; on the contrary, we are taught that God does not live in temples made with hands, but that the Holy Spirit uses the believer's body as a tabernacle or dwelling place (1 Corinthians 6:19, 20). The fact that Israel rebuilds the temple demonstrates that she has not received the Lord Jesus Christ as Messiah, but rather has turned to Antichrist and his false prophet (chapter 13) because of the initial peace they bring to their nation and to the world. It is worth noting that the longer Antichrist and his false prophet can keep the Jewish people deceived and focused on their OT worship, the more Jewish souls that will ultimately fail to recognize and turn to their true Messiah, the Lord Jesus Christ.

11:1 – 2: John is now told: *"Go and measure the temple of God and the altar, and count the worshipers there. But exclude the outer court; do not measure it, because it has been given to the Gentiles. They will trample on the holy city for 42 months."* With the discovery in recent years of the western gate precisely opposite the eastern gate, we have more reason now to believe the original location of the temple is north of the present day Dome of the Rock. That would locate the Dome of the Rock in the middle of the Court of the Gentiles, thus fulfilling this prophecy (see end-of-chapter illustration entitled, *The Temple Mount*). Although the Temple Mount is in Israeli hands, the politics of the area forbid the Jews from actual entry onto the mount. Regardless, the likely site for the rebuilding of the temple is known and available. A fund has been created and a temple priesthood of Jews from the tribe of Levi is currently in training to conduct worship based on OT ritual. In light of the evidence, it seems the path is being cleared for the remarkable events described here by the Apostle John.

The fact that John is told to measure the temple suggests he may find it sadly lacking as compared to Solomon's temple, which was inspired by God. The word "measure" refers to the fact that God is about to deal with the nation of Israel (Jeremiah 31:38, 39; Zechariah 2). The word "rod" speaks of chastisement and judgment (Psalm 2:9 KJV), but it also speaks of comfort (Psalm 23:4). Israel will be severely judged for her rejection of the Lord Jesus Christ as Messiah in spite of the 144,000 servants of chapter 7 and the testimony of the two witnesses of this chapter.

The prophet Zechariah revealed the devastating result of God's historic dealing with His rebellious people: *"And it shall come to pass in all the land that two-thirds in it shall be cut off and die, but one-third shall be left in it: I will bring the one-third through the fire, will refine them as silver is refined, and test them as gold is tested. They will call on My name, and I will answer them. I will say, 'This is My people'; and each one will say, 'The Lord is my God'"* (Zechariah 13:8, 9 NKJV). The scattered flock of Israel will face dire judgment during the Great Tribulation in which only one-third will survive to the end to witness the return of Jesus Christ, the Messiah. However, the remnant that does survive will be purified through faith in the Messiah, Jesus Christ and spiritually restored in their covenant relationship with God.

The Two Witnesses

11:3 – 6: *"I will give power to my two witnesses, and they will prophesy for 1,260 day, clothed in sackcloth. These are the two olive trees and the two lampstands that stand before the Lord of the earth ...."* During the first half of the 7-year Tribulation Period (1,260 days/42 months), God will establish two divine witnesses in Jerusalem. Sackcloth is the usual attire of the OT prophets and reminds us of Elijah and John the Baptist. The two olive trees immediately suggest the vision in Zechariah 4. Those two were Joshua and Zerubbabel, both anointed and enabled by the Holy Spirit to stand against insurmountable difficulties. Throughout history, it has been the responsibility of the nation of Israel to declare and proclaim to the world the one, true living God. The lampstand is symbolic and represents an individual who brings God's light (word/truth) to the world, as it was with the Lord Jesus Christ. The olive trees provide the oil (fuel) for the lamp, which symbolizes the work of the Holy Spirit through that individual. The Holy Spirit will be present during the Tribulation Period as well. These two witnesses will be endowed with supernatural powers, similar to prophets from the OT, and for the following three purposes:

1) They will prophesy (v.6), which means they will preach concerning things to come.
2) They will witness (v.6), meaning they will demonstrate God's power in contrast to that of the emerging world powers (Antichrist and his false prophet).
3) They will testify (v.7), meaning they will preach the Gospel of Jesus Christ.

These two witnesses are lights before the powers of darkness. They are immortal and immune to all attacks until their mission is completed. They are yet another illustration that God is so keenly interested in the souls of His children that He will even send two supernatural witnesses to convince lost humanity. Scripture has always required two or more witnesses to bear testimony to anything before it is to be heard (Matthew 18:16). Is it possible that all believers are immortal as well until their God-given purpose is fulfilled on earth; and only then will God call each home to heaven to be with Him?

We can only offer a suggestion as to the identity of these two witnesses. The prophet predicted that Elijah would come before, *"... that great and dreadful day of the Lord comes"* (Malachi 4:5).

Furthermore, we find that the use of fire in the OT was given to Elijah, who called down fire to consume the altar in the days of King Ahab and Jezebel (2 Kings 18:20 – 40). Elijah also withheld rain from the earth for three years. There are three reasons why some commentators suggest that Moses may be the second witness:

1) When the Lord Jesus was transfigured before His Jewish witnesses – Peter, James, and John – the two representatives of the OT that were brought before them to see were Moses and Elijah (Matthew 17:1 – 4).
2) Moses manifested the power to bring plagues onto the earth and to turn water into blood during the days of Pharaoh.
3) To this day, Moses remains an important part of Jewish family tradition.

It seems logical that Moses and Elijah combined would represent the entire OT to the Jewish nation.

Another possibility to consider would be the only two OT patriarchs that did not taste death, but were raptured (taken up) to heaven. The first one being Enoch who was taken directly to heaven by God (Genesis 5:24); and the second one, again, being Elijah, who was carried bodily to heaven in a whirlwind (2 Kings 2:11). Whether you choose to accept the writings from *The Lost Books of the Bible,* or not, it is interesting to read the following: *"Here we [Enoch and Elijah] have up to now been and have not tasted death, but are now about to return at the coming of Antichrist, being armed with divine signs and miracles, to engage with him in battle, and to be slain by him at Jerusalem, and to be taken up alive again into the clouds, after three days and a half"* (Gospel of Nicodemus 20:4). The descriptive language in this passage is clearly specific, and leaves no doubt as to its relevance to what we read here in these verses of chapter 11. This scenario would liken Enoch as a representative to the Gentile nations and Elijah as a representative to the Jewish nation in the kingdom of God that will be established on earth at Christ's return.

Others, still, suggest that John the Baptist might be the second witness. He was the forerunner to Christ at His First Coming. He was similar to Elijah in manner and message. Both knew what it was like to oppose the forces of darkness and to stand alone for God against impossible odds. John the Baptist would be the witness of the NT, where Elijah would be the witness of the OT.

11:7: *"Now when they have finished their testimony, the beast that comes up from the Abyss will attack them, and overpower and kill them …."* The expression, "the beast," is used here for the first time. The fact that he will come up out of the Abyss is a reference to the death and apparent resurrection of Antichrist, as we will study in greater detail later. The beast (Antichrist), or man of lawlessness, as the Apostle Paul describes him, (2 Thessalonians 2:3), will hate the two witnesses, make war against them, and eventually kill them, only after they have finished their testimony.

11:8: *"Their bodies will lie in the street of the great city …."* These men are not even given a decent burial. This demonstrates an extremely cruel and barbaric-like culture in existence during this time. The Holy City, Jerusalem, where the Lord Jesus was crucified, will have become so immoral and corrupt spiritually that she will be called Sodom and Egypt. Jerusalem was called Sodom by the Prophet Isaiah (Isaiah 1:10); Sodom being symbolic of immorality and rebellion against God. In contrast, Egypt is symbolic of materialism and the love for worldly wealth.

11:9 – 10: After Jesus Christ was crucified, even the Roman governor Pilate permitted His disciples to take down the body and give Him a respectable burial according to Jewish custom, but not so with the two witnesses. With the help of modern television media via satellite, 24-hour cable news networks, and the internet, ours is the first generation that will literally see the fulfillment of this prophecy by allowing people from every tribe, language, and nation to witness such a gruesome spectacle.

Not content to just look on them, the inhabitants of the earth will enjoy a Christmas-like celebration, giving and receiving gifts because these preachers of righteousness are now dead. This is Satan's Xmas. The world will celebrate what Antichrist has done instead of the coming of Christ to Bethlehem. Their treatment of these two men demonstrates the worst humiliation imaginable by a depraved and godless society.

11:11 – 12: *"But after three and a half days a breath of life from God entered them, and they stood on their feet …."* In the Greek, the scriptural word for resurrection used here is the verb *histemi* which means "to make to stand." In a loud voice directed at the two deceased witnesses, the Lord again uses the phrase, *"Come up here"* (v.12). These are the same words Jesus used earlier in chapter 4, which we said represented the Rapture and resurrection of the Church. A cloud will receive them out of sight as their enemies, again with the help of modern video technology, look on. The cloud of glory is associated with both the ascension and return of Christ. It is no wonder the people were struck with terror. The resurrection of these men will be the final confirmation that they were men of God, and another illustration that God does not forget His children.

11:13: *"At that very hour there was a severe earthquake and a tenth of the city collapsed. Seven thousand people were killed …."* This judgment is a result of the shocking treatment of the two faithful witnesses of God by the inhabitants of the city of Jerusalem. This event apparently triggers a revival, for the passage continues, *"… the survivors were terrified and gave glory to the God of heaven."* Although the people did acknowledge God, the text does not indicate that they repented and turned to Christ.

11:14: *"The second woe has passed; the third woe is coming."* This verse serves as our transition verse ending the interlude and bringing us back in time to the final trumpet judgment and the third woe of the Tribulation Period.

The Seventh Trumpet Judgment

11:15: The seventh trumpet – the third woe: The blowing of the seventh trumpet does not initiate anything on the earth. It may be much like the breaking of the seventh seal in that it merely introduces the next series of judgments, the seven bowls, which we will study starting in chapter 15. This coincides with the tossing of Satan from heaven and confining him to earth, as we will see in chapter 12. Satan's banishment to earth and assault during the second half of the Tribulation Period will be, without a doubt, the third woe.

It may be noteworthy that the following verses are inserted here for the encouragement of the saints remaining on earth (those who are sealed). These verses give us a glimpse of the eternity ahead when all rebellion to God is finally crushed and Christ reigns victorious.

Following the blowing of the seventh trumpet, John hears loud voices, evidently angelic voices in chorus. This is in contrast to the breaking of the seventh seal when there was silence in heaven. It is a time of joy, for God's entire created heavenly host can now anticipate the coming end and termination of all wickedness. They announce two things:

1) *"The kingdom of the world has become the kingdom of our Lord and of his Christ."* This is a view of the kingdom of Antichrist at the time of the Revelation (14:1) when Christ returns to earth to defeat Antichrist, overthrow his one-world empire, and establish His earthly Millennial Kingdom.

2) *"... and He will reign for ever and ever."* This indicates that once Christ comes to earth, there will be no interruption of His government despite the rebellion that will break out when Satan is released from his prison (Revelation 20:7). Our glorified Lord will extinguish it so fast it will not interfere with His kingdom.

11:16 – 18: The twenty-four elders fall on their faces before God and worship Him, announcing His eternity with the following words: *"The One who is and who was ..."* (v.17). This is a song of thanksgiving, indicating that they anticipate in heaven the final stage of God's activity on the earth, as they rejoice over the eventual consummation of His kingdom. They make three predictions on the basis of Christ's return:

1) Verse 18: *"The nations were angry; and your wrath has come."* Because of their stubborn rebellion against God, mankind will be angry and will resent the Lord's coming. The hearts of unrepentant men will be hardened all the way up to the end of the Tribulation Period.

2) *"The time has come for judging the dead, rewarding your servants the prophets, and your saints and those who reverence your name ..."* This is a clear reference to the resurrection of the OT saints and the slain Tribulation saints. These are the saints under the altar mentioned earlier (6:9). They are included in the first resurrection. This does not refer to unbelievers, who will be resurrected (the final resurrection) and judged at the end of the Millennium (Revelation 20:11 – 15). The resurrection of these OT saints is also promised in Psalm 50:1 – 6 and Daniel 12:1 – 2.

3) *"... and for destroying those who destroy the earth."* The word "destroy" is translated from the Greek word *diaphtheiro*, which means those who "ruin" or "corrupt," and refers to both man and Satan. The NT teaches that those who die without receiving Christ as their Savior will go in soul and spirit to the place of torment (as did the rich man in Luke 16:23) to await the judgment of the great white throne, as we will study later in chapter 20. At that time, they will stand before Christ, the Judge, for their final judgment.

11:19: When we see the Church again, it will be in the New Jerusalem, and we are definitely told that there is no temple there; however, there is a temple in heaven. The temple (tabernacle), which Moses made, was made after the pattern in heaven (Exodus 25:9, Hebrews 8:5). Therefore, the phrase, "God's temple in heaven was opened," means that here God is dealing with the nation of Israel. The vision of the ark of the covenant could be a reminder to Israel that they are dealing with a covenant-keeping God, and on the basis of His past faithfulness the redemption of the remnant of the nation of Israel is guaranteed. The writer of Hebrews tells us, *"The time is coming, declares the Lord, when I will make a new covenant with the house of Israel and with the house of Judah"* (Hebrews 8:8). At that time the Law will be written on their hearts instead of hard cold tablets of stone.

The lightning, rumblings, peals of thunder, earthquake, and great hailstorm are dreadful occurrences of nature that speak of judgment yet to come.

This chapter is a reaffirmation of God sending His final witnesses and making one last attempt to say to the nation of Israel that there is one, true God, Jehovah, and Jesus is His Christ (Messiah).

In view of the destruction and misery that awaits the earth during the Tribulation Period, any reasonable person today is left with only one decision: Avoid this dreadful period in the world's future by repenting and receiving Jesus Christ as your Lord and Savior by personal invitation.

Review Questions

1) The nation of Israel will finally rebuild their temple during the first half of the 7-year Tribulation Period most likely as a result of _____

_____.

2) In our discussion of the proposed site plan of the third temple, it locates the present day Dome of the Rock in the middle of _____.

3) The lampstand is symbolic of _____.

4) The olive oil provides the fuel for the lamp, which symbolizes _____.

5) The two witnesses are endowed with supernatural power for the purposes of _____

_____.

6) The two witnesses will be killed by Antichrist and after three and a half days these men will be

_____.

7) The blowing of the seventh trumpet is much like the breaking of the seventh seal in that it

_____.

Up For Discussion

"And there was given me a reed like unto a rod: and the angel stood, saying,
Rise, and measure the temple of God, and the altar,
and them that worship therein."
(Revelation 11:1 KJV)

According to our analysis (vv.1 – 2), it appears possible that Israel's third temple could be located and constructed without any displacement of the Muslim Dome of the Rock. Of course it would take a miracle of politics to make that happen, a miracle in the form of a covenant of peace confirmed by the ruler to come (Daniel 9:27). John calls him the Antichrist. We will study him further in chapter 13.

Using the illustration entitled, *Jerusalem's Four Temples*, review on your own or as a class. Discuss each block, moving from left to right, and read the Scripture references associated with each. Review the illustration, *The Temple Mount*, for further discussion.

Some folks believe the identity of the two supernatural witnesses of this chapter is irrelevant. What is more important is the message of grace through the Gospel of Jesus Christ to an unrepentant world in tribulation. Do you agree, or do you find it interesting or challenging to speculate as to their identities based on various writings aside from our Bible?

Jerusalem's Four Temples

First Temple	Second Temple		Tribulation Temple	Millennial Temple
King Solomon's	Zerubbabel's and Herod's	Dome of the Rock	Antichrist Desecrates	Christ's Memorial Temple

Shekinah Present
(Glory of God)
1 Kings 5-8

Roman Insignia
Ezra 3:7-6:18

Mosque dominates the Temple Mount, Jewish Dispersion

Church Age
Gentile Inclusion
Romans 9-11

"Abomination that causes Desolation"
Daniel 9:27
2 Thessalonians 2:4
Revelation 13:14-15

Glory Returns
Ezekiel 43:1-5

Jesus Christ Reigns
Ezekiel 40-43
Isaiah 56:7

70 Year Exile

374 Years	586 Years	"Age of Grace"	7 Years	1,000 Years

Israel's Monarchy
1st Temple built by Solomon 960 B.C.
Temple destroyed by Babylon 586 B.C.

Gentile Domination
2nd Temple built by Zerubbabel 516 B.C.
Temple enlarged by Herod 19 B.C.

The Church
Believer's body as the temple
1 Corinthians 3:16 and 6:19
Temple destroyed by the Romans 70 A.D.

Tribulation Period
3rd Temple
Temple is desecrated by Antichrist.
Matthew 24:15

Midpoint

Millennium
Messianic Age
Isaiah 2:2-4
Jeremiah 23:5-6
Zechariah 14:9-21
Acts 3:16-24
Revelation 20
4th Temple built by the Lord Jesus Christ

The Temple Mount and the Tribulation Temple Under the Covenant of Antichrist

Many things coincide with the mid-point of the Tribulation Period, one of which is Antichrist's persecution of the nation of Israel. It is at this time that Antichrist breaks his covenant of peace with Israel as his false prophet initials idol worship in the newly rebuilt temple in Jerusalem. It may be that Israel, who does not accept Jesus Christ as her Messiah during the first half of the Tribulation Period, will embrace Him in the second half, thereby rejecting the deceiving, idolatrous religion of Antichrist.

The nation of Israel will become the dividing line for the entire world during the second half of the Tribulation Period. Those who receive the mark of the beast and worship Antichrist will assist him worldwide in his persecution of the Jews and Christians. Those who have received Jesus Christ as Lord and Savior (Tribulation saints) will provide aid and protection to the redeemed Jewish remnant, while sharing with them the long anticipated message of mercy and grace from their true Messiah, Jesus Christ. Below is an example of how the Temple Mount might appear under Antichrist's coexistent covenant.

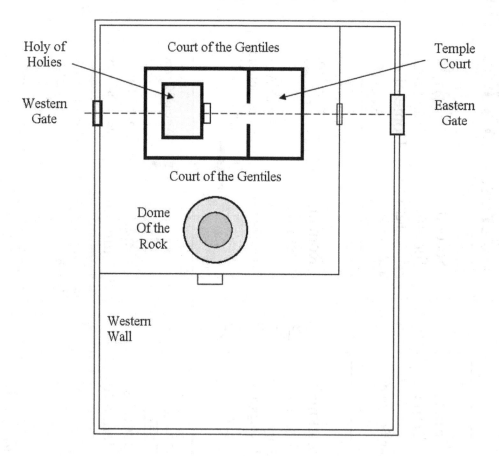

*Sketch is for illustration proposes only and not to precise scale.

Chapter 12

Please follow along in your Bible.

This chapter introduces the second half of the 7-year Tribulation Period by giving a heavenly recap of the great conflict of the ages. It brings us up-to-date in our study. In chapters 12 and 13, we will take a close look at seven key personalities/groups. The identification and clarification of these are essential for a proper understanding of the book of Revelation. Please keep in mind that what John is seeing here is past, present, and future.

1) The Woman – Israel

12:1 – 2: John calls the woman he sees, "a *great and wondrous sign … in heaven*" (v.1). The word "sign" clearly indicates that the woman is not to be taken literally as a woman, but as a symbol of something else. At its most basic level, the Roman Catholic Church symbolically views the woman as the Blessed Mother – the Virgin Mary. The pain is viewed on a deeper level in her suffering, as that of the mother of the Lord Jesus as she stood beneath the cross upon which her Son died. However, literally speaking, it seems impossible to imagine Mary giving birth to her child in heaven. Instead, I agree with the interpretation that the woman described here represents the nation of Israel, which gave birth to the Messiah, Jesus Christ. From Abraham to the days of Mary, the nation of Israel was preparing to bring forth a man-child that would bless the entire world. The fact that this woman is seen, "*… clothed with the sun, with the moon under her feet*" (v.1), emphasizes enlightenment. The sun as a generator of light and the moon as a reflector are both symbolic of Israel's responsibility to bring God's light (word/truth) to mankind. The sun, moon, and stars also belong to Israel as seen in Joseph's dream (Genesis 37:9). The crown of twelve stars is representative of the twelve tribes of Israel.

Remember in our previous chapter we learned that it was the responsibility of the nation of Israel to be light to the pagan Gentile world and to proclaim the one, true God (11:3 – 6). However, when Israel rejected Jesus Christ as her Messiah, God gave that responsibility over to the Church for an undetermined time period.

2) The Red Dragon – Satan

12:3: Next, John sees another sign, which again means we are not to take it literally. Satan is identified by name in verse 9 and is here described as: *"an enormous red dragon …."* The KJV uses the word "great," meaning he is very powerful. He is red because he is the motivating force behind all of the bloodshed throughout human history. He is called a dragon because of the viciousness of his character. Satan is the most dangerous being in all of God's creation. It is not certain, but many commentators suggest that the seven-crowned heads likely represent governmental powers – that is, the empires or kingdoms throughout history that Satan has used to enslave, persecute, and war against the nation of Israel and to blaspheme God. First was the kingdom of Egypt during the time of Moses. Second was the Assyrian Empire during the time of the divided kingdom. The Prophet Daniel identified the next four great empires as Babylonia, Media/Persia, Greece, and Rome. In fact, Roman government or Imperialism is still today in its sixth stage (or head symbolically) and governs a great deal of the earth's population. Any dictatorial government belongs to this category. The seventh head belongs to the future kingdom of the end-times Antichrist – the revived Roman Empire.

The ten horns refer to ten kings who will be dominant during the Tribulation Period, from whom Antichrist (the seventh head) will receive his power and authority. Antichrist is the human pawn of Satan himself, for throughout history Satan has stirred up and used governmental power to accomplish his purpose. Nothing has brought more havoc and evil to mankind than government. Political power in the hands of evil men has given license to torture, murder, and war, resulting in famine, pestilence, and suffering beyond human comprehension. Satan's intent has always been to keep nations fighting one another, and his energy has always been directed at the nation of Israel. This is why the Middle East will never be at peace – they will always be in conflict. During the second half of the 7-year Tribulation Period (forty-two months of Gentile rule), Satan will have the nations of the earth raging war against the nation of Israel. All of his efforts will be directed at Israel.

12:4: *"His tail swept a third of the stars out of the sky and flung them to the earth …."* Because of Satan's pride, which encourages rebellion, we see the casting from heaven of one-third of the angels, those who chose to rebel against God and follow the dragon (cf. Matthew 25:41; Jude 6).

The original casting of Satan out of heaven was not his final overthrow, for although his forces have been limited to the atmospheric heaven around the earth; Satan himself still has access, even today, to the throne of God to accuse believers. In the book of Job, we are told that Satan came with other angels to appear before God (Job 1:6; 2:1). This fact is further confirmed by the words of the Lord Jesus to Peter: *"Simon, Simon, Satan has asked to sift you as wheat"* (Luke 22:31).

The vision of Satan standing before the woman, *"… who was about to give birth, so that he might devour her child the moment it was born,"* refers to Satan's hatred of the Male Child. It was predicted from the very beginning that this Child would be his downfall (Genesis 3:15). Satan initiated what biblical scholars call the *conflict of the ages*, attempting to stamp out the seed of the woman from the time of Adam and Eve to the end of the Tribulation Period – that is, from the beginning of Genesis through the end of Revelation.

3) The Male Child – Jesus Christ

12:5: Only the Lord Jesus Christ fits this description. The male child, *"... who will rule all the nations with an iron scepter,"* refers to Christ's rule during the Millennium, when He will be the absolute, sovereign ruler of the world. The persecuted Christians of the early church quoted the second Psalm, identifying the Lord Jesus as the One to rule with a rod of iron (Acts 4:25, 26). His identity is further clarified by the phrase, "her child was snatched up to God and to his throne." This is exactly what happened to Jesus forty days following His death and resurrection. Luke, the Gospel writer, was witness to Christ's ascension: *"... he was taken up before their very eyes, and a cloud hid him from their sight"* (Acts 1:9). Ten days later, the Apostle Peter preached to the crowd at Pentecost proclaiming, *"God has raised this Jesus to life and ... Exalted to the right hand of God"* (Acts 2:32 – 34). The book of Revelation is the unveiling of the ascended Christ, the glorified Christ, and the Christ who is to return to earth one day in glory. The writer of Hebrews tells us: *"Let us fix our eyes on Jesus, the author and perfecter of our faith, who for the joy set before him endured the cross, scorning its shame, and sat down at the right hand of the throne of God"* (Hebrews 12:2). The KJV translates the expression as, "finisher of our faith."

12:6: *"The woman fled into the desert to a place prepared for her by God, where she might be taken care of for 1,260 days."* This verse brings us up-to-date in our study and to the mid-point of the Tribulation Period. We are not told specifically where the nation of Israel will flee; the important thing to keep in mind is that God will protect and provide for her. Recall how God provided for the Israelites during the forty years in the desert after their exodus from Egypt. Remember also how God protected and provided for Joseph and Mary following the birth of Jesus when they fled into the desert to escape the murderous decree of Herod. During the second half of the Tribulation Period (1,260 days), God will protect and provide for the remnant of the nation of Israel. The redeemed Jewish remnant will flee from persecution during the greatest anti-Semitic crusade Satan has ever unleashed against them.

4) The Angel – Michael

12:7 – 9: There are two angels whose names are given in our Bible: Gabriel and Michael. Gabriel is the announcing angel, and Michael is the commanding angel of the heavenly host. We are told in the book of Jude (v.9) that Michael is the archangel. In the sixth century B.C., the Prophet Daniel had a vision and wrote the following: *"At that time Michael, the great prince who protects your people, will arise. There will be a time of distress such as has not happened from the beginning of nations until then. But at that time your people – everyone whose name is found written in the book – will be delivered"* (Daniel 12:1). The phrase, "your people," means Daniel's people – the nation of Israel. We can thereby conclude that Michael is the angel specifically assigned by God to work for the protection of the nation of Israel. In the middle of the 7-year Tribulation Period, the conflict between Michael, with his army of heavenly host and Satan, with his demons will reach its climax. When God gives the order, Michael will cast the great dragon (Satan) down to earth, *"... and his angels with him"* (v.9). Satan and his demonic host will then be banished and confined to earth. He will no longer have access to the throne of God. His fury will know no limitations, except the power of God. This passage details several things about Satan:

1) He is first referred to as the ancient serpent. This refers to the first time he is seen in Scripture, in the Garden of Eden (Genesis 3:1).

2) He is also called the devil. This is the name used in the Gospels for this enemy of God. It means "slanderer" or "false accuser." In verse 10, he is called the accuser of our brothers. This is the reason all believers need an *Advocate* in heaven and why the apostle wrote: *"But if anyone does sin, we have one who speaks to the Father in our defense – Jesus Christ, the Righteous One"* (1 John 2:1).

3) Lastly, he is called Satan. This name means "adversary." Satan is the enemy of God and the adversary of everything that is good, including God's people.

4) He is described as the one who leads the whole world astray. Satan is the great deceiver. The Apostle Paul wrote on this very point: *"The god of this age has blinded the minds of unbelievers, so that they cannot see the light of the gospel of the glory of Christ, who is the image of God"* (2 Corinthians 4:4).

12:10: The fact that Satan is once and for all cast out of heaven along with his evil host and confined to earth will be cause for great rejoicing in heaven. This opens the way for the coming of four precious heavenly blessings when Christ returns to earth:

1) **Salvation**: Salvation is consummated in the Person of Christ. Our salvation (sanctification) is made complete when we finally come into the presence of Christ. For the surviving Tribulation saints, this speaks of Christ's physical return to earth.

2) **Power**: Throughout history, the nations have corrupted and abused power. However, when Christ returns to earth, He will abolish all wickedness and assume all worldly power. True righteousness and justice will finally reign over all the nations.

3) **The kingdom of our God**: When Christ returns to establish His Millennial Kingdom on earth, only then will there be true peace, harmony, and freedom for all of God's creation.

4) **Authority**: This refers to the governmental authority that Christ will establish upon His return. His authority will be absolute and final.

12:11: The rejoicing in heaven continues in these verses that give us three sources of victory for the saints over Satan the accuser:

1) *"They overcame him by the blood of the Lamb ..."* The blood of the Lamb, which takes away the sins of the world, is the only true means of victory. The continued mention of the blood of the Lamb in the book of Revelation is not to be taken lightly, because it is our sin which made it necessary for Jesus Christ to shed His blood. It is only through the blood of the Lamb that any of us overcome Satan.

2) *"... by the word of their testimony ..."* Another way to overcome Satan is with a decisive testimony for Jesus Christ. The place to give your testimony is not in a well-fed church, but out in the world. Let the world and those around you know that you belong to Christ and that the love of Christ lives in you. Before sending out his disciples, the Lord told them, *"Whoever acknowledges me before men, I will also acknowledge him before my Father in heaven"* (Matthew 10:32).

3) *"... they did not love their lives so much as to shrink from death."* Those who overcome are more concerned with obeying and glorifying God than they are with pleasing men or saving their own lives. When we put Jesus Christ first, others second, and ourselves last, we find that our love is the very basis of Christian service. The Lord questioned Peter saying: *"Do you love*

me ... Feed my sheep" (John 21:15 – 17). The Lord afterward used Peter in a mighty way. As a result of his preaching to the crowd on the day of Pentecost, about three thousand believers were baptized and added to their numbers (Acts 2:41).

The Third Woe

12:12 – 13: *"Therefore rejoice, you heavens and you who dwell in them! But woe to the earth and the sea, because the devil has gone down to you! He is filled with fury, because he knows that his time is short ...."* Although heaven will rejoice because Satan is cast out, the earth will not share in this rejoicing. This is the third woe of the book of Revelation. Satan's confinement to earth extends through the final set of judgments and up to the final day of the Tribulation Period. Satan will now personally take command of the earth and step up his crusade against his greatest enemy, the nation of Israel. Christians must keep in mind that it is through the nation of Israel that we have our blessed Savior Jesus Christ, our Holy Scriptures, the ministry of the apostles, and everything else associated with the faith we hold so dear. Pastor and best-selling author, John Hagee wrote: "Judaism does not need Christianity to explain its existence while Christianity cannot define its existence without Judaism." Satan and all his energy will be directed at Israel and all of God's children. Knowing he has but a short time, he will be filled with rage and hatred.

12:14: *"The woman was given the two wings of a great eagle ...."* This imagery has become a symbol to Israel representing that God will deliver her to safety, for this is the same symbolism used by God in His past deliverance of Israel from Egypt. God told Israel through His servant Moses: *"You yourself have seen what I did to Egypt, and how I carried you on eagles' wings and brought you to myself"* (Exodus 19:4). The important thing is not the specific place in the desert Israel will flee to or how they will get there, but the fact that God will protect them from persecution by His mercy and grace. The phrase, "time, times, and half a time," means three and a half years. The Prophet Daniel used the same expression (Daniel 12:7) in describing his vision of this future time of distress for the people of Israel. During the second half of the 7-year Tribulation Period, God will care for, or nourish (KJV) the nation of Israel as He did in the days of Moses when He rained manna from the sky and streamed water from the rocks.

12:15 – 16: *"Then from his mouth the serpent spewed water like a river, to overtake the woman and sweep her away with the torrent ...."* Since this chapter has already used various symbols, i.e., the woman and the enormous red dragon, the word "torrent" is likely a symbol as well. This word might be likened to the word flood as used by the Prophet Isaiah (59:19) in his description of the enemies of God and their massive armies advancing from the west and the east. As in the days of the rebellion of Korah (Numbers 16:31 – 33), so also during the Tribulation Period, the earth will swallow up the satanic-driven armies of Antichrist.

5) The Remnant of Israel

12:17: *"Then the dragon was enraged at the woman and went off to make war against the rest of her offspring ...."* Who is the rest of Israel's offspring a reference to? The KJV uses the phrase, "remnant of her seed." Throughout the OT, the prophets spoke of a remnant of the house of Israel that would survive. The Prophet Jeremiah wrote: *"I myself will gather the remnant of my flock out of all the countries where I have driven them and will bring them back to their pasture, where they will be fruitful and increase in number"* (Jeremiah 23:3). Centuries later, the Apostle Paul wrote: *"So too, at the present time there is a remnant chosen by grace"* (Romans 11:5). Hence, in every age, God has chosen to protect and save a remnant of Israel, His covenant people. Earlier in this chapter we read about a remnant of the nation of Israel that will flee into the desert to escape persecution by the satanic forces of Antichrist. Apparently, the remnant in this passage is a different group. Frustrated by his failed attempt to destroy the fleeing Israelites (vv.15, 16), Satan will turn his rage to every follower of Christ scattered throughout all the nations – Jew and Gentile. This would also include the 144,000 servants of God (chapter 7) that are evangelizing the world. We know that they are the redeemed of the Tribulation Period because John describes them as follows: *"… those who obey God's commandments and hold to the testimony of Jesus."* Even though Satan will make war against all of God's people and ultimately fail, he will never stop trying to eradicate them from the face of the earth. Satan's final fate is exposed later in chapter 20.

Review Questions

1) The woman is symbolic of _____.

2) Her crown of twelve stars represents _____.

3) The enormous red dragon is identified as _____.

4) The male child who will rule all the nations with an iron scepter refers to _____

   _____.

5) Why does the woman flee into the desert in the middle of the Tribulation Period? _____

   _____.

6) What is the third woe? _____

   _____.

7) The two wings of a great eagle have become a symbol to Israel representing _____

   _____.

Up For Discussion

"And there appeared another wonder in heaven; and behold a great red dragon …."
(Revelation 12:3 KJV)

Read on your own or as a class the following related lessons entitled, *The Dragon* and *The Sovereignty of God*. Consider how they reinforce or give added insight to the message of the book of Revelation.

In *The Dragon*, we look at the origins of Satan and how his fall from grace was the result of a prideful heart. As we move further into our study of the book of Revelation, we will see Satan's rise to power during the second half of the Tribulation Period and his final doom when Christ returns to reclaim the earth from all unrighteousness.

In *The Sovereignty of God*, we emphasize that God is in complete control, nothing happens outside of His permissive will, and whatever He allows, He will turn to our good. Indeed, we are to live our lives with that understanding.

The Dragon

The dragon is introduced to us in chapter 12, beginning in verse 3. He is later identified by name – Satan, "*… that ancient serpent called the devil … who leads the whole world astray*" (Revelation 12:9). John described the dragon first as a sign and then as an enormous, red dragon. This sign was symbolic of his character, not his physical appearance. Satan is a created being. He was created as an angel. In fact, the Lord called him a guardian cherub (Ezekiel 28:14). By nature, angels are spiritual beings (Hebrews 1:14) and exist in the spiritual realm where they remain unseen by mankind, unless God allows otherwise.

The origin of Satan is found in the Word of God given to the Prophet Ezekiel (28:12 – 17). In these verses we find the judgment of the king of Tyre. However, there was never a king of Tyre in the Garden of Eden. This prophecy looks beyond the local ruler to the one who is behind the kingdoms of the world – Satan. Recall that Satan offered the kingdoms of the world to the Lord Jesus during His temptation in the wilderness (Luke 4:5 – 7). The Lord rejected Satan's offer. Apparently, Satan had the authority to make the offer – at that point in time. Ultimately, as John reveals, Christ will rule over the kingdoms of the world, but not as some prince of Satan. Unfortunately, Satan still functions today, in the words of our Lord, as "the prince of this world" (John 12:31, 14:30, and 16:11). Satan is the one behind all the kingdoms of the world. He has always used governmental power – that is, kings and kingdoms to accomplish his purpose. Please follow along in your Bible as we take a brief look at the Word of God given through the words of the prophet:

Ezekiel 28:12: Satan was created as, "*… the model of perfection, full of wisdom ….*" Satan is the wisest creature God ever created. He is smart, clever, and wise. You and I are no match for him. We will be overcome if we try to stand in our own strength against him. This is why the Apostle Paul counsels believers to "*… be strong in the Lord and in his mighty power. Put on the full armor of God so that you can take your stand against the devil's schemes*" (Ephesians 6:10, 11).

Satan was also created, "*perfect in beauty.*" He is not some creature with horns, a forked tail, and webbed feet as might be found in Greek mythology. No, the Word of God presents him as perfect in beauty. When God says perfect, that is exactly what He means. If you could see him, I suspect you would find him to be the most beautiful creature imaginable.

Ezekiel 28:13: "*You were in Eden, the garden of God …*" Satan was the ancient serpent who, millennia ago, enticed Eve into disobeying God's command not to eat the fruit from the tree in the middle of the Garden of Eden (Genesis 3:1).

"*… every precious stone adorned you: ruby, topaz … Your settings and mountings were made of gold.*" Imagine what a beautiful creature he must be.

The NIV omits the following passage: "*… The workmanship of your timbrels and pipes was prepared for you on the day you were created*" (Ezekiel 28:12 NKJV). As you can see, Satan was also created as the pinnacle of music itself for the purpose of singing praises to his Creator.

Ezekiel 28:14: Satan was, "*… anointed as a guardian cherub …*" meaning he protected the throne of God. This is not Eden on earth. Apparently, the holy mount of God mentioned here is a picture of heaven itself. You might ask, "Why does the throne of God need a guardian, and protected from what?" Yes, God is all-powerful and all-knowing. He simply has to speak, and His will is accomplished. Angels, like mankind, were created for God's pleasure and His good purpose. We were all created to praise, worship, and serve our Creator; and just as with mankind, angels, too, were evidently given free will. Consequently, we learn that a third of the angels in heaven choose to rebel against God and follow Satan (Revelation 12:4). As a result, the war between the forces of God and the forces of Satan – that is, the war between the forces of good and evil has continued down through the ages.

Ezekiel 28:15: Satan protected God's throne. He had the highest position a created being could have. So, what was it that brought him down? Ezekiel will tell us shortly in verse 17, but even before Ezekiel, the Prophet Isaiah has already told his story (Isaiah 14:12 – 15; read aloud for class discussion).

The thing that corrupted Satan was pride. He wanted to, *"… raise his throne above the stars of God"* (Isaiah 14:13). He wanted to separate himself from God and become God. He was in rebellion against God. However, God cannot tolerate rebellion. So, what is He going to do?

Ezekiel 28:16: *"… you sinned. So I drove you in disgrace from the mount of God …."* Satan will be judged for his sin. He is only a creature. This should be comforting to us all. Although we are no match for him, we can be thankful God is going to deal with him. John will reveal his ultimate fate in chapter 20 of our study.

Ezekiel 28:17: *"Your heart became proud on account of your beauty, and you corrupted your wisdom because of your splendor …."* Pride is number one on God's hate list: *"There are six things the Lord hates, seven that are detestable to him: haughty eyes …"* (Proverbs 6:16, 17). *"To fear the Lord is to hate evil, I hate pride and arrogance"* (Proverbs 8:13). King Solomon, who was considered the wisest man to have ever lived, became prideful. Although God had forbidden the Israelites to intermarry, he took on wives from all the surrounding nations. Subsequently, those wives caused him to sin against God by seducing him into worshiping their gods and idols. Here in Ezekiel, we have the greatest creature God ever created, perfect in wisdom and beauty, but prideful and in rebellion against his Creator. God says He is going to make a spectacle of Satan someday. At some time in the future, God is going to banish Satan from His universe.

In our study of Revelation 12, we learned that at the mid-point of the 7-year Tribulation Period the conflict between good and evil reaches its climax. At that time, when God gives the order, Michael, the archangel, and his forces will cast Satan and his demons down to earth. They will no longer have access to the heavenly realm, but will be confined to earth.

As a preview, Revelation 13 opens with Satan standing on the shore of the sea. You may ask yourself, "If I was standing on that beach, would I see him?" The answer is no. Satan is still an angelic being, but of the fallen order. He still operates in the spiritual realm, unless God allows otherwise. Satan will then enter the slain body of Antichrist causing a fake resurrection. At the mid-point of the Tribulation Period, Antichrist will become the incarnation of Satan: *"The dragon gave the beast his power and his throne and great authority"* (Revelation 13:2). The beast is the end-times Antichrist. The dragon's power and throne is a reference to the kingdoms of the world. The false prophet, Antichrist's religious leader, will also be given power and authority by Satan to perform great and miraculous signs (Revelation 13:13), erect an idol image of Antichrist, and to give breath to the image (Revelation

13:15). These are just a few illustrations of the supernatural powers that Satan possesses in order to accomplish his evil plan.

In his vision, John says he saw, *"… three evil spirits that looked like frogs; they came out of the mouth of the dragon, out of the mouth of the beast, and out of the mouth of the false prophet"* (Revelation 16:13). These evil spirits are deceiving spirits, and they again operate in the spiritual realm. The Lord Jesus was referring to Satan when He proclaimed the following: *"When he lies, he speaks his native language, for he is a liar and the father of lies"* (John 8:44). All lies originate from Satan, and here Satan is the power and authority behind both Antichrist and the false prophet. They will use their powers of speech, represented by these evil spirits, to deceive the invading armies from the East. They will deceive these kings into coming over to their side to assist them in their efforts to further persecute God's people and to oppose the Lord.

All of Satan's efforts will ultimately come to naught. He has already been judged and condemned by the God of heaven, and his fate, as we will see in chapter 20, has been recorded for the comfort of God's children. Satan's fate, and the fate of all who choose to reject and rebel against God in favor of pride and self-reliance, will be an eternity spent in everlasting torment and separation from the God that created them, and gave His worldly life to demonstrate just how much He loved all of His creation.

"Therefore rejoice, ye heavens, and ye that dwell in them.
Woe to the inhabiters of the earth and of the sea!
For the devil is come down unto you, having great wrath,
because he knoweth that he hath but a short time."
(Revelation 12:12 KJV)

The Sovereignty of God

The message given to John in Revelation is that God will be victorious. God has made promises to the nation of Israel throughout history and has kept every one. There is not one single unconditional promise in the OT that God has not kept, unless it is something that has to do with future events and times such as those we are studying in the book of Revelation which He will keep in due course. If God has been that faithful to the nation of Israel, which historically has been a stiff-necked people (Exodus 34:9), wicked, idolatrous, sinful, and disobedient, to keep His promise to a small remnant, then what does that say to Christians today? It assures all believers that God will also be faithful to keep every NT promise in His Word, no matter what goes on around us.

The truth is – God is sovereign.

God is sovereign. He is in complete and absolute control of everything. If at any point in our lives we believe ourselves to be victims of circumstance, then God ceases to be sovereign. If God is sovereign, then we are not victims of anything. He may allow some tragedy to attack, afflict, or harm us – as it may appear – but if God is sovereign, then He will turn it to our good. Therefore, God is faithful and keeps His promises. God is sovereign and in complete control of our lives. The wisest thing we can do as children of God is to walk in His perfect will day by day, obeying His Word and giving thanks for His grace. If we do so, then we can take every single promise in His Word and claim it for ourselves.

He is the sovereign God of this universe. He is the ultimate and final authority, and nothing happens outside of His permissive will. Therefore, we can walk every single day with complete confidence and assurance that nothing is going to happen to us unless God allows it; and, if He allows it, then He has a purpose that is higher and far wiser than ours. Whatever God allows, He will turn to our good. That is how the child of God should live.

We must also realize God works His sovereign plan through our choices and decisions. This should motivate and encourage us. God uses our choices to direct us – that is, our wise choices to bless us, our unwise choices to teach us. This is known as the doctrine of providence; and it teaches us, as believers, that we are never in the grip of blind forces such as luck, chance, or fate. Everything that happens to us is divinely planned; and each event should come as a summons to trust, obey, and rejoice.

The Apostle Paul wrote these comforting words: *"And we know that in all things God works for the good of those who love him, who have been called according to his purpose"* (Romans 8:28).

It bears repeating – whatever is going to happen, God is going to turn it to our good, no matter what.

To live our lives any other way is to say that God is not sovereign. The essence of the Christian life can be summed up in these words: trust and obey. If you believe God is sovereign then you will trust God wholeheartedly – you are not going to worry about anything or let anything upset you. God will allow us to go through all kinds of trials in life, but He will ultimately turn them to our good.

Why, then, do Christians suffer in many of the same ways as the rest of the world? Christians die of cancer, in automobile accidents, at the hands of terrorists, and in some parts of the world, are persecuted for their faith. Jesus made it very clear: *"I have told you these things, so that in me you may have peace. In this world you will have trouble. But take heart! I have overcome the world"* (John 16:33). The Apostle Peter likewise wrote: *"Dear friends, do not be surprised at the painful trial you are suffering, as though something strange were happening to you"* (1 Peter 4:12).

God allows us to go through suffering for a purpose. Sometimes, He wants to teach us about ourselves. At other times, He may want to build deeper character and faith in our lives so we may be of comfort to others in similar times of suffering. Perhaps, He wants to show us His goodness in the midst of the trial. There may be times when He just wants to move us to a new place. Regardless, God always has a specific purpose for hardships in our lives.

Knowing our troubles are part of God's plan for us, we can be grateful and thank Him for leading us through times of trial. He is with us at all times. Does this make the pain of hardship any less? Sadly, oftentimes, it does not. However, because God is at work, we can nonetheless rejoice that He is using the hard time to bring us closer to spiritual maturity.

The book of Revelation tells us when Jesus Christ returns to earth, sin will be judged and brought to an end. Until that time, pain and death will be the experience of all who live in this fallen world, without exception. The book of Revelation also reminds us that our Lord will wipe away every tear from the eyes of His children and death will be no more.

God is sovereign, and if He has kept a remnant of the nation of Israel down through history, then He will keep you and me as well.

The Word of God that was given to Moses and spoken to Joshua just before he was to lead the nation of Israel across the Jordan to take possession of the Promised Land comforts us even today: *"The Lord himself goes before you and will be with you; he will never leave you nor forsake you. Do not be afraid; do not be discouraged"* (Deuteronomy 31:8).

Chapter 13

Please follow along in your Bible.

As we begin this chapter of God's Word, we find the dragon (Satan), having been cast out of heaven, angry and standing on the shore of the sea. It is Satan who will bring the beast out of the sea and dominate him. We are now at the mid-point of the 7-year Tribulation Period, also referred to by the Lord Jesus as *the great tribulation* (Matthew 24:21 NKJV).

6) The Beast Out of the Sea – Antichrist

13:1 – 2: *"And I saw a beast coming out of the sea. He had ten horns and seven heads, with ten crowns on his horns, and on each head a blasphemous name. The beast I saw resembled a leopard …."* Since chapter 13 is a continuation of chapter 12, both using symbols to describe personalities, and since there are no seven-headed beasts, we can conclude that this composite picture of a leopard, bear, and lion must be a symbol as well. This is not the first time the Holy Spirit has used the symbol of these three beasts to describe either a king or a kingdom. In chapter 7 of Daniel, these same three beasts are used to represent and describe the vicious character of three former world empires. Some details about this beast can apply only to an individual, while others apply to his kingdom. These verses begin our description of the end-times king and his kingdom. This first beast is Antichrist and his one-world government.

The beast rose out of the sea. In Scripture, the sea is symbolic of the nations of the world (Isaiah 17:12). The Prophet Daniel tells us: *"After the sixty-two 'sevens,' the Anointed One will be cut off and will have nothing. The people of the ruler who will come will destroy the city and the sanctuary"* (Daniel 9:26). The phrase/title, "Anointed One," is a reference to Jesus Christ, Israel's rejection of Him as her Messiah, and His subsequent crucifixion. Who destroyed the city and the sanctuary? It was the Romans. Therefore, Antichrist, the ruler who will come, will arise, as most commentators believe, out of the nations of Europe to establish a new one-world government – the revived Roman Empire.

The ten horns represent the tenfold division of this new global government and the leaders of those ten nations who give Antichrist their power during the Tribulation Period. The seven heads of this beast are mentioned later in chapter 17 (v.10) as kings of the Roman Empire. They represent five kings up to the time of the Apostle John. The sixth king, Domitian, was the Roman emperor at the time of John. Lastly, John skips forward to the end-times for the seventh king (head), Antichrist. All seven kings are guilty of blasphemy. Blasphemy manifests itself in two ways:

1) Making oneself equal to God.
2) Slandering and taking God's name in vain.

At the time of John and his writing, much of the prophecy of Daniel 7 had been fulfilled. The first three beasts (kingdoms) – Babylon, the lion, Media-Persia, the bear, and Greece, the leopard, had all come to pass. John's focus is on the prophet's fourth beast and upon the little horn because the fourth beast, the Roman Empire, had appeared. The emphasis of the book of Revelation is on the rule of the *little horn* of Daniel 7:8. The little horn of Daniel 7 and the beast out of the sea of this chapter are one and the same, the man who becomes the final dictator of the world during the Tribulation Period. Take a moment and read Daniel's description of Antichrist, *The King Who Exalts Himself* (Daniel 11:36 – 45).

The Apostle John wrote extensively about Antichrist in his epistles, and he is the only writer in Scripture to use this term. John speaks of two characteristics of Antichrist:

1) Antichrist is one who is against Christ.
2) Antichrist is one who imitates Christ.

This beast, Antichrist, will exhibit both of these characteristics. The apostle wrote: *"Little children, it is the last hour; and as you have heard that the Antichrist is coming, even now many antichrists have come, by which we will know that it is the last hour"* (1 John 2:18 NKJV). Note that John not only said that there is going to be an Antichrist, but there were many antichrists already present in his day. The apostle stated one key characteristic that identifies an antichrist: *"Who is the liar? It is the man who denies that Jesus is the Christ. Such a man is the antichrist – he denies the Father and the Son"* (1 John 2:22). John gave some additional facts concerning antichrist: *"Dear friends, do not believe every spirit, but test the spirits to see whether they are from God, because many false prophets have gone out into the world … but every spirit that does not acknowledge Jesus is not from God. This is the spirit of antichrist, which you have heard is coming and even now is already in the world"* (1 John 4:1 – 3). In other words, any person, organization, or publication that denies the deity of Jesus Christ is antichrist. Last of all, John warned: *"Many deceivers, who do not acknowledge Jesus Christ as coming in the flesh, have gone out into the world. Any such person is the deceiver and the antichrist"* (2 John 7). Antichrist is a deceiver – he pretends to be Christ.

The Lord Jesus told His disciples: *"For many will come in my name, claiming 'I am the Christ,' and will deceive many"* (Matthew 24:5). Believers ought to be testing every little group or organization that they might be interested in these days. Instead of being faith-based, some may actually be following an antichrist. Can you identify any antichrist today?

13:3 – 4: *"One of the heads of the beast seemed to have had a fatal wound, but the fatal wound had been healed …."* These verses indicate that the beast – that is, Antichrist, will be given a deadly wound. Antichrist will apparently be killed. Revelation 17:8 indicates that his spirit will go down into the Abyss where it belongs, but that it will also return; in other words, he will be resurrected. We must keep in mind that this beast is the end-times Antichrist, and Satan will use this beast to duplicate things Jesus Christ has done. In the words of Jesus: *"I tell you the truth, a time is coming and has now come when the dead will hear the voice of the Son of God and those who hear will live"* (John 5:25). My brethren, only He who created life can resurrect life – the Lord Jesus Christ. This resurrection of Antichrist is a fake resurrection, a ruse. It is accomplished through an embodiment of Antichrist by the dragon, Satan, in order to imitate the resurrection of Jesus Christ. In other words, at the midpoint of the Tribulation Period, Antichrist will be slain, at which time, Satan will evidently enter the body of Antichrist, in spirit, in order to resurrect him back to life. I cannot imagine any other way Satan can duplicate a resurrection. There may very well be things that we are not meant to know, but remember that Satan is the most dangerous and deceitful being in all of God's creation. Presumably after his resurrection, millions of people worldwide, previously undecided about Antichrist, will fall down and worship him. This is the very moment Satan has waited millennia for – that is, to be worshiped. Antichrist becomes the incarnation and pawn of Satan, for John tells us, *"The dragon gave the beast his power and his throne and great authority"* (v.2), meaning all the kingdoms of the world that he once offered Christ (Matthew 4:8, 9).

13:5 – 6: *"The beast was given a mouth to utter proud words and blasphemies and to exercise his authority for forty-two months …"* (forty-two months is three and a half years). Satan has long been the source of blasphemy against God. He is against Christ and His Church, which are in heaven. During the second half of the 7-year Tribulation Period, Antichrist will seem to manifest even greater supernatural powers. People will worship the dragon, as the Apostle Paul predicted: *"He will oppose and will exalt himself over everything that is called God or is worshiped, so that he sets himself up in God's temple, proclaiming himself to be God"* (2 Thessalonians 2:4). This prophecy is also foretold by the Prophet Daniel (9:27) and by the Lord Jesus Christ in His Olivet Discourse (Matthew 24:15). Antichrist's claim of deity is the big lie that the Apostle Paul was referring to when he wrote: *"For this reason God sends them a powerful delusion so that they will believe the lie and so that all will be condemned who have not believed the truth but have delighted in wickedness"* (2 Thessalonians 2:11 – 12). Paul used the word "them" to refer to unrepentant mankind. Take a moment and read Paul's full revelation concerning the coming of Antichrist, the man of lawlessness (2 Thessalonians 2:1 – 12).

13:7: *"He was given power to make war against the saints and to conquer them. And he was given authority over every tribe, people, language and nation."* During this time many believers, whom we refer to as Tribulation saints, will suffer martyrdom at the hands of this brutal beast. These will be, without a doubt, the darkest hours in the history of the world. I call it a dictatorship on steroids!

13:8: *"All inhabitants of the earth will worship the beast – all whose names have not been written in the book of life belonging to the Lamb …."* Today the world is being prepared for a one-world government philosophy. That philosophy, inspired by Satan and promoted by the atheistic and progressive, secular leaders of world governments today, is rapidly spreading across the earth. During the Tribulation Period, Satan will provide a visible god with seemingly divine powers. On the basis of this verse alone it seems the majority of people on the earth will worship Antichrist rather than the Lord Jesus Christ.

The book of life is mentioned in several passages of Scripture, particularly in Revelation: *"If anyone's name was not found written in the book of life, he was thrown into the lake of fire"* (Revelation 20:15). When a child is born, God records that infant's name in His book. If he/she matures and dies without receiving His Son Jesus Christ as their Savior, then that person's name is blotted out of the book (Revelation 3:5). The names remaining make up the book of life belonging to the Lamb. There is no doubt as to the identity of the Lamb, for John the Baptist pointed to Jesus and said, *"Look, the Lamb of God, who takes away the sin of the world!"* (John 1:29) The Lamb's book of life contains only the names of those who have accepted, through faith, the Lamb of God. Jesus Christ offers us eternal life if we simply receive Him into our hearts as Savior and Lord. Once that happens, the angels in heaven rejoice in knowing that another soul's name has been sealed in the Lamb's book of life, from which it can never be blotted out.

13:9 – 10: John is speaking here to God's saints who will be in the world at this time. He is telling them that they are going to have to bear, with patience and faith, the awful trials and sufferings that come even upon God's people.

7) The Beast Out of the Earth – The False Prophet

The first beast, Antichrist, is a political leader, and his power will become worldwide. Satan will provide another leader to promote his own form of worship. This second beast is a religious leader, and he is called the false prophet (Revelation 16:13; 19:20). During the second half of the Tribulation Period, the false prophet will command and facilitate global worship of the first beast – Antichrist.

13:11 – 12: These verses give us five characteristics of the false prophet:

1) Verse 11: *"Then I saw another beast, coming out of the earth …."* Unlike the first beast, the earth from which the second beast arises is symbolic of the Middle East and, more specifically, it is thought that he will rise out of the nation of Israel. This beast, the false prophet, is apparently prophet-like in some manner. The Jewish people would not trust him unless he came from their land and was of Jewish descent. He will lead Israel into signing the covenant with Antichrist, (chapter 6) which triggers the 7-year Tribulation Period. This covenant of peace, as we said earlier, is likely the instrument which permits the rebuilding of the Jewish temple on the Temple Mount.

2) *"He had two horns like a lamb …"* Lambs do not have horns, which are symbolic of power and/or authority. As with Antichrist, the false prophet will also be given certain power and authority from Satan; therefore, he will also imitate things Jesus had done. The resurrection of the first beast, Antichrist, imitates Jesus Christ; thus, he possesses the characteristic of antichrist as described by John. As a Jew who has not accepted Messiah, this second beast, the false prophet, is opposed to Christ; thus, he also possesses the characteristic of antichrist. Jesus warned His disciples: *"Watch out for false prophets. They come to you in sheep's clothing, but inwardly they are ferocious wolves"* (Matthew 7:15).

3) *"… he spoke like a dragon."* This indicates that the false prophet will derive powers of speech from Satan and deceive human beings by acting like a lamb; but in reality, he speaks the words of the devil.

4) Verse 12: *"He exercised all the authority of the first beast on his behalf …"* The false prophet will be given authority by Antichrist (Satan incarnate). During the second half of the Tribulation Period, his purpose will be to work toward the extermination of the apostate (false) church (the prostitute of chapter 17) left on earth after the Rapture of the true Church. The reason for eliminating the apostate church is touched on next and explained in greater detail in chapter 17.

5) *"… made the earth and its inhabitants worship the first beast, whose fatal wound had been healed."* He will not exalt himself, but will work solely for the purpose of facilitating global worship of the first beast, Antichrist. The phrase, "whose fatal wound had been healed,"

indicates that both beasts will be capable of various kinds of counterfeit miracles, signs, and wonders, all enabled by Satan and which make up the powerful delusion, of which the Apostle Paul so boldly wrote (cf. 13:5, 6).

13:13 – 15: *"And he performed great and miraculous signs …."* The false prophet will be equipped by Satan/Antichrist with authority and power to do such supernatural and miraculous signs so as to deceive the populace of the earth. The fact that he will cause fire to come down from heaven should not be surprising, for Satan, the real force behind the false prophet, brought fire down from heaven and burned up Job's sheep and servants (Job 1:16). The Lord Jesus Christ warned His disciples concerning the last days: *"For false Christs and false prophets will appear and perform great signs and miracles to deceive even the elect – if that were possible"* (Matthew 24:24).

The false prophet will cause an image (the Greek word is *eikon* which means likeness) of Antichrist to be built and erected in the new temple in Jerusalem. This is the abomination that causes desolation as foretold by the Prophet Daniel (9:27) and by the Lord Jesus Christ (Matthew 24:15). He will even be, *"… given power to give breath to the image …"* (v.15). An idol that speaks! How many times have the OT prophets and the NT apostles told us that idols, made by men of gold, silver, stone, and wood, cannot hear or speak? Evidently this one will, and it will issue an order that all who do not worship it will be killed. We are told later that these martyrs will suffer decapitation (Revelation 20:4).

Many things coincide with the mid-point of the Tribulation Period, one of which is Satan's persecution of the nation of Israel. When the false prophet erects this idol image in the newly rebuilt temple in Jerusalem and decrees universal idol worship of Antichrist, it may well be that the nation of Israel, who does not seem to receive Jesus Christ as her Messiah in the first half of the Tribulation Period, will embrace Him in the second half, thereby rejecting the deceiving, idolatrous religion of Antichrist and his false prophet.

The Mark of the Beast

13:16 – 18: *"He also forced everyone, small and great … to receive a mark on his right hand or on his forehead … so that no one could buy or sell unless he had the mark … His number is 666."* Six is the number of a human being. It is one short of the complete and perfect number seven; and mankind was created on the sixth day. Therefore, in Bible numerology the number six is used to refer to mankind. We cannot be certain as to why three digits are used. Perhaps it is to emphasize man's identity; nevertheless, it has been a puzzling source of speculation to biblical scholars throughout history. John also suggests that it will somehow mathematically represent the name of the beast, Antichrist. What is more important than the meaning of 666, is that the false prophet will use this as a means of forcing people to worship Antichrist. Additionally, he will mandate that everyone have this mark on his/her forehead or right hand in order to buy or sell. One can hardly imagine the pressure of having to possess such a mark to secure the necessary food for his family.

Physically speaking, it will be necessary for every human being to have the mark of the beast. Spiritually speaking, it will be fatal. We have seen that those who are redeemed by the Lamb, those who have the seal of God, have made the choice to receive Jesus Christ as their Lord and Savior.

However, those who receive Antichrist's mark will have made their final decision for eternity to reject Christ and worship his enemy (Satan); and thus share in his fate.

The nation of Israel becomes the dividing line for the world during the second half of the Tribulation Period. Those who receive the mark of the beast and worship Antichrist will assist him worldwide in his persecution of God's people – Jews and Christians. Those who receive Jesus Christ as Lord and Savior (Tribulation saints) will provide aid and protection for the redeemed Jewish remnant, while sharing with them the message of mercy and grace from their true Messiah, Jesus Christ.

Instead of wasting time trying to identify a person by this number 666, I would rather spend my time getting to know Jesus Christ as my Savior, following the example of the Apostle Paul, whereby he wrote: *"I want to know Christ and the power of his resurrection and the fellowship of sharing in his sufferings, becoming like him in his death, and so, somehow, to attain to the resurrection from the dead"* (Philippians 3:10).

Review Questions

1) The seven-headed, ten-horned beast out of the sea symbolically represents _____ _____.

2) In Scripture, the sea is symbolic of _____.

3) Blasphemy manifests itself in what two ways? _____ _____.

4) What are the two characteristics of Antichrist described by John? _____ _____.

5) How does Satan fake the resurrection of Antichrist? _____ _____.

6) The second beast, the false prophet, is a religious leader. He will promote a religion that solely worships _____.

7) The mark of the beast will be used as a means of forcing people to _____ _____.

Up For Discussion

"And all the world wondered after the beast."
(Revelation 13:3 KJV)

How much do you follow the news and current world events? Discuss any actions and/or policies that may appear as though the world, including the United States, is moving closer to a one-world governmental order. One example might be our nation's massive debt resulting in the eventual devaluation of the U.S. dollar and the call for a global currency. In 1999, the euro was introduced and is today the single currency shared by eighteen of the European Union's Member States, which together make up the euro area.

Other examples might be: 1) the continued overall growth in the size of government, 2) an administration's overt decision to not enforce or even disobey certain laws for ideological reasons thereby placing its citizens in danger, and 3) the decline in religious liberties and protections, specifically the nullification of conscience protection policies in regard to religious beliefs for healthcare workers, private companies, and the military. All of these examples are the result of an ever increasing secular, progressive agenda.

Keep in mind this is an area of great debate, so be sensitive and tolerant of the opinions of others in the class.

Do more: Take a moment and read the following related lesson entitled, *Ezekiel's Latter Days Vision*, on your own. Compare God's judgments upon the enemy that invades Israel with the six seal judgments of chapter 6 and the first four trumpet judgments of chapter 8.

Ezekiel's Latter Days Vision
(Ezekiel chapters 37 – 39)

In chapter 37, the Prophet Ezekiel describes his vision of the valley of dry bones which concerns the future restoration of the nation of Israel. Ezekiel was among the Jews exiled to Babylon by Nebuchadnezzar in 597 B.C. This vision was given to Ezekiel to reassure the exiles that God would be faithful to His promises – that is, to give them hope. Israel's restoration not only had to do with them as a national entity, but also with their spiritual revival which the Lord had promised as well (Ezekiel 36: 24 – 27; Hebrews 8:8 – 10).

In his vision, the valley (37:1) represents the world where the Jewish people have been scattered. God told Ezekiel to prophesy, which means to speak or give out the Word of God. The Word of God is trustworthy; it is faithful and true, and His Word endures forever (Matthew 24:35). Ezekiel was faithful and obedient to God's call.

The restoration of the nation of Israel occurs in stages as represented by the coming together of these bones that were dead and dry and then coming to life. There are three distinct stages:

1) The scattered bones (37:1, 2) represent Israel's dispersion throughout the world and being dead in their relationship to God because of their disobedience and rejection of God's Son, Jesus Christ, the Messiah.
2) The coming together of the bones with tendons, flesh, and skin (37:8) represent Israel's regathering. This began with their pre-1948 return and extends to their present state as a nation, and even further into the future including the Tribulation Period of the latter years.
3) Breath entered them (37:9, 10), representing their final conversion as a nation. They are made alive when they choose, at the midpoint of the Tribulation Period, to turn in faith to Jesus Christ as Messiah rather than worship Antichrist and take his mark. The breath can also be viewed symbolically as the Holy Spirit. The restoration of a person (or nation) into a right relationship with God, through His Son Jesus Christ, results in the Holy Spirit indwelling that once spiritually lifeless person (or nation).

God has made it very clear: *"He who has the Son has life; he who does not have the Son of God does not have life"* (1 John 5:12).

The kingdom of David split in two after the reign of Solomon and became the northern kingdom of Israel and the southern kingdom of Judah. The joining together of the two sticks marked Judah and Ephraim (Israel, the northern kingdom, was often called Ephraim after its largest tribe) is another assurance to the Jewish people that all twelve tribes will be represented when the nation of Israel is finally united and restored during the Millennium. The earthly reign of Jesus Christ, the Messiah, over the children of Israel begins with the resurrection of David as their prince (Ezekiel 37:24, 25) along with the rest of the OT saints (Daniel 12:1).

Invasion of Israel during the Tribulation

As we can see, God has a definite plan and purpose for the nation of Israel in the future, and chapters 38 and 39 focus on stage two of their restoration and specifically during the Tribulation Period. The prophet's message tells of an enemy that will come against Israel in future years, or the latter years (KJV). The brazen nation that will invade Israel is thought to be Russia.

Gog is the leader of this coalition. Magog (land of) is the territory and is identified with the land north of Israel around and above the Black and Caspian Seas. Magog was one of the sons of Japheth (Genesis 10:2), and his descendants occupied lands from Spain to southern Russia and were later called Scythians. This is from whom the Slavic people are thought to have descended. The Hebrew word for chief is *Rosh*, and has been translated "chief of Rosh." When taken as a proper name, this identifies Rosh with the inhabitants of Scythia. Meshech and Tubal were also sons of Japheth; thus making the coalition in Ezekiel's vision inclusive and led by people descended from Japheth. In addition, Russia was originally called Muscovy which was thought to be derived from Meshech. Other nations will ally with Gog. Persia is Iran, and Cush and Put are nations from North Africa. These are nations with radical Islamic factions and leadership, and are long-time enemies of Israel. Finally, Gomer and Togarmah, from the far north, will also join the alliance and again represent descendants of Japheth (1 Chronicles 1:6).

God is in absolute control of this invasion. God says He will *"… turn you around, put hooks in your jaws and bring you out with your whole army"* (Ezekiel 38:4).

We have already seen the beginning of this – that is, the preparation. That occurred in 2014 when Russia invaded and took possession of Crimea during the unconcerned administration of President Barak Obama. Now, during another indecisive U.S. administration, that of President Joe Biden, Russia is emboldened again and invading the small, sovereign country of Ukraine. Although his efforts have been met with brave and unexpected resistance from Ukrainian forces and its people, Russia, led by its godless President Vladimir Putin, is making progress in taking land, especially in the east. We do not know for certain the political/military reasons as to why Russia is currently on such an illegal and aggressive campaign against Ukraine; however, one objective seems to be to establish a land bridge from Russia to the Black Sea in order to secure a warm-water port with access to the world's waterways. There is also the expressed vision of Vladimir Putin to reestablish the Soviet Union to its former size and glory. It appears as though God has started bringing Russia onto the world stage to deal with this ruthless nation according to His plan.

The prophet says that these nations, led by Gog, will invade Israel in future years, or latter years (KJV) during a time when the people (the Jews) are gathered from many nations to the mountains of Israel and living in safety (Ezekiel 38:8). Our first clue as to the timing of this assault is the phrase, "latter years," which, according to the OT prophets, is a reference to the future time of the end, the 7-year Tribulation Period of Revelation (cf. Jeremiah 23:20; Daniel 10:14; Hosea 3:5 KJV). Our second clue is the fact that the Jewish people will have returned from their national dispersion to Jerusalem and will be living in safety, meaning in peace. This could only be possible during the first half of the Tribulation Period when the people of Israel are living under the covenant of peace and dominion of Antichrist (Daniel 9:27). During this time the temple will be rebuilt and the Jewish people that have long been scattered throughout the globe will flock back to Israel *en masse*. The attack will likely come sometime in the first year of the Tribulation Period when the rebuilding of the temple is well underway and the gathering of the Jewish people is near complete. Russia and its Islamic allies will come against the nation of Israel like a storm (Ezekiel 38:9).

I would suggest the following four reasons why this confederation of nations would invade Israel:

1) The first reason is given to us by the prophet – that is, to plunder and loot Israel's wealth (Ezekiel 38:12, 13).
2) The second reason would be to gain territorial control of the Middle East.
3) The third would be to wipe Israel off the face of the earth, which is the ultimate desire expressed time and again by the leaders of Iran and their Islamic brethren.
4) The last reason would be to challenge the authority of Antichrist (Daniel 11:40 – 44). Israel will be living under his covenant of peace; therefore, an attack against Israel will be viewed as a direct attack against Antichrist as well.

Antichrist will muster his armies against the invading threat from the North and the South; however, unbeknownst to him, God is orchestrating this entire ordeal. God will deal with Russia.

As war breaks out, God will deliver His covenant people by destroying the invading forces with the use of four judgments:

1) A great earthquake (Ezekiel 38:19, 20).
2) The troops will turn against one another (Ezekiel 38:21), as did the armies that invaded Judah during the reign of Jehoshaphat (2 Chronicles 20:22, 23).
3) A judgment of plague and bloodshed (Ezekiel 38:22).
4) Torrents of rain, hailstones, and burning sulfur (Ezekiel 38:22). God will even send fire upon Magog, the homeland of the invaders as a final consequence (Ezekiel 39:6).

This is God's judgment. After the armies of the Russian/Islamic alliance are supernaturally destroyed, the birds and wild animals will feast on the dead, the weapons will be burned for fuel for seven years (inclusive), and the dead will be buried in the valley (Ezekiel 39:4 – 11). Israel will rejoice in the Lord's deliverance all the way up to the mid-point of the Tribulation Period.

The second half of the Tribulation Period (42 months/3½ years), referred to by our Lord Jesus Christ as the Great Tribulation (Matthew 24:21 KJV) then begins. With the defeat of his enemies, Antichrist becomes the first global ruler of the united world. Empowered by Satan, Antichrist's tyrannical reign begins, and his first action will be to break his covenant of peace with Israel and invade her himself (Daniel 11:41 – 44). He will put an end to the daily sacrifice and erect his idol image in the newly rebuilt temple in Jerusalem. Antichrist will exalt himself as god and demand that everyone worldwide worship him and take his mark – 666. The whole world under the rule of Antichrist becomes a battleground of war, persecution, fear, and distress. It is no wonder our Lord said, *"If those days had not been cut short, no one would survive, but for the sake of the elect those days will be shortened"* (Matthew 24:22). The elect are believers, Jew and Gentile. As a result of Antichrist's deceit and persecution, the people of the nation of Israel will reject Antichrist and turn instead to Jesus Christ. Finally, as a united people and as a nation, they will accept the Lord Jesus Christ as their long-awaited Messiah.

During the first half of the Tribulation Period, God will use the covenant of peace signed between Israel and Antichrist along with the reconstruction of the temple as an incentive to gather all the

Jewish people from around the world back to Israel once more. Then, as a nation, they will stand and watch as Almighty God, through a series of judgments, completely destroys the invading hoards descending from opposite directions, leaving them nothing more than smoldering ruins scattered throughout the valley. *"I will display my glory among the nations, and all the nations will see the punishment I inflict and the hand I lay upon them"* (Ezekiel 39:21). The nations will witness God's deliverance of His people, and Israel will acknowledge God's protective power and sovereign plan for them as a nation. Israel's rebellion against God is finally broken (Daniel 12:7) as she rejects the rule of Antichrist and turns wholly as a nation in faith to Jesus Christ, her true Messiah.

God will fulfill all His promises to Israel, including her restoration: *"Therefore, this is what the Sovereign Lord says: 'I will now bring Jacob back from captivity and will have compassion on all the people of Israel, and I will be zealous for my holy name … I will no longer hide my face from them, for I will pour out my Spirit on the house of Israel, declares the Sovereign Lord'"* (Ezekiel 39:25 – 29).

God's plan for His people will be accomplished with the return of His Son Jesus Christ to earth at the end of the Tribulation Period (Daniel's Seventieth Seven) to put an end to all wickedness and rebellion and establish His eternal kingdom of righteousness. *"Then the sovereignty, power and greatness of the kingdoms under the whole heaven will be handed over to the saints, the people of the Most High. His kingdom will be an everlasting kingdom, and all rulers will worship and obey him"* (Daniel 7:27).

Chapter 14

Please follow along in your Bible.

This chapter is yet another interlude in our chronology and contains several events. The contrast between chapters 13 and 14 is remarkable. From the wicked and rebellious scene of earth during the Great Tribulation, John's vision is fast forwarded in time to the end of the Tribulation Period, where Jesus Christ's name is honored rather than profaned, and all voices are raised in praise and adoration. It is apparent from chapter 13 that the Lamb of God will not be on earth in the midst of the Tribulation Period. The scene in this chapter is on earth, and these first five verses offer us a rare glimpse into the days immediately following the end of the Tribulation Period and the return of Christ to earth. John's vision begins with a scene in the Holy City that opens the Millennium upon the earth, when heaven and earth are finally brought into beautiful harmony.

The Lamb and the 144,000

14:1: *"Then I looked, and there before me was the Lamb, standing on Mount Zion, and with him 144,000 who had his name and his Father's name written on their foreheads."* The Lamb is the Lord Jesus Christ. Mount Zion is Jerusalem, and the Lord Jesus is going to reign from Jerusalem as the Psalms proclaim (Psalm 2:6 – 9; 9:11, 12; 48:1 – 3; 110:1, 2, to name a few).

The 144,000 standing with Jesus are the same ones who were sealed back in chapter 7. Although Jesus is called the Lamb here, we also know Him as the good shepherd (John 10:11). Our Lord started out with 144,000 servants, and He came through seven years of tribulation with 144,000. He didn't lose a single one! In the words of the late pastor and radio commentator, J. Vernon McGee: "They came through the Great Tribulation like the three Hebrews came through the fiery furnace."

14:2 – 3: The 144,000 Tribulation servants join the heavenly chorus during the Millennium. They *"... had been redeemed from the earth"* (v.3) in the same way that all are redeemed – through faith in Jesus Christ. They, too, were purchased by His precious blood so they may enter the Millennial Kingdom on earth. *"No one could learn the song ..."* (v.3), simply refers to the fact that no one can sing praises to God except those who love God – those who are redeemed. Songs of the heart are only learned through personal faith experience. The psalmist proclaims: *"Give thanks to the Lord, for he is good; his love endures forever. Let the redeemed of the Lord say this – those he redeemed from the hand of the foe, those he gathered from the lands, from the east and west, from the north and south"* (Psalm 107:1 – 3). The redeemed from all corners of the earth are the result of the 7-year evangelizing efforts of these 144,000 bold servants for Jesus Christ, the Lamb of God.

14:4 – 5: These verses give us additional characteristics of the 144,000 servants as they endured through the entire Tribulation Period:

1) Verses 4: They were morally pure because they did not defile themselves with women. This may mean that they either kept their marriage vows; or more likely, they were never married in the first place and therefore viewed their obedience to God's commission to evangelize the world to be paramount above all else. During the Tribulation Period there will be an exaggerated emphasis upon sex and, as we mentioned in chapter 9, immorality will abound. The 144,000 servants keep themselves separated from these sins. Consequently, in the eyes of God, they were considered pure or, as the KJV translate, virgins. This probably refers to chastity in both the literal and spiritual sense.

2) Verse 4: *"They follow the Lamb wherever He goes."* This means they were obedient to the Lord.

3) They were offered as firstfruits to God and the Lamb. This phrase has definite reference to the nation of Israel. Israel (and especially the 144,000 servants) is described as the firstfruits by the Apostle Paul: *"For if their rejection is the reconciliation of the world, what will their acceptance be but life from the dead? If the part of the dough offered as firstfruits is holy, then the whole batch is holy; if the root is holy, so are the branches"* (Romans 11:15, 16). These 144,000 Tribulation servants will evidently hold some special or unique position alongside the Lamb when He establishes His Millennial Kingdom on earth.

4) Verse 5: *"No lie was found in their mouths …"* means that they did not participate in the big lie of the beast and his false prophet. They simply did not fall for it.

5) They lived blameless lives. This does not mean they were perfect (without sin), but in their desire to serve Jesus Christ and walk with Him, they leaned on His power to live holy, consecrated lives. They are considered blameless because they possessed the righteousness of Christ through faith.

This ends our brief fore-glimpse of the bright days beginning the Millennium as John's vision now returns in time to the mid-point of the dreadful Tribulation Period.

The Three Angels

14:6 – 7: *"Then I saw another angel flying in midair, and he had the eternal gospel to proclaim to those who live on the earth …."* One of God's faithful practices in all generations has been to send adequate warning prior to judgment. Another angel suggests a change in the matter in which God will communicate with those remaining on earth. This angel is the first of six we will find in the remaining verses of this chapter. The eternal gospel is the message of Jesus Christ's sacrificial death for the sins of the world and His resurrection to conquer death. During this current age, the Gospel has been committed to men – that is, the Church as the messenger of it. In the OT, angels, as well as men, were messengers of God. The writer of Hebrews tells us: *"The message spoken by angels was binding"* (Hebrews 2:2).

We have already seen that God will use 144,000 sealed servants and two supernatural witnesses to evangelize the world during the Tribulation Period. However, the times are so intense that even an angel is needed to help spread God's message of salvation to the world. Why do you suppose God would go so far as to use an angel? One suggestion might be that angels are spiritual creatures, and as such, they are immortal and cannot be harmed by men, unlike the two supernatural witnesses of chapter 11. In addition, the physical and visual manifestation of a spiritual being to a stiff-necked, unbelieving population would be the final positive proof of a divine reality and a loving God reaching out to lost humanity. In a loud voice, this angel will warn the people to fear God and give Him glory instead of Antichrist, and to worship Him instead of Antichrist, for He created all things. Scripture reminds us: *"The fear of the Lord is the beginning of knowledge"* (Proverbs 1:7). This seems to be God's final call to mankind to flee the wrath to come before accepting Antichrist and his mark.

14:8: Our second angel announces that which is yet to come: *"Fallen! Fallen is Babylon the Great, which makes all the nations drink the maddening wine of her adulteries."* The book of Revelation makes reference to two Babylons; both are termed, *Babylon the Great.* They are:

1) Religious Babylon: This is the apostate (false) church, and it represents a false religion that promotes idolatry and sexual immorality.
2) Governmental and commercial Babylon: This is the literal ancient city of Babylon in present day Iraq that becomes the global headquarters of the end-times Antichrist.

As we briefly touched on in chapters 2 (v.13) and 9 (v.14), Babylon has been Satan's headquarters from the very beginning. Babylon is the place where idolatry began. Semiramis was the wife (some say the mother) of Nimrod. She was queen of Babel, which later became Babylon. She devised a story (a lie) in which she stepped fully grown out of an egg in the Euphrates River, thus beginning a whole system of idolatry. The worship of Semiramis introduced the female deity of false religion. This identifies Babylon as the birthplace of all false religions. In this verse, John gives us a fore-glimpse of the judgment of religious Babylon. It takes place in the middle of the Tribulation Period and is explained in greater detail in chapter 17. The prediction of the destruction of the literal city of Babylon is found in chapter 16 (vv.18, 19), and the judgment upon governmental and commercial Babylon is vividly described in chapter 18.

14:9 – 11: *"A third angel followed them and said in a loud voice: 'If anyone worships the beast and his image and receives his mark … he, too, will drink the wine of God's fury ….'"* In chapter 13, we saw that the awful consequence for not having the mark of the beast was starvation. On the other hand, this third angel announces that anyone who does receive the mark will bring down upon his/her head the wrath of God in full strength. The wine of God's fury is symbolism taken from the OT. The psalmist wrote: *"In the hand of the Lord is a cup full of foaming wine mixed with spices; he pours it out and all the wicked of the earth drink it down to its very dregs"* (Psalm 75:8). This angel issues a warning of the dire consequences to those who worship the beast and receive his mark. During the second half of the Tribulation Period, not only will they experience the cataclysmic judgments sent by God upon the earth as revealed in the bowl judgments of chapter 16; but even worse, they will be, *"… tormented with burning sulfur"* (v.10) for eternity. I do not know anyone who enjoys teaching eternal damnation for lost souls, but Scripture presents no explanation other than the lake of burning sulfur (Revelation 20:10) as being literal and eternal, and those who are condemned and sent there will be tormented for eternity. John even says that this torment will be visible to the holy angels and Christ. This is not something I care to witness.

14:12 – 13: *"This calls for patient endurance on the part of the saints ...."* One of the consistent chords of Scripture is the concept that present-day sufferings are inconsequential in view of the eternal blessings prepared for those who love the Lord. The phrase, "for their deeds will follow them" (v.13), reveals that the saints (believers) will be rewarded for their faithfulness, patience, and their good deeds to others during the Tribulation Period. God does not save anyone by his/her deeds (good works), but only through faith in His Son Jesus Christ. Just as crowns are heavenly rewards for good works done while on earth for those who make up the Church, so, too, will God reward these Tribulation saints for their good works. The greatest reward of all will be entry into the earthly kingdom Christ will establish and reign from at the conclusion of the Tribulation Period.

The Harvest of the Elect

14:14: In these last two sections, John gives us another prophetic fore-glimpse of events to come. John first sees, *"... a white cloud, and seated on the cloud was one like the son of man."* This is obviously a vision of the Lord Jesus Christ as He returns to earth at the end of the Tribulation Period. The cloud aids us in our identification for the Lord told His disciples: *"At that time the sign of the Son of Man will appear in the sky, and all the nations of the earth will mourn. They will see the Son of Man coming on the clouds of the sky, with power and great glory"* (Matthew 24:30). The crown of gold on his head refers to the fact that when Jesus returns to earth, He will return as King, the King of kings – not as a prophet. The sharp sickle speaks of the judgment that is to come upon the wicked.

14:15 – 16: *"Then another angel came out of the temple and called in a loud voice ... 'Take your sickle and reap ....'"* This fourth angel announces the first harvest – the harvest of the elect. These are believers, Tribulation saints who have survived all the way to the end of the Tribulation Period when Christ returns to earth. Our Lord foretold of this event: *"And he will send his angels with a loud trumpet call, and they will gather his elect from the four winds, from one end of the heavens to the other"* (Matthew 24:31). The harvest has long been associated with Christian witnessing. After Jesus had completed His first journey through the region teaching the good news of the kingdom, and just before sending His disciples out to preach to the lost sheep of Israel, He encouraged them with these words: *"The harvest is plentiful but the workers are few. Ask the Lord of the harvest, therefore, to send out workers into the harvest field"* (Matthew 9:37, 38; Luke 10:2). Today however, believers are not urged to harvest, but to sow – sow the message of the Gospel of Christ and the Word of God.

The Harvest of the Wicked

14:17 – 19: *"Another angel came out of the temple in heaven, and he too had a sharp sickle. Still another angel, who had charge of the fire ... called in a loud voice ... 'Take your sharp sickle and gather the cluster of grapes from the earth's vine, because its grapes are ripe.' ...."* The fifth and sixth angels announce the second harvest – the harvest of the wicked. These are all who have rejected Christ and followed Antichrist. The fifth angel also has a sharp sickle, and the sixth angel, likely the same angel we saw in chapter 8 (v.3), has charge of the fire from the altar. Both are symbolic references to the judgment of the wicked. Here we continue in our fore-glimpse with a preview of Armageddon. The expression, "great winepress of God's wrath," is a picture of the fullness of the cup of God's wrath against the wicked left on earth. The Prophet Joel set the time of the harvest with these words: *"Swing the sickle, for the harvest is ripe. Come, trample the grapes, for the winepress is full and the vats overflow — so great is their wickedness! Multitudes, multitudes in the valley of decision! For the day of the Lord is near in the valley of decision"* (Joel 3:13, 14). What makes it possible that the time to reap has come? The Lord Jesus answered that question when He told His disciples: *"The harvest is the end of the age, and the harvesters are angels. As the weeds are pulled up and burned in the fire, so it will be at the end of the age. The Son of Man will send out his angels, and they will weed out of his kingdom everything that causes sin and all who do evil. They will throw them into the fiery furnace, where there will be weeping and gnashing of teeth"* (Matthew 13:39 – 42).

14:20: *"They were trampled in the winepress outside the city, and the blood flowed out of the press ...."* Outside the city means outside Jerusalem – that is, in the valley of decision (see Joel reference above). The blood of the wicked flowed as high as the horses' bridles, which would imply about four feet deep, and for a distance of 1,600 stadia, which is equal to about 184 miles. It is interesting to note, when using the mileage scale on a map of modern-day Israel, the distance from the northern point of the Golan Heights to the southern point of the Gaza Strip, north to south, is right around 180 miles. This is the scene of the final war between Jesus Christ and the evil forces of Antichrist.

There is some debate among biblical scholars regarding verses 14 – 20. Many, including myself, see two harvests – that of the righteous and that of the wicked. This harvesting of the earth is also explained by our Lord in His parable of *The Sheep and the Goats* (Matthew 25:31 – 46). However, there are others that see only the harvest of the wicked. Whichever way you choose to believe, just know that you are in exceedingly good company. When Christ returns to earth at the end of the Tribulation Period, He will judge all those remaining; and He will separate those who will enter into His Millennial Kingdom from those who will not.

Review Questions

1) All 144,000 servants survived the 7-year Tribulation Period because they had _____ _____.

2) The first angel's proclamation was _____ _____.

3) The second angel proclaims the judgment and fall of _____.

4) The third angel issues a warning of the dire and eternal consequences to those who_____ _____.

5) The one sitting on the white cloud and referred to as like a son of man is _____ _____.

6) The fourth angel announces the harvest of the _____.

7) The fifth and sixth angels announce the harvest of the _____ _____.

Up For Discussion

"And I saw another angel fly in the midst of heaven, having the everlasting
gospel to preach unto them that dwell on the earth."
(Revelation 14:6 KJV)

The events of the book of Revelation are directed by the Lord Jesus Christ from heaven and are executed on earth, for the most part, through the ministry of His angels. We have seen the four angels that control the winds of wrath. We have witnessed the angel seal the 144,000 Tribulation servants. In chapters 8 and 9 we saw seven angels with seven trumpets execute their judgment on mankind. Further, in chapter 8 we saw the angel who had the golden censer that ministers before the altar in heaven. Now, in this chapter, we witnessed a parade of six more angels, each with a specific duty. Just as Gabriel is known as the announcing angel, the first three angels of this chapter are also sent, each to make a dreadful announcement to an unrepentant world in turmoil. The remaining three angels represent a fore-glimpse of the angels who will accompany and assist Christ when He returns to earth at the end of the Tribulation, to judge the earth and those surviving to the end.

Obviously, angels play an important role throughout the book of Revelation; but, how about in our lives? While teaching in the temple, the Lord Jesus told His disciples: *"See that you do not look down on one of these little ones. For I tell you that their angels in heaven always see the face of my Father in heaven"* (Matthew 18:10). Have you ever sensed the supernatural presence and/or assistance of an unseen force – a guardian angel? Does it give you a sense of comfort, hope, and/or security? Share with the class any experience that you have had that you feel may have involved a supernatural presence or intervention.

Chapter 15

Please follow along in your Bible.

In this chapter we will see the preparation for the final set of judgments of the Great Tribulation. Chapters 15 and 16 belong together, for in them we have the pouring out of the seven bowls of God's wrath. We have already seen the seven seal judgments and the seven trumpet judgments. However, the coming seven bowls of God's wrath, as we will see, are the most intense and devastating of them all.

Seven Angels with Seven Plagues

15:1: *"I saw in heaven another great and marvelous sign: seven angels with seven last plagues ...."* The phrase, "great and marvelous sign," indicates that this may be the most significant of all signs revealed to this point. The word "sign" means a symbol of revelation; in other words, it represents something that will be revealed in greater detail later, just as we saw in chapters 12 and 13 with the seven personalities/groups. From chapter 12 to the return of Christ, there are a series of events or elements that are inexorably intertwined. This does not mean they are in a precise chronological order, but rather a logical order used to retrace them with added detail. We mentioned this at the onset in our introduction. John, however, immediately identifies the sign as the seven angels with the seven last plagues. The apostle makes it clear that this will be the last or final set of judgments of the Great Tribulation before the return of Christ. The psalmist wrote: *"The Lord says to my Lord: Sit at my right hand until I make your enemies a footstool for your feet"* (Psalm 110:1). Keep in mind that these judgments are the wrath of God upon the earth. These judgments proceed from heaven and are directed by the Lord Jesus Christ as Judge of the earth, and not from Satan or the beast.

15:2: *"And I saw what looked like a sea of glass mixed with fire and, standing beside the sea, those who had been victorious over the beast ...."* This sea of glass is most likely the same sea of glass observed before the throne of God in chapter 4 (v.6). We said it represented the Word of God, and here, the vision includes the Tribulation saints who held firm to God's Word. The fire refers to the trial of fire, i.e., persecution endured by these slain saints of the Great Tribulation, *"... those who had been victorious over the beast and his image and over the number of his name."* This is why the Lord Jesus responded to John, a disciple at the time, with the following words: *"I tell you the truth, anyone who gives you a cup of water in my name because you belong to Christ will certainly not lose his reward"* (Mark 9:41). During the second half of the 7-year Tribulation Period, Antichrist and the false prophet will persecute those who refuse to worship his idol image and receive his mark. These saints suffered through the fires of persecution on the earth and never lost faith. The harps, given to them by God, indicate that they are playing the heavenly instrument in a beautiful symphony of praise and worship.

15:3 – 4: They *"sang the song of Moses the servant of God and the song of the Lamb …."* These Tribulation saints are singing the song of victory over their enemy. The song of Moses, found in Exodus (15:1 – 21), speaks of God's deliverance, salvation, and faithfulness. They combine it with the song of the Lamb we saw in chapter 5 (vv.9 – 12) which praises the Lord Jesus Christ as the Redeemer. Let me remind you that the book of Revelation is Christ-centered. Do not let anything else we study distract your focus from Christ. In this book, we have the unveiling of Jesus Christ in His holiness, His power, and His glory. The songs of Moses and the Lamb here clearly identify the Lord Jesus Christ with the attributes of God the Father. While teaching in the temple, the Lord Jesus told those standing around Him, including the Jews: *"I and the Father are one"* (John 10:30). Let's look at the divine characteristics attributed to the Lamb – the Lord Jesus Christ:

1) Verse 3: **Great and marvelous are your deeds, Lord God Almighty**. This refers to the Lord Jesus Christ as the Creator.
2) **Just and true are your ways, King of the age**. This refers to His reign during the Millennium. He will rule with perfect justice and true righteousness.
3) Verse 4: **Who will not fear you, O Lord, and bring glory to your name?** This speaks of Christ as omnipotent, meaning all-powerful, and the object of universal worship. This is the primary purpose of God the Father – to glorify His Son, Jesus Christ, in His created universe!
4) **For you alone are holy**. This is a reference to the Lord's purity and holiness. Only Jesus lived a sinless life. It is only through faith in His death, as the perfect, blameless sacrifice, and subsequent resurrection, that we too are made holy.
5) **All nations will come and worship before you, for your righteous acts have been revealed**. This refers to His absolute and sovereign rule during the Millennium. As their righteous King, all the nations on earth will eagerly journey to Jerusalem, the place of His throne, to worship Him.

The book of Revelation clarifies who Jesus Christ truly is. This book is worthy of our study because it does exactly that, it announces – the revelation of Jesus Christ (Revelation 1:1). The late pastor and radio host, J. Vernon McGee, once stated: "The Man Christ Jesus is wonderful! Only He can put one hand in the hand of God and the other in the hand of man and bring them together. He can do this because He is God." What awesome insight!

15:5 – 6: *"After this I looked and in heaven the temple, that is, the tabernacle of the Testimony, was opened …."* Beginning with chapter 4, the scene of the throne and/or temple in heaven is referred to many times. Its prominence cannot be ignored. There is no temple in the New Jerusalem (where the Church is going) because the Church is never identified with a temple. This fact makes itself abundantly clear that God is dealing with the nation of Israel, for only they had a temple. Both the temple and the ark of the covenant were patterned after the originals in heaven (Exodus 25:9, 40). Recall John's earlier vision when he saw God's temple in heaven opened, and within His temple was the ark of his covenant (11:19). The tabernacle of the temple of God is the Holy of Holies, the dwelling place of God during the desert wandering of the Israelites. Great significance should be given to this scene. The testimony that radiates from the tabernacle is seen in the ark of the covenant. The action of God here is based on Israel's violation of His covenant – that is, their disobedience resulting in the broken Law. God is righteous in what He is about to do. He will judge, and then He will fulfill His New Covenant with the nation of Israel.

When you read the OT prophets, you cannot miss the fact that God is going to return the children of Israel back to their land. The Prophet Jeremiah wrote extensively concerning the restoration of Israel in chapters 30 and 31. The writer of Hebrews (8:8 – 12) quotes Jeremiah's prophetic announcement and definition of the New Covenant. The writer goes further to state that the New Covenant is established upon better promises with Christ as the Mediator (Hebrews 9:15).

The temple of the tabernacle in heaven is opened so that the seven angels with the seven last plagues could go forth. Created as holy beings, angels are permitted entrance into the true tabernacle in heaven. These seven angels depart from the presence of God, who dwells upon the mercy seat. But now, God acts in justice instead of mercy. These angels, *"… dressed in clean, shining linen and wore golden sashes around their chest"* (v.6), are described in priest-like attire (Exodus 28); however, as servants of the Lord Jesus Christ, they are used to bring judgment upon the earth.

15:7: Seven is God's number for completeness, and in the book of Revelation we see a series of sevens that all represent completeness. We have seen that the seven churches represent Christ's complete message to the Church of all ages. After the Church is removed from the earth, we have a complete 7-year Tribulation Period that includes seven seal judgments and seven bowl judgments. With these last seven angels and seven golden bowls filled with God's wrath, God's judgment upon the earth will be complete.

The bowl reminds us again of the temple wherein bowls were used in the service of the temple. Once a year, a bowl of blood was taken by the high priest into the Holy of Holies on the Day of Atonement. That bowl of blood represented redemption for sins. A world that has rejected the blood of Jesus Christ must now bear the judgment of its sin. The Apostle Paul warned: *"But because of your stubbornness and your unrepentant heart, you are storing up wrath against yourself for the day of God's wrath, when his righteous judgment will be revealed"* (Romans 2:5).

15:8: *"And the temple was filled with smoke from the glory of God and from his power, and no one could enter the temple until the seven plagues of the seven angels were completed."* From this time forward, no created being will have access to the presence of God on His throne until the end of the Tribulation Period. God will not be dealing with humanity in mercy, as is His usual custom. During the second half of the 7-year Tribulation Period, referred to by the Lord as the *great tribulation* (Matthew 24:21 NKJV), God will deal with mankind in judgment.

Even though our evangelical responsibility may include warning the world of the coming judgment of God, it is of greater importance we offer them the Gospel of grace – that is, the message that God loves them and is willing to save them through faith in His Son Jesus Christ. I truly believe more people are brought to salvation by the love of God than by the judgment of God. God has shown His love for the world for almost two thousand years of the Church Age (the dispensation of grace). These last three and a half years of the Tribulation Period are God's final attempt, through judgment, to save a rebellious people.

Review Questions

1) In Scripture, the word sign means _____.

2) The sea of glass in heaven represents _____.

3) The fire refers to _____.

4) The song of Moses speaks of _____.

5) The song of the Lamb speaks of _____.

6) The visions of the temple in heaven indicate that _____.

7) With the seven angels and the seven bowls of God's wrath, God's judgment upon the earth will be

_____.

Up For Discussion

"And after that I looked, and, behold, the temple of the tabernacle
of the testimony in heaven was opened."
(Revelation 15:5 KJV)

Up to this point in our study, we have witnessed the scene of God's temple in heaven several times. John has given us his vision of the glory of God (*Shekinah*) on His throne. He has described for us the rainbow-like crystal sea and the four seraphim that surround the throne. We have seen the twenty-four elders, a multitude of angels, and the souls of Tribulation saints before the throne singing praises to God and to the Lamb. In addition, John shares his vision of the temple opened in heaven and of the ark of the covenant. Now, at the conclusion of this chapter, the temple is emptied (except for the glory of God) until the last seven plagues are completed. God is using these visions of the temple in heaven to emphasize His message to the nation of Israel. During this time of tribulation and judgment on earth, He is still working out His plan of redemption for the Jewish remnant – His chosen people.

In speaking of the future nation of Israel, God told Abram: *"I will bless those who bless you and whoever curses you I will curse"* (Genesis 12:3). Israel remains one of America's closest allies in the world. Do you believe we have been blessed as a nation because of our past alliance with Israel? Do you think recent political events have strengthened or damaged America's relationship with Israel? Cite some examples where we, as a nation, have disregarded Israel in favor of others in the region. One example might be the 2015 Iran Nuclear Deal. Cite some examples where America has honored Israel as a nation. One example might be moving our embassy from Tel-Aviv to Jerusalem in 2018 in recognition of its capital.

Chapter 16

Please follow along in your Bible.

16:1: The seven angels, each holding a bowl containing the wrath of God, are obedient to the loud voice of the Lord Jesus when He speaks: *"Go, pour out the seven bowls of God's wrath on the earth."* The Father has committed all judgment to the Son, as we have already confirmed (John 5:22). The power, the glory, and the majesty belong to Him. The Lord Jesus Christ is in complete control. He is the One who gives the command from heaven, and the seven angels execute His command on earth.

The Bowl Judgments

Should we take these judgments as literal? It is worth noting that four of these seven judgments occurred among the ten plagues in Egypt; and as such, the plagues of Egypt have never been viewed by credible commentators of God's Word as anything but literal. In addition, part of the sixth judgment, the drying up of the Euphrates River and the menacing frogs, was literally fulfilled as well during the time of Israel's exodus from Egypt. Hordes of frogs were generated in the second plague of Egypt, and both the Red Sea and Jordan River were driven back and stilled (Exodus 14:21; Joshua 3:16) so God's people could walk forth on dry ground. If the plagues of Egypt were literal (and we certainly believe they were), then we should also expect these awful judgments to be literal as well.

16:2: The first bowl: *"The first angel went and poured out his bowl on the land, and ugly and painful sores broke out on the people who had taken the mark of the beast and worshiped his image."* This judgment causes grievous and painful sores to come upon the wicked. This parallels the sixth plague of Egypt (Exodus 9:8 – 12). It is interesting to note that Moses predicted coming judgment upon Israel similar to this, and it has yet to be fulfilled (Deuteronomy 28:27, 35). This judgment identifies two important points:

1) The time: This judgment occurs at the time when the beast, i.e., the Antichrist is worshiped. This is further confirmation that the three judgments (seals, trumpets, and bowls) are sequential, not concurrent as some might suggest. This judgment will fall on mankind because of their worship of Antichrist, which only occurs after the mid-point of the Tribulation Period as we learned in chapter 13.

2) The recipients of the judgment – the people who had taken the mark of the beast and worshiped his image. This indicates that God in His amazing grace will not bring judgment on believers during the second half of the Tribulation Period, but will protect them as He did the Israelites in Goshen during the plagues of Egypt.

16:3: The second bowl: *"The second angel poured out his bowl on the sea, and it turned into blood like that of a dead man, and every living thing in the sea died."* We have already seen that God caused one third of the sea to turn to blood as a result of the second trumpet judgment; therefore, the second bowl judgment afflicts the remaining oceans. It does not take much imagination to see that when all living creatures in the sea die, they will swell up and start floating to the top. Their decaying bodies, discharging an unbearable stench and lining the shores, will produce widespread disease and pestilence. People worldwide will die as a result. This judgment will obviously put an end to commercial shipping and destroy what is left of the fishing industry. This judgment is very similar to the first plague of Egypt, which was the turning of the waters of the Nile River to blood (Exodus 7:20 – 25).

16:4 – 7: The third bowl: *"The third angel poured out his bowl on the rivers and springs of water, and they became blood …."* With the third bowl judgment, God will destroy the only remaining sources of water, the rivers and springs, by turning them to blood. This will breed disease and pestilence as well and result in more human death on an even greater scale. People simply cannot live without water. Symbolically speaking, this may also represent corrupt blood. Antichrist will have shed the blood of so many Christian martyrs that he will, in return, get exactly what he deserves. His quest for the blood of God's saints will result in his water supply turning to blood in the second half of the Tribulation Period. The altar response (v.7) is from the souls under the altar of chapter 6; here their prayers are answered. Their response is the result of God's earthly vindication of suffering martyrs from the time of the early (first century) Church to the present.

The angel in charge of water reveals yet another ministry of angels in charge of the physical elements of the universe. We have already seen four angels that control the winds (7:1). This angel declares that God is holy and just in His judgments. My brethren, whatever God does is righteous and just; that is without question.

16:8 – 9: The fourth bowl: *"The fourth angel poured out his bowl on the sun, and the sun was given power to scorch people with fire …."* When the fourth bowl is poured out, mankind will suffer from a sun-induced heat wave, the likes of which has never been experienced. This is global warming in the true sense, not some deceptive political talking point. Even though one third of the sun will have been darkened as a result of the fourth trumpet judgment, the remaining sun light will be so powerful it will scorch people with fire. Even worse, without water to quench their thirst, we see that the people will be scorched by the intense heat, and literally tasting the torments of hell as described by the Lord Jesus: *"In hell, where he was in torment, he looked up and saw Abraham far away, with Lazarus by his side. So he called to him, 'Father Abraham, have pity on me and send Lazarus to dip the tip of his finger in water and cool my tongue, because I am in agony in this fire'"* (Luke 16:23, 24). Jesus also predicted: *"There will be signs in the sun, moon, and stars. On the earth, nations will be in anguish and perplexity at the roaring and tossing of the sea"* (Luke 21:25). The OT prophets had a good deal to say regarding this specific judgment of the Great Tribulation (cf. Deuteronomy 32:24 (KJV); Isaiah 24:6; Malachi 4:1).

Instead of driving people to their knees in repentance to God, we see the first of three occasions when people *"cursed the name of God ... but they refused to repent and glorify him"* (v.9). This proves that the human heart is incurably wicked and by this time no amount of punishment will change it. This is God's judgment upon an unrepentant world. Believers, however, during the Great Tribulation, will find comfort in the Word of God spoken through the psalmist: *"The Lord watches over you – the Lord is your shade at your right hand: the sun will not harm you by day, nor the moon by night"* (Psalm 121:5, 6).

16:10 – 11: The fifth bowl: *"The fifth angel poured out his bowl on the throne of the beast, and his kingdom was plunged into darkness ...."* The fifth bowl is a special judgment that centers on the headquarters of Antichrist, for it is poured out on the throne of the beast and his kingdom, resulting in vast darkness. This is comparable to the darkness that covered all of Egypt (Pharaoh's dominion) for three days during the ninth plague (Exodus 10:21 – 23). The OT prophets foretold of this same judgment (cf. Joel 2:1, 2, 31; Amos 5:18; Zephaniah 1:15). Jesus, as well, warned His disciples concerning the distress of those days: *"The sun will be darkened, and the moon will not give its light"* (Matthew 24:29; Mark 13:24). Keep in mind that since the water supply has been turned to blood, mankind may well be incapable of producing electrical power and illumination from the rivers and bodies of water. Subsequently, battery operated, fuel generated, or other types of light generation will be supernaturally rendered useless as well. When God says darkness, He means darkness!

In response to this judgment of darkness, men gnawed their tongues because of the pain. Can you imagine the intensity of the suffering? Yet, for the second time, instead of falling down before God in repentance, the people only *"... cursed the God of heaven because of their pains and their sores"* (v.11). We must understand that those who reject the Lord do so not because of philosophical doubts, but as a result of hardness of their hearts. We read earlier the Apostle Paul's warning: *"But because of your stubbornness and your unrepentant heart, you are storing up wrath against yourself for the day of God's wrath, when his righteous judgment will be revealed"* (Romans 2:5). This is God's righteous judgment.

16:12: The sixth bowl: *"The sixth angel poured out his bowl on the great river Euphrates, and its water was dried up to prepare the way for the kings from the East."* The sixth bowl judgment comes in two parts:

1) The drying up of the Euphrates River, which will be in preparation for the battle on the great day of God Almighty (v.14).
2) The three, frog-like, demon spirits (v.13) that will bring the rebellious armies of the world to the Valley of Megiddo for the purpose of opposing the Lord.

As mentioned earlier (9.14), the Euphrates River is one of the most prominent rivers in Scripture. It has always stood as a natural barrier between east and west. The sixth bowl judgment will dry up that river to make way for the kings from the East. The literal meaning is, "the kings from the sunrising," a reference to the kings of the Oriental nations of the world. This Oriental alliance may be preparing to oppose Antichrist, whose capital lies in Babylon. However, because of the lying tongues of the three demonic spirits described in the next two verses, the armies will instead be deceived into coming across onto the side of Antichrist in opposition to the Lord. The bulk of the world's population is in the east, and there is very little Gospel there. They will choose Antichrist. No wonder the blood of the wicked will flow and rise as high as the horses' bridles (14:20).

16:13 – 14: *"Then I saw three evil spirits that looked like frogs ...."* These three evil spirits are deceiving spirits, because they will come from the mouths of the dragon, the beast, and the false prophet. They should not be taken literally as frogs, because John only says they looked like frogs. They are to be interpreted spiritually as demonic creatures (visible or invisible – it is not certain) that will perform miraculous signs – that is, work miracles before the kings of the earth. In some deceitful manner, they will convince these kings into joining sides with the forces of Antichrist for the battle on the great day of God Almighty. The timing of this event must be the last days of the Great Tribulation, since the next bowl concludes the Tribulation Period with, what is believed to be, the literal destruction of governmental and commercial Babylon.

16:15: The words of the Lord Jesus Christ: *"Behold! I come like a thief! Blessed is he who stays awake and keeps his clothes with him, so that he may not go naked and be shamefully exposed."* This verse represents another interlude. As we have seen before with the seal and trumpet judgments, this also occurs between the sixth and seventh bowl judgments. This is the Lord's challenge to all the saints still living during the closing days of the Great Tribulation to continue faithfully to the very end.

Christ will never come as a thief to the Church. The Apostle Paul wrote: *"But you, brothers, are not in darkness so that this day should surprise you like a thief"* (1 Thessalonians 5:4). A thief is someone you shut out; you don't welcome him. However, the Lord Jesus Christ does come like a thief to the world at the end of the Great Tribulation. As we read earlier, the earth will mourn because of Him (1:7). The world does not want the Lord to come. Christ's challenge to these saints to stay awake and keep their clothes on is a command to continue faithfully, clothed with the righteousness of Christ through faith.

16:16: *"Then they gathered the kings together to the place that in the Hebrew is called Armageddon."* This is the only occurrence of the word *Armageddon* in Scripture; it means "Mount of Megiddo." It stands on the southwestern edge of the *Esdraelon* (Greek for Jezreel) Valley. The Valley of Jezreel is a major travel route through the rugged Palestinian hills. It also separates the province of Galilee from the district of Samaria. Armageddon is an expression often used to describe the decisive battle between the God-opposing forces of Antichrist and the Lord Jesus Christ upon His return to earth. The actual scriptural expression is, "the battle on the great day of God Almighty" (v.14). It takes place in the Valley of Megiddo. This valley is a place where many battles have been fought in the past, from the OT account of the thirty-one kings conquered by Joshua (Joshua 12:21), to the devastating march of Napoleon Bonaparte from Egypt to Syria. It was Napoleon who was said to have stated with deep emotion after his first sight of this great valley: "This is the ideal battleground for all the armies of the world." The pronoun "they" mentioned in this verse refers to the dragon trinity (Satan, Antichrist, and the false prophet) with their deceptive tongues; nevertheless, they unknowingly fulfill the Word of God.

16:17 – 18: The seventh bowl: *"The seventh angel poured out his bowl into the air ...."* The expression, "into the air," means into the atmosphere or heavens, and at no specific location or target. The Lord Jesus Christ controls the heavens, and He is getting ready to come through them. Verse 17 continues, *"... out of the temple came a loud voice from the throne, saying, 'It is done!'"* The loud voice is that of the Son of God, the Lord Jesus Christ conveying a most welcome message. This is the second time we have heard Him say this. As He hung from the cross, Jesus murmured these final words: *"It is finished"* (John 19:30). The word "finished" is translated from the Greek word *teleo*, which means "complete" or "discharge" (a debt). At that point in history, redemption was made and salvation became available to all mankind. There is nothing more mankind can do to add to its salvation, but to simply receive it in faith as the miraculous gift from a loving God.

Here, the expression, "it is done," is most welcomed because it signifies the end of the Great Tribulation, the conclusion of the day of God's wrath on the ungodly, and the end of the time of Jacob's (the nation of Israel) trouble (Jeremiah 30:7).

Earlier, John saw proceeding from the throne in heaven flashes of lightning, rumblings, and peals of thunder which began the Tribulation Period and announced the coming judgments (4:5). Here, at the conclusion of the Great Tribulation, the scene is repeated; however, this time with the addition of a severe earthquake. Likewise, John saw that the opening of the sixth seal brought about a great earthquake (6:12), and that men hid from the wrath of the Lamb. This final judgment of God will include an even greater earthquake which will apparently shake the entire world, for John says: *"No earthquake like it has ever occurred since man has been on earth, so tremendous was the quake"* (v.18).

16:19 – 20: This earthquake will destroy the great city. There is much debate about the meaning of the expression, "the great city." Some believe it to be Jerusalem. But, why did John not say Jerusalem since he was well familiar with that city? Others identify it as governmental and commercial Babylon, the capital of the world at that time. I agree with the latter, for two reasons:

1) Governmental Babylon is referred to as the great city several times in chapter 18.
2) In chapter 18, Governmental Babylon is destroyed by a cataclysmic judgment from God. In fact, the next two chapters will give us the details concerning both great Babylons and their destruction.

"… the cities of the nations collapsed" (v.19). The word "nations" refers to the nations of the world, thus referring to all the cities of the world and their ultimate destruction. Additionally, John says, *"Every island fled away and the mountains could not be found"* (v.20). We can only conclude that what John is witnessing is a complete renovation of the earth's surface. We will discuss this further in chapter 20.

16:21: If this were not enough catastrophes, John also describes huge hailstones of about one hundred pounds each falling from the sky upon men. Recall that the Lord told his servant Job: *"Have you entered the storehouses of the snow or seen the storehouses of the hail, which I reserve for the times of trouble, for the days of war and battle?"* (Job 38:22, 23)

"And they cursed God on account of the plague of hail, because the plague was so terrible" (v.21). It is hard to imagine human beings so rebellious that they lift their faces in final defiance to God even in the midst of such disaster. All hopes and dreams will be ended with this final judgment because people will have chosen to worship Antichrist.

The hailstorm ends the Great Tribulation.

Review Questions

1) The first bowl judgment produced ugly and painful sores upon all who _____

   _____.

2) The second bowl judgment turned the remaining parts of the sea into blood resulting in

   _____.

3) The third bowl judgment turned the remaining fresh water supplies to blood. The angel said
   Christ was justified because _____

   _____.

4) The fourth bowl judgment was poured out on the sun and as a result _____

   _____.

5) The fifth bowl judgment of darkness affected only _____.

6) The sixth bowl judgment dried up the _____ so that the three demonic
   spirits could deceive the kings of the East into coming together to assist Antichrist in his
   opposition to _____.

7) The seventh bowl judgment was poured out into the air resulting in _____

   _____.

   _____.

Up For Discussion

"And men blasphemed God because of the plague of hail ...."
(Revelation 16:21 KJV)

Imagine the magnitude of grief and suffering on human beings. The people on earth recognized that
these judgments were from God, but they still refused to repent and turn to Him. When they rejected
God and all the warnings He sent, and accepted the mark of the beast, their decision was cemented for
eternity. God hardened their hearts just as He did Pharaoh's at the time of Israel's exodus from Egypt.
Is this fair? Can you reconcile their decision with their fate and agree that God is just and righteous?

Read on your own or review as class time permits the FAQ: *Tribulation Saints.*

Read on your own or review as class time permits the FAQ: *God Hardens the Heart.*

Take a few minutes and look over the map of Ancient Israel and Judah. Locate and discuss:

1) Jerusalem: The capital city and worship center of the southern kingdom of Judah.
2) Samaria: The capital city of the northern kingdom of Israel.
3) Bethel: The location where Abraham first pitched his tents and built an altar to the Lord. This is also where Jacob dreamed of the ladder reaching to heaven and referred to it as *the house of God* and *the gate of heaven*. This city was earlier recognized as the worship center of Israel because the ark of the covenant was located there; but later, after the death of Solomon and the division of his kingdom, it became a great center of idolatry in the northern kingdom.
4) Megiddo: The site of the battle between the forces of Antichrist and the Lord Jesus Christ upon His return to earth.

If you have traveled to the Holy Land, share with the class some of your experiences and the sites you enjoyed seeing the most. If time allows, bring some photos to share with the class as well.

ANCIENT ISRAEL & JUDAH

Damascus

Zarephath

Tyre

TYRE

Dan

Hazor

SYRIA

Aphek

Sea of Galilee

Megiddo

Beth-shean

Ramoth-gilead

ISRAEL

Samaria ✪

Tirzah

Shechem

Penuel

Jordan River

Joppa

AMMON

Beth-horon

Bethel

Rabbah

Jerico

Gezer

Jerusalem ✪

Ashdod

Heshbon

Shaphir

Bethlehem

Gath

Adullam

Ashkelon

Moresheth-gath

Achzib

Mareshah

Gaza

PHILISTIA

Lachish

Hebron

Dibon

Dead Sea

Engedi

JUDAH

MOAB

Beersheba

Kir-hareseth

EDOM

Kadesh-barnea

Bozrah

N
↑

FAQ: Tribulation Saints

We learned in chapter 7 that 144,000 Jewish servants received the seal of the living God from an angel so as to protect them from the judgments of the Tribulation Period as they evangelize the world.

Question: Are the Tribulation saints protected from God's judgments as well?

We defined Tribulation saints as those who had not accepted the Lord Jesus Christ during the Church Age and were thus left behind on earth after the Rapture. They, in turn, will accept Jesus Christ as Lord and Savior during the dreadful days of the Tribulation Period as the result of the faithful witness of the 144,000 Jewish servants. Most commentators believe that the only way these Tribulation saints will die is by martyrdom – that is, persecuted and slain by Antichrist and his forces because of their faith in Jesus Christ and refusal to worship Antichrist and his idol image. Apparently, they will not suffer death as the result of the divine judgments that are coming upon the earth and its inhabitants. God will protect them as He did the Israelites in Goshen during the plagues brought upon Pharaoh. The Tribulation saints, however, will have to persevere during and through these dark days of judgment.

Revelation 12:6: Here we are told that the redeemed remnant of Israel will flee persecution by Antichrist into the desert to a place prepared for her by God, where she might be taken care of for 1,260 days. This occurs at the mid-point of the Tribulation Period when the Jewish remnant rejects the idolatrous religion of Antichrist and turns as a nation to the one, true Messiah, Jesus Christ. God will protect and provide for them just as He did during their exodus from Egypt.

Revelation 13:7: Here we are told that the beast, i.e., Antichrist, will be given power to make war against the saints and to conquer them. This is a reference to the above mentioned persecution and martyrdom of God's people by Antichrist.

Revelation 20:4b: Sadly, we are told that these Tribulation saints are beheaded because of their testimony for Jesus and the Word of God; they had not worshiped the beast and his image. They held fast to their new-found faith in the Savior and became martyrs for Christ.

On the other hand, the unrighteous (nonbelievers) suffer as a direct result of the judgments (wrath) from God coming upon the earth.

From our study of the seal judgments, we learned that Hades, the spiritual abode of the unrighteous dead, followed close behind Death (6:8). Additionally, from our study of the trumpet judgments, we learned that the rest of mankind that were not killed by the plagues still did not repent of the works of their hands; they did not stop worshiping demons and idols and committing other wickedness (9:20). Therefore, we can conclude that these judgments only affected the wicked – that is, nonbelievers.

In our explanation of the bowl judgments of chapter 16, we learned that John spoke of these judgments and their punishment as only being *poured out* upon the unrighteous – that is, those who had the mark of the beast and worshiped his image (16:2).

Revelation 16:9: Here John says the people cursed the name of God. This is obviously a reference to the unrighteous, because a child of God would never curse God's name. Unrepentant mankind becomes progressively worse in its rebellion against God on account of the bowl judgments.

Revelation 16:10: *"The fifth angel poured out his bowl on the throne of the beast and his kingdom was plunged into darkness."* This judgment is directed specifically onto the wicked governmental and commercial headquarters of Antichrist.

Revelation 16:11: Here again, mankind cursed the God of heaven because of their pain and their sores and refused to repent of their sinful deeds. These are the wicked, unrighteous, and corrupt associates of Antichrist and his kingdom.

Revelation 16:21: Lastly, we learned that the wicked cursed God on account of the plagues. Three times in chapter 16 alone, the unrighteous – that is, unrepentant mankind curses God. When you live your life in complete rebellion to God, apparently no amount of judgment will cause you to turn around and repent.

Please do not misunderstand me; the dark days of the Tribulation Period will be a time of extreme suffering for everyone, including Tribulation saints. Sadly, those who do die, their death will be the result of some dreadful persecution by Antichrist and not by any judgment from God. What about natural causes or accidental death? We cannot determine that from our study. However, it is certain that God will use every resource – the 144,000 servants (chapter 7), the two supernatural witnesses (chapter 11), angels (chapter 14), and every saint in every underground church across the globe to reach and convert as many souls as possible for the sake of His Gospel of grace and His Son Jesus Christ.

FAQ: God Hardens the Heart

Up to this point, we have discussed the fact that these divine judgments are poured out on and affect only unrepentant mankind. The righteous – that is, those who have made the decision to accept Jesus Christ as Lord rather than Antichrist – will be protected from God's judgments despite the extreme conditions of the times. We highlighted the fact that three times the people cursed the name of God and refused to repent. Recall the words of the Apostle Paul as he warned the Church concerning the man of lawlessness: *"For this reason God sends them a powerful delusion so that they will believe the lie and so that all will be condemned who have not believed the truth but have delighted in wickedness"* (2 Thessalonians 2:11, 12). Thus, for a great many people who have lived their entire lives in rebellion to God and in favor of self-reliance, God will eventually harden their hearts, just as He did Pharaoh's during the time of Israel's exodus from Egypt.

Question: Why does a loving God harden the hearts of men against Him?

This is a great question and one that has likely been the subject of debate as much as the meaning of 666. In past Revelation Bible studies, we have discussed as a class the fact that some people are indoctrinated from childhood into other religions or raised with non-religious beliefs. Consequently, as adults, they refuse to accept Jesus and believe the Gospel message despite hearing and/or reading the truth from the Word of God. That probably has a great deal to do with the answer to the question. However, during the dreadful Tribulation Period, God will use 144,000 servants, two supernatural witnesses, and a number of angels to get the message of the Gospel of Jesus Christ out to the entire world, i.e., every nation, tribe, people, and language (7:9). Every single person on earth will hear the Gospel and be given the opportunity to make a choice – Jesus Christ or Antichrist.

As I pondered this question, God kept bringing my thoughts back to the Lord's words of rebuke to the Pharisees when they said that it was only by Beelzebud that He was able to drive out demons: *"He who is not with me is against me, and he who does not gather with me scatters. And so I tell you, every sin and blasphemy will be forgiven men, but the blasphemy against the Spirit will not be forgiven. Anyone who speaks a word against the Son of Man will be forgiven, but anyone who speaks against the Holy Spirit will not be forgiven, either in this age or in the age to come"* (Matthew 12:30 – 32). This message is highly significant since it is repeated again in both the Gospels of Mark (3:28, 29) and Luke (12:10). The phrase, "this age," is a reference to this present day up through the return of Christ at the end of the Tribulation Period. The phrase, "the age to come," refers to the Millennium – that is, the Messianic or Kingdom Age (chapter 20).

We learned in chapter 13 that blasphemy manifests itself in two forms: 1) making oneself equal to God, and 2) slandering the name of God. The context of the above statement by Jesus was in response to the Pharisees attributing the miracles of Jesus to Satan's power and not that of the Holy Spirit – that is, making Satan equal to God. However, the statement has greater scope for us in regards to slandering the name of God. Once a person hears the Gospel of Jesus Christ, it is the work of the Holy Spirit that woos and leads that person into a commitment and, subsequently, a personal relationship with Jesus Christ as their Savior and Lord. If that person denies or rejects the message of the Gospel, or even worse curses God, then they have slandered or blasphemed the Holy Spirit. They have rejected God's grace; and that, my brethren, is the unpardonable sin that the Lord forbids.

Our lesson makes it abundantly clear that all people remaining on earth after the Rapture will hear the message of salvation through faith in the Lord Jesus Christ during the 7-year Tribulation Period. By the time we get to the second half of the Tribulation and into the bowl judgments, most people will have made their decision. Unfortunately, those who choose Antichrist and take his mark will have made an irreversible decision; and thus, God will harden their hearts.

Chapter 17

Please follow along in your Bible.

Religious Babylon (the Apostate Church) Destroyed

Historians tell us that Babylon is the cradle of civilization. Located on the shores of the Euphrates River, the ruins of this city have uncovered some of the most ancient documents of past generations. This was the first city established after the flood by Nimrod, grandson of Ham, son of Noah, and who grew to be a mighty warrior (Genesis 10:8 – 10). However, Nimrod rebelled against God. He initiated some of the greatest evils ever to fall on mankind. In those days Babylon appeared to be the capital of Satan's evil operation. It became the birth place of all false religion. From here, a system of false religion originated which emphasized idolatry and sexual immorality. Babylon was also the beginning of mankind's attempt at self-governance in defiance of God's will, and structures were built for commercial and social purposes contrary to God's laws and statutes.

In chapter 14, John witnessed another angel who proclaimed: *"Fallen! Fallen is Babylon the Great, which made all the nations drink the maddening wine of her adulteries"* (v.8). This chapter describes in detail the coming judgment from God on this evil, religious system, also referred to by commentators as the apostate or false church. It will acquire its members from all the great systems of the world, especially pagan religions and the occult. Even in our churches today there are those who are not true believers. During the first half of the Tribulation Period, they will join this organization that may call itself a church, but is not. God calls it *the great prostitute* (v.1).

These verses symbolically portray two great institutions: One religious (the prostitute, i.e., the apostate or false church) and the other governmental (Antichrist and his revived Roman Empire). Together they describe a powerful global religious system which gains a controlling influence in Antichrist's government during the first half of the Tribulation Period. Leaders of false religions of the world have always competed with political leaders for dominance over their countries or empires. This is in contrast to the *authentic* first century Apostolic Church (and the universal Church of Christ in America as we know it today) which has never sought political power; in fact, Jesus told the Roman Governor, Pontius Pilate: *"My kingdom is not of this world"* (John 18:36).

17:1 – 2: John is told by one of the seven angels: *"Come, I will show you the punishment of the great prostitute, who sits on many waters …."* The great prostitute is, in part, that faction of the church which will be left on earth after the true Church has been raptured. It will be made up of those who have never trusted Jesus Christ as Savior. This is the group that enters into the Tribulation Period. Just as the bride (19:7) represents Christ's raptured and resurrected Church, the prostitute represents an evil, religious system that emphasizes idolatry and sexual immorality. Later in this chapter, the angel defines the meaning of the phrase, "many waters," as the *"… peoples, multitudes, nations, and languages"* (v.15) of the world. This phrase is used here to designate all of humanity. This prostitute is a worldwide system that has control over all people. This is why she is portrayed as sitting on them. We must understand that when a person rejects the genuine, they become wide open to the counterfeit. Let me reiterate the words of the Apostle Paul: *"For this reason God sends them a powerful delusion so that they will believe the lie and so that all will be condemned who have not believed the truth but have delighted in wickedness"* (2 Thessalonians 2:11, 12).

The phrase, "punishment of the great prostitute," refers to the fact that God's judgment will come down upon her. How will God put an end to this false church? During the first half of the Tribulation Period the beast, i.e., Antichrist tolerates it; and even though he hates it, he will use this apostate church to control the masses. However, during the second half of the Tribulation Period, God will use the beast and the false prophet to destroy the great prostitute so that they may set up a religion making Antichrist the sole object of worship as he proclaims himself to be god. This is the big lie of which Paul warned.

This religious system will have gained worldwide dominance during the first half of the Tribulation Period, causing the, *"… kings of the earth to commit adultery"* (v.2) and making the, *"… inhabitants of the earth intoxicated with the wine of her adulteries"* (v.2). This clearly demonstrates a corrupt union – that is, an unholy alliance between church and state during the first half of the Tribulation Period.

17:3: *"Then the angel carried me away in the Spirit into a desert …."* Recall in chapter 4 that John was carried in Spirit to heaven to prepare him for the vision of the glorified Christ. Here, the meaning might refer to John's spiritual need for additional anointing from the Holy Spirit to prepare him for the awesome visions still to come.

In his vision, John's focus is now on a woman sitting on a scarlet beast. We identified the beast in chapter 13 as the end-times Antichrist and his revived Roman Empire. John identifies the woman later as the great city that rules over the kings of the earth (v.18). Hence, the woman is also a city, and that city is most likely present-day Rome (Vatican City contained therein), considered by some to be the religious capital of the world. The woman is religious Rome, who at that time will have merged and incorporated all religions of the world. The city is further identified as follows: *"The seven heads are seven hills on which the woman sits"* (v.9). Any internet search today would identify Rome, Italy as the city set on seven hills.

The phrase, "covered with blasphemous names," refers to the irreverent and profane nature that has been characteristic of all world governments that continue in opposition to God's ways.

17:4: *"The woman was dressed in purple and scarlet …."* Purple is the color of royalty and the predominant color of Roman imperialism. It was worn by every senator and consul in recognition of their position. In the Roman Catholic Church, scarlet is the color worn by a cardinal and is associated with the blood of Christ and Christian martyrs. She was also dressed in items of glittering gold, precious stones, and pearls. These things detail a lavish outward appearance reminiscent of the Pharisees. Recall our Lord's rebuke of the Pharisees: *"Woe to you, teachers of the law and Pharisees, you hypocrites! You clean the outside of the cup and dish, but inside they are full of greed and self-indulgence"* (Matthew 23:25).

Lastly, the woman is described as holding, *"... a golden cup filled with abominable things and the filth of her adulteries."* This depicts the religious intoxication – that is, the lure or enticement of the false church and its religion that emphasizes idolatry and sexual immorality. This is the cup that intoxicated the inhabitants of the earth (v.2). The prophet foretold this: *"Babylon was a gold cup in the Lord's hand; she made the whole earth drunk. The nations drank her wine; therefore they have now gone mad"* (Jeremiah 51:7).

17:5: The woman did not wear a crown, but a title, the mark of her profession, on her forehead: *"MYSTERY BABYLON THE GREAT..."* The false church is a mystery because it was not revealed until John wrote about it here. The true Church is a mystery because it was never revealed in the OT. After the true Church is removed from earth at the Rapture, only false members are left. As mentioned earlier, they are but a part of many factions that will make up the false church remaining on earth during the first half of the Tribulation Period. However, God does not call Babylon a church, but a prostitute. The Apostle Paul wrote about the wickedness in the Church: *"For the secret power of lawlessness is already at work; but the one who now holds it back will continue to do so till he is taken out of the way"* (2 Thessalonians 2:7). Lawlessness is at work in the Church today, just as it was in Paul's day. The Lord spoke of this in His *Parable of the Sower*, (Matthew 13:3 – 23). Here Jesus compares lawlessness to thorns or weeds that come up among the wheat (believers). Who is the one who now holds lawlessness back? It is the Holy Spirit. When will He be taken out of the way? The answer to that question is at the Rapture. Does that mean the Holy Spirit will not be present during the Tribulation Period? Of course, He will. The Holy Spirit will continue in His same mission, to woo people to Christ through the evangelizing efforts of the 144,000 servants and the two supernatural witnesses; however, He will not hinder evil. Satan will have his day for a while.

"... THE MOTHER OF PROSTITUTES AND OF THE ABOMINATIONS OF THE EARTH." This is one of the most expressive and vivid descriptions of abominable sin to be found in the Word of God. Sex, idolatry, and false religions go hand-in-hand. Abomination in the OT refers to the worship of idols and that is exactly the form of religion Satan has used throughout the ages to deceive mankind and lead people away from a relationship with God.

17:6 – 7: *"I saw that the woman was drunk with the blood of the saints, the blood of those who bore testimony to Jesus ...."* The prostitute not only makes others drunk, as we saw above, with her doctrine which emphasizes idolatry and sexual immorality, but she is also intoxicated by her own acts of persecution. The saints, mentioned here, may refer to OT saints where the phrase, "those who bore testimony to Jesus," is a reference to NT saints. Religious Babylon is a composite system made up of all religions, groups, and cults that remain on earth after the Rapture of the true Church. It was in Babylon where three Hebrew exiles were thrown into a fiery furnace because they would not worship the king's golden statue. Even today, our greatest fears come from unpredictable acts of terrorism throughout the world perpetrated by religious extremists.

When John saw the vision of the woman sitting on the scarlet beast, he confessed that he was greatly astonished. John was in great amazement, or maybe even confused. His question might be: "Is the emphasis here on the kingdom of the beast or on Antichrist himself – the revived Roman Empire or the king?" As we look at the next few verses we will see that this is an area of debate among commentators.

17:8 – 10: We have already seen a description of the death of the beast (Antichrist) and his apparent resurrection by the dragon (Satan) at the mid-point of the Tribulation Period (13:3 – 6). Many commentators feel these verses reinforce that explanation. However, for the purpose of comparison, let me suggest another view that places the emphasis on the kingdom, the revived Roman Empire aspect of the beast rather than Antichrist himself.

The expression, "once was," speaks of the past history of the Roman Empire. The expression, "now is not," refers to the present condition of the fragmented Empire. The Roman Empire did not die; it just fell apart becoming the nations of Europe as seen today. The phrase, "will come out of the Abyss," speaks of the restoration of the Roman Empire by Antichrist during the Tribulation Period. Lastly, the phrase, "go to his destruction," refers to the destruction of the Roman Empire by the return of Christ at the end of the Great Tribulation. As a result, all the unredeemed inhabitants of the earth will be astonished. The reestablishment of the Roman Empire in its great power and glory will win the admiration of all the unrepentant, unredeemed of humanity remaining on earth. They will respect and worship Antichrist for his brilliant accomplishment.

The seven heads of the beast are also described as seven kings and are likely representative of kings of the Roman Empire throughout John's lifetime, thus reinforcing the above-mentioned explanation. They are:

1) Augustus
2) Tiberius
3) Caligula
4) Claudius
5) Nero
6) The expression, "one is," would refer to the ruling king at the time of the writing of John's Revelation – Domitian.
7) The expression, "other has not yet come," refers to the future ruler of the revived Roman Empire – Antichrist.

Others commentators, however, view these kings as representative forms of government as we discussed in our study of the dragon in chapter 12 (v.3). Regardless, the end in view is the same – Antichrist rules over the revived Roman Empire until it is destroyed by the coming of the Lord Jesus Christ.

17:11: *"… an eighth king … belongs to the seven and is going to his destruction."* This suggests that king number eight is the same as king number seven. Thus, this clearly identifies the last head (king), the final emperor of the world as Antichrist, the resurrected, incarnation of Satan, with his dictatorial manifestation of the revived Roman Empire.

17:12 – 14: The ten horns are the same ten kings we saw in chapter 13 (v.1) who give their power and authority to Antichrist during the Tribulation Period. These are the same as the ten horns of Daniel 7:7. The fact that they, for one hour, will receive authority as kings likely indicates that they will reign with Antichrist, but will be subservient to him.

The fate of these ten kings is revealed here. Although they will follow Antichrist and make war against the Lamb – the Lord Jesus Christ – they will fail miserably in their efforts. The Lord will ultimately triumph, because He is Lord of lords and King of kings (cf. 19:15, 16). At His return to earth, Christ will be accompanied by, "… *his called, chosen and faithful followers*" (v.14). It is believed that this expression represents the entire host of heaven, including the redeemed and glorified Church making up the bride of Christ. We will discuss this in greater detail in chapter 19 (v.14).

17:15: As mentioned earlier, this verse defines for us the phrase, "many waters" (v.1).

17:16 – 17: "*The beast and the ten horns you saw will hate the prostitute ….*" Antichrist will allow the prostitute (the apostate church) to govern his actions during the first half of the Tribulation Period while he gathers and consummates his power. However, in the middle of the Tribulation Period, when he firmly establishes his revived Roman Empire and lifts himself up as world dictator (and god), he and the ten kings will eliminate the prostitute. Antichrist not only breaks his treaty with the nation of Israel, but he also terminates his relationship with the false church.

In reality, while sharing in their exalted position, the beast and the ten horns will hate the prostitute. Why? They hate the prostitute because the power and the glory is divided. When it is no longer necessary, Antichrist and the ten kings will, "… *bring her to ruin and leave her naked …*" (v.16), meaning they will destroy her temples and seize her many riches. This hatred is so violent that the passage further states that, "*they will eat her flesh and burn her with fire*" (v.16). This great hatred destroys the false church. In contrast to the true Church in heaven, the false church on earth has no victory.

In bringing her to ruin, Antichrist and his ten allies will unknowingly be instruments of God in destroying this dreadful Babylonian system of false religion once and for all: "*For God has put it into their hearts to accomplish his purpose …*" (v.17).

From then on the world does not worship Mystery Babylon, but the image of the beast. As mentioned earlier, Mystery Babylon is likely Rome, and when it is destroyed in the middle of the Tribulation Period, the religious center shifts to Jerusalem. It is in the newly rebuilt temple in Jerusalem that the false prophet will erect an idol image of Antichrist to be worshiped (Daniel 9:27; Matthew 24:15). The false prophet will do away with all religion except the worship of Antichrist (Satan), which he will mandate and enforce. The reign and worship of Antichrist will be the darkest time earth will ever know. Having rejected the truth, the only alternative left for mankind is to believe the big lie.

17:18: The woman who rides the beast and gets her power from the beast is mentioned here by the Holy Spirit to illustrate how intertwined religious and governmental Babylon are during the first half of the Tribulation Period. However, they are destroyed at different times. Religious Babylon is destroyed in the middle of the Tribulation Period. Governmental Babylon, as we will see in the next chapter, will be destroyed at the end.

Review Questions

1) What are the two basic tenets associated with false religions? _____.

2) The great prostitute, or false church, is that part of the church that is left on earth after _____
_____.

3) This false church is made up of those who _____.

4) During the first half of the Tribulation Period, Antichrist will tolerate this false church because he will use it to _____.

5) Religious Babylon is destroyed when? _____.

6) Who destroys religious Babylon? _____.

7) Why was religious Babylon destroyed? _____
_____.

Up For Discussion

"And the habitants of the earth have been made drunk with the wine of her fornication."
(Revelation 17:2 KJV)

Religious Babylon, the false church, is that part of the church left on earth after the Rapture of the true Church. It consists of those who have never placed their faith and trust in Jesus Christ as Savior and Lord. I once read the following: "Take the simple Gospel of Jesus Christ: God manifest in the flesh at the Virgin birth, lived a sinless life, died on the cross for the sins of all mankind, on the third day rose from the dead, and now sits at the right hand of God, the Father in heaven. If you add to or take away from this simple Gospel, then what you have is religion" (paraphrased, author unknown). There are many books available today written on the subject of world religions and false teachings. You might have read some, and if so, you may have even been surprised at some of the organizations listed in them. Is it spiritually healthy for Christians to read and study the tenets of other worldly religions?

Or, is it of greater importance to prayerfully read and study our Bibles daily so we are better prepared, at a moment's notice, to defend the faith we hold so dear?

Share with the class any experiences you have had in another church and/or social organization that conflicted with your faith in the Gospel of Jesus Christ. How did you respond?

Chapter 18

Please follow along in your Bible.

Governmental and Commercial Babylon Destroyed

In chapter 16, we read: *"God remembered Babylon the Great and gave her the cup filled with the wine of the fury of his wrath"* (v.19). In this chapter, we will discuss in greater detail the judgment of governmental and commercial Babylon, and the reaction of both earth and heaven to it. *Babylon the Great* is ancient Babylon rebuilt as the governmental and commercial capital of the world. This city is the final capital of the political power of Antichrist. Its judgment will not take place until the end of the Tribulation Period. The following four reasons establish the distinction between the destruction of Babylon in chapter 17 and that of chapter 18:

1) In verse 1, the expression, "after this," indicates that the events described in chapter 18 will not take place until sometime after the events of chapter 17 have been fulfilled.
2) Religious Babylon, the prostitute of chapter 17, will be destroyed by Antichrist and the kings of the earth. Governmental Babylon will be destroyed by a cataclysmic judgment from God.
3) The kings who destroyed religious Babylon rejoice because they hated the prostitute. In this chapter concerning governmental and commercial Babylon, those same kings and merchants will lament and weep over her destruction.
4) If the events of chapters 17 and 18 both took place during the last days of the Tribulation, then there would be no time remaining for Antichrist and the false prophet to do away with the false church in order to mandate and enforce universal worship of Antichrist and his idol image as described in chapter 13.

18:1: *"After this I saw another angel coming down from heaven ...."* We begin our chapter with yet another awesome angel. Thus far, we have seen the phrase, "mighty angel," described and used twice by John (cf. 5:2; 10:1). Since this angel has such great authority, he may likely be of a higher order than other angels we have previously seen, including the seven angels who had the seven bowls of God's wrath. These great or mighty angels may well be of the order of archangel, since they allegedly number seven in all. Michael and Gabriel are two who are mentioned by name in Scripture. If it is true that the archangels total seven, then should we not expect each to play a prominent role in these final chapters of earth's history leading up to the return of Christ? The fact that the earth was illuminated by his brilliance seems to further illustrate the magnificence of this angel.

18:2: The message of this angel who cries with a mighty voice is: *"Fallen! Fallen is Babylon the Great! She has become a home for demons and a haunt for every evil spirit, a haunt for every unclean and detestable bird."* The OT prophets predicted that Babylon would be the place where wild beast and dragons, and unclean birds would dwell following its destruction (cf. Isaiah 13:19 – 22 KJV; Jeremiah 50:39) – that is, during the Millennium. These prophecies find their final fulfillment in this chapter with the destruction of the literal city of Babylon. Babylon, the great commercial center of the world, will be destroyed because it is in God's plan to do so.

Since this chapter describes the destruction of a literal commercial city, the governmental capital of the world during the Tribulation Period, we naturally ask ourselves the question, "Where is this city?" Commentators are not in agreement on this either, but, I agree with those who follow the OT prophecies that point to the literal rebuilding of Babylon. God woos us through His Word and His Spirit to walk by faith; Satan woos us through government, commerce, and religious idolatry to walk by sight. There are several reasons for believing that the literal city of Babylon in modern-day Iraq must be rebuilt that relate to prophecies concerning her destruction that are yet unfulfilled:

1) Isaiah 13 – 14 and Jeremiah 50 – 51 describe the destruction of Babylon as being at the time of the day of the Lord. These verses refer to the overthrow of Babylon (the enemy of Israel) on the final day of their atonement and referred to as the day of the Lord, marking the end of the 7-year Tribulation Period.

2) Contrary to the writings of the Prophet Jeremiah, the ruins of Babylon have been used to build other cities. It is reported that at least six cities bear the marks of having used stones from ancient Babylon in their building, including Baghdad, fifty miles north of the site of ancient Babylon. This fact alone demands the rebuilding of Babylon because, when God destroys it, the prophet tells us: *"No rock will be taken from you for a cornerstone, or any stone for a foundation"* (Jeremiah 51:26).

3) Jeremiah also foretold that, *"Babylon will suddenly fall and be broken"* (51:8). Likewise, the Prophet Isaiah wrote: *"Babylon, the jewel of kingdoms, the glory of the Babylonians' pride, will be overthrown by God like Sodom and Gomorrah"* (Isaiah 13:19). History reveals that ancient Babylon was never destroyed like that.

4) Furthermore, Isaiah foretold that the ruins of Babylon were never to be inhabited: *"She will never be inhabited or lived in through all generations; no Arab will pitch his tent there, no shepherd will rest his flocks there"* (Isaiah 13:20). Again, a look at history reveals that this prophecy regarding Babylon has never been fulfilled.

Much has happened in recent years in both Iraq and Babylon. Saddam Hussein, the former dictator of the country, spent over $800M on reconstruction and the reestablishment of ancient Babylon, which may well be taken over some day by Antichrist, renamed New Babylon, and made the political and commercial center of the world. Saddam was trying to restore ancient majesty to the city and his rebuilding program was progressing. It is interesting to note that among his first projects was the rebuilding of the monumental staircase in the temple of Marduk, also called the Ziggurat. This should not be difficult to understand, as Saddam Hussein was a committed Satanist. He was a Muslim for political reasons, but at heart he worshiped the supreme god of the Babylonians. He also built a lavish palace for himself, which was featured in many televised news reports following his downfall and capture in 2003. In addition, he commissioned over 60 million bricks to be placed in the walls behind the Southern Palace, each dedicated to the memory of King Nebuchadnezzar and engraved with the inscription: "In the reign of the victorious Saddam Hussein, the president of the Republic, may God keep him the guardian of the great Iraq."

18:3: *"For all the nations have drunk the maddening wine of her adulteries ...."* As similarly noted in chapter 17 (v.2), this case illustrates an unholy alliance between government and business. The word "merchants" used here means "those who travel." It is not those who produce or manufacture goods; but those who are brokers, engaging in business for a big profit. God will judge godless commercialism. Man has always used business as the biggest excuse for not having any time for God. This is God's judgment on big business, which denies God's authority and promotes corruption.

18:4: John hears another voice from heaven. This is the voice of the Lord Jesus Christ calling God's people out of the city of Babylon before its destruction. The Lord's summons makes it clear that God's people are going to be in the world to the very end. Just as Lot was warned to get out of Sodom to escape the judgment of fire (Genesis 19), so too are these people of God warned. Such was also God's warning to Israel (cf. Isaiah 48:20; Jeremiah 51:5, 6, 45). In these prophetic verses, the Lord warns Israel to have no fellowship with the sins of Babylon and to flee before judgment falls.

Who are these people referred to as My people, and what are they doing in the capital city without the mark of the beast? They may be Jew/Gentile believers, or they could be Jews who have not yet received Christ as their Savior. Christ's command to, *"Come out,"* is typical of God in His call to His elect (those who will choose to believe) to flee this evil, world system before it is destroyed. The mercy and grace of God is forever available. In every age, God receives those who, through faith in His Son Jesus Christ, are willing to repent of their sin and look to Him for mercy. I believe this may also be a warning to us today to separate ourselves from the world and our old sinful nature, and walk by the Spirit.

18:5: *"... for her sins are piled up to heaven."* Babylon is the oldest city in the history of mankind. With the exception of Jerusalem, Babylon is mentioned more than any other city in the Bible, roughly 260 times. Babylon has a long history of accumulating sins, and God has kept a record, for John says, *"God has remembered her crimes."* Finally God's judgment will come upon this city.

18:6: *"Give back to her as she has given ...."* God is just in what He does. Listen to the words of the OT prophet: *"The day of the Lord is near for all nations. As you have done, it will be done to you; your deeds will return upon your own head"* (Obadiah 15). Consequently, Babylon's own cup of iniquity will be pressed in double portion back onto her and all who have joined with her in sin and wickedness.

18:7: *"Give her as much torture and grief as the glory and luxury she gave herself ...."* The riches and fame of Babylon blinded her to the coming judgment of God. The fact that she boasts in her heart refers to her arrogance – her pride. Such glory and luxury are often short-lived in life. Self-gratification – that is, the pursuit of prosperity, success, and self-realization characterized the spirit of this godless city. Recall the humble prophets from chapter 11, the two supernatural witnesses in Jerusalem who preached a warning to a world in rebellion – repent and turn to God. They, on the other hand, were hated and eventually killed.

18:8: The expression, "in one day," illustrates the suddenness of her destruction, for John says that she will be completely destroyed in flames. Her grief is so great that mourning is counted as a plague along with death and famine. Her destruction is total and final. The long history of this sinful city ends with the judgment of God upon her.

"... *For mighty is the Lord God who judges her.*" It is God who destroys this city because He alone is able to do so. It is believed that He does this as part of the seventh bowl judgment and just prior to the return of Christ to earth (cf. 16:19 – 21). This occurs in the final days or even hours of the Tribulation Period. In His return to earth, Christ is seen coming from Edom (Isaiah 63:1 – 4). It is my opinion He returns by way of Babylon, after executing judgment upon that wicked city. Christ is coming to rescue the redeemed remnant of Israel that has fled Jerusalem and the persecution of Antichrist (12:6). We will discuss Christ's Second Coming in the next chapter.

In this next section, John describes the reaction to the destruction of this great city. There are two distinctly opposite views to her destruction. There will be anguish in the world and rejoicing in heaven because of the judgment upon Babylon.

18:9 – 10: "*When the kings of the earth who committed adultery with her and shared her luxury see the smoke of her burning, they will weep and mourn over her ....*" In that day, Antichrist will have established the first global dictatorship, and his capital will be Babylon. Babylon will dominate and rule the world. Everything will center in Babylon. Everything in that city will be in rebellion against Almighty God, and it centers on Antichrist. The kings of the earth love commercial Babylon. The expression, "committed adultery," is a reference to the revenue she brought to these kings – that is, corrupt profits. No one ever expected this great city to be judged. In spite of her splendor, this will be the most short-lived capital of the world, for by the end of the day, Babylon is nothing but smoldering ruins. When the word goes out, the world will weep and mourn over her and will be terrified at her suffering. As stated earlier in our introduction to this chapter, one of the contrasts between the destruction of religious and commercial Babylon is that the kings who destroyed religious Babylon rejoiced, where here they will stand in awe and weep.

18:11 – 17a: These verses illustrate the products of an affluent society. These are articles of a society accustomed to the finer things of the material world. However, with the destruction of Babylon, the merchants are left without a buyer for their goods. Let's take a brief look at the costly products mentioned in these verses and try to categorize them:

1) Gold, silver, precious stones and pearls are monetary currencies and fine jewelry.
2) Fine linen, purple, silk, and scarlet cloth refers to luxurious garments and soft lines.
3) Citron (cedar) wood, ivory, costly wood, bronze, iron and marble would refer to gift items and costly building materials.
4) Cinnamon and spice, incense, myrrh, and frankincense are spices and cosmetics.
5) Wine and olive oil, fine flour and wheat refer to expensive wines and alcoholic beverages, oils, flour and grains.
6) Cattle and sheep not only refer to expensive cuts of meat produced for the wealthy, but also leather and wool products.
7) Horses and carriages refer to certain types of ground transportation.

This merchandise covers every phase of business. Even the bodies and souls of men were traded. Slavery becomes acceptable everywhere and apparently is big business during the Tribulation Period. Unfortunately, I have sat in church and, on more than one occasion, been told by a Bible study teacher that the Word of God does not condemn slavery as such, but simply overlooks this cruel and degrading institution as a common part of ancient society. I disagree, and this verse, written by John in the first century, makes it abundantly clear that God is going to judge slavery. If He is going to judge it, then it is wrong and it is sinful – in John's day as well as in any other day.

"The merchants who sold these things and gained their wealth from her will stand far off, terrified at her torment. They will weep and mourn" (v.15). The merchants sit in front of their television screens and cry, for in one hour wealth so great lay desolate.

18:17b – 19: The last group of mourners are those who are engaged in transportation. John describes those who travel by ship and earn their living from the sea. Although we concluded earlier (chapter 16) that oceanic shipping would be shut down due to the second bowl judgment turning the remainder of the sea to blood, this must be a reference to other modes within the transportation industry in operation at the time, i.e., airline carriers, railroad, and trucking. In today's language, these are all considered ships. The sea, as we stated in chapter 13 (v.1), is symbolic of the nations of the world. They all became rich by transporting the merchandise of Babylon. Like the others, they weep and mourn, and marvel as well at the sudden destruction of the great city.

The truth is: The things of this earth are passing away. Would it break your heart if you saw the things of this earth go up in smoke? Is your heart fixed on Christ and things in heaven? Pastor, author, and renowned photographer, Dr. Charles Stanley, once stated: "If you cannot part with a penny out of every dime, then you are materialistic, and to be materialistic is to be sinful." We are living in a Babylonian society today. Take a moment and read what the Lord Jesus Christ said regarding materialism and storing up treasures (Matthew 6:19 – 21), and on the subject of handling worldly wealth (Luke 16:10 – 12).

18:20: *"Rejoice over her, O heaven …."* The scene is entirely different in heaven – there is rejoicing. It is the celebration of a long awaited event. The saints prayed for it; the OT prophets and the NT apostles predicted it. Now that it is fulfilled, there is joy in heaven because God has vindicated His name. Judgment has come upon Babylon.

18:21: *"Then a mighty angel picked up a boulder the size of a large millstone and threw it into the sea …."* This action symbolizes the suddenness and permanence of the destruction of Babylon. Just as a huge boulder makes a big splash and then disappears beneath the water, so too will Babylon come to an end. The expression, "never to be found again," coincides with the prophecies of Isaiah 13 as mentioned earlier, and is yet another illustration of the permanence of her destruction.

18:22 – 23: The music will be silenced, the storerooms and warehouses will be destroyed, and the bright lights will go out. It is all over. No more marrying or being given in marriage here. The expression, "led astray," means that this city deceived the nations of the world with the worship of Antichrist. This is the strong delusion – the big lie of which the Apostle Paul warned. The tragedy of the ages is the millions of souls Satan has deceived about God and His grace. There is nothing in Scripture to even suggest they will not suffer forever for allowing themselves to be deceived.

18:24: *"In her was found the blood of the prophets and of the saints, and of all who have been killed on the earth."* Babylon will be solemnly and finally judged because of her slaughter of the prophets and the saints and those who would communicate God's truth to the world. Just as God chose Jerusalem as His city to win the souls of people, Satan chose Babylon as his capital to destroy them. This was Satan's city, and he was a murderer from the beginning.

This marks the final ruin of the most destructive religious and governmental system in the history of mankind, and the demise of the most godless and influential city ever built. With her destruction and the darkness in which Babylon will be permanently entombed, she will bear testimony to her lifelessness for eternity as we will see in chapter 19 (v.3).

This chapter brings to a conclusion the frightful period referred to by the Lord Jesus Christ as the Great Tribulation. In the next chapter we will see the Lord coming to earth to bring to an end this dark period of unrighteousness and to establish His Millennial Kingdom.

Review Questions

1) Commercial Babylon, also considered the political capital of Antichrist, is believed by most commentators to be located _____.

2) The Lord Jesus calling His people out from Babylon before her destruction is consistent with God's warning to Israel _____.

3) The fact that Babylon boasts of her glory and luxury refers to _____.

4) The adulteries committed with the kings of the earth refer to _____

   _____.

5) Her destruction is sudden and is accomplished in only _____.

6) Commercial Babylon is destroyed by a cataclysmic judgment of God, most likely as a result of _

   _____.

7) Her destruction concludes the frightful period referred to by the Lord as _____.

   _____.

Up For Discussion

*"The kings of the earth have committed fornication with her, and the merchants
of the earth are waxed rich through the abundance of her delicacies."*
(Revelation 18:3 KJV)

Throughout history Satan has stirred up and used governmental power to accomplish his purpose. We mentioned in chapter 12 that nothing has caused more grief to humanity than government. Power in the hands of evil men, in the form of government, has literally given license to war, torture, and genocide resulting in famine, death, and human suffering beyond comprehension. The history books testify to it. However, let us take a closer look at our state and local governments. Satan has used them to inflect pain and suffering on people in both an economic and emotional sense. Corruption in government abounds; you need only watch the nightly newscast on television. Lobbyists and special interest groups take priority over real needs and desires of constituents. Taxpayers' money is oftentimes mismanaged and wasted on enormous salaries, perks, and pet projects. As a result, good, hard-working people are laid off or furloughed, and legitimate needs and programs are cut out of budgets everywhere.

As our country continues to endure through recession after recession, has your family been impacted in any way by the irresponsible and/or corrupt actions of your local government? Examples may include: 1) increased taxes to compensate for mismanagement, 2) cutting education and/or law enforcement budgets for ideological reasons, 3) the covert implementation of progressive ideology and teaching in our children's classrooms, i.e., CRT and/or gender identity curriculums. This may be another hot button topic; but if you are willing, please share your thoughts or experiences with the class.

Chapter 19

Please follow along in your Bible.

The destruction of Babylon, the capital city of Antichrist's kingdom, marked the end of the 7-year Tribulation Period and the Great Tribulation of the latter days. Chapter 19 begins a remarkable transition in our study. The shift is from darkness to light and from dreadful days of judgment to bright days of blessing. This chapter is the link between the Great Tribulation and the Millennium. Here we will see two great and significant events. The first is the wedding of the Lamb. The second is the return of Christ to earth to abolish all wickedness and to execute judgment upon Antichrist, the false prophet, and all who are in rebellion to God and who persecuted His children. The hallelujahs open this chapter and the opening of hell concludes it. There are also two great suppers recorded in this chapter. The first is the wedding supper of the Lamb, and the second is the cannibalistic feast of the birds called *the great supper of God* following the conclusion of the battle of Armageddon.

The Heavenly Hallelujahs

19:1: *"After this I heard what sounded like the roar of a great multitude in heaven shouting: 'Hallelujah!....'"* The *Hallelujah Chorus* from Handel's *Messiah* (1741) is considered to be the grandest and most majestic expression of praise and worship in the field of music. However, this praise will be completely surpassed by the magnificent heavenly *Hallelujah* chorus of the future that John describes here. The apostle's words were actually the source of Handel's inspiration.

This chapter gives us a spectacular view of the rejoicing in heaven now that God's judgment has finally come upon the earth; no longer will anyone be permitted to rebel against Him. This heavenly chorus results from the final triumph of good over evil, Christ over Antichrist, God over Satan, and the Holy Spirit over the deceptive and destructive spirit of evil. The great multitude mentioned here is distinct from the other beings in heaven for they are singing a song that includes salvation. This incorporates all believers – OT saints, Church Age saints, and the Tribulation saints. This is the first time they can all join together in this great chorus, proclaiming, "Hallelujah!"

In the NT, the word "Hallelujah" is only found here; it occurs four times in these opening six verses. It is an OT word taken from the Psalms and means "praise the Lord." Hallelujah is an exclamation of praise as the final phase of salvation is coming to pass. The Apostle Paul wrote explicitly about this in his letter to the Romans (8:18 – 23). This is that great day which is coming when the earth will be released from the bondage of sin.

Two additional divine attributes are used to express this praise to the Lord our God. The first is glory, which refers to God's moral glory in judgment. The second is power, which speaks of His omnipotence displayed in the execution of His judgment upon the earth and its corrupt rulers.

19:2 – 3: *"He has condemned the great prostitute who corrupted the earth by her adulteries ...."* These verses establish the cause for the judgment brought upon the great prostitute, thus referring here to religious Babylon of chapter 17. Furthermore, the term prostitute, as used here, may refer to all three forces, or adulteries, that corrupt and lead a person away from a personal relationship with the one, true God and Creator:

1) False religions which advocate pagan rites including idolatry, ritualized acts of immorality, and the sacrifice of children (present-day abortion).
2) Pride – a lust for power through government.
3) Greed – a lust for money and material possessions.

Recall from chapter 17 that the kings of the earth and Antichrist destroyed religious Babylon, the prostitute; yet, here we are told it was God who judged it. God uses different instruments, and He will even use Satan to accomplish His purpose. Those in heaven who have more perfect knowledge than you and I are able to say that God's judgments are true and just. My brethren, whatever God does is true and just!

All the iniquities of past ages will be justified in this ultimate destruction when God, in righteous judgment, avenges the blood of His servants.

As Christians, we are not to seek revenge on those who do harm to us for the Apostle Paul wrote: *"Do not take revenge, my friends, but leave room for God's wrath, for it is written: It is mine to avenge; I will repay, says the Lord"* (Romans 12:19). God will take care of vengeance for you and me. The extent of God's judgment on the prostitute and the kingdom of Antichrist is illustrated by the phrase, "the smoke from her goes up for ever and ever" (v.3), indicating that the judgment on Babylonian religion, politics, and commerce will be eternal.

19:4: Five times in the book of Revelation the twenty-four elders express themselves, each time in praise and rejoicing, and this time along with the four living creatures of chapter 4. Recall from chapter 4 that we said the twenty-four elders are representative of the Church in heaven. This is the last time the elders appear as such, for the Church is to become the bride of Christ. The word "church" is translated from the Greek word *ekklesia* which means "called out." While on earth, believers who make up the Church are the called out ones – that is, separated from the darkness of the world to be light and Christ's ambassadors (2 Corinthians 5:20). However, when the Church leaves the earth, it will become Christ's bride in heaven.

19:5: *"Then a voice came from the throne saying: Praise our God ...."* Notice the call to praise and worship comes directly from the throne of God, because the Lord Jesus Christ is preparing to take control of His world. This great heavenly chorus will be a mixture of human and angelic voices as they sing, "Hallelujah!" They all share one thing in common; through faith, they have all voluntarily become God's servants.

19:6: *"... Hallelujah! For our Lord God Almighty reigns."* This proclamation reminds us of the OT covenant that God made with David when the Lord declared: *"Your house and your kingdom will endure forever before me; your throne will be established forever"* (2 Samuel 7:16). The united song of all those in heaven anticipate the reign of the Lord God Almighty, Jesus Christ. For almost two thousand years, Christians have prayed in obedience to our Lord, *"Your kingdom come, your will be done on earth as it is in heaven"* (Matthew 6:10). That prayer will finally be answered and the covenant that God made with David fulfilled when Christ returns physically to earth to rule forever.

The Wedding of the Lamb

19:7 – 8: *"Let us rejoice ... For the wedding of the Lamb has come ...."* The phrase, "wedding of the Lamb," beautifully describes the final and complete union of Jesus Christ and the Church. It expresses an intimacy of relationship between Christ and believers that in this life has never been experienced, and one that will never be compromised or broken. While on earth, Jesus spoke often about weddings and wedding suppers in His teachings. The wedding takes place in heaven after the Lord Jesus raptures His Church from the earth.

In *The Parable of the Wedding Banquet*, the Lord Jesus taught: *"The kingdom of heaven is like a king who prepared a wedding banquet for his son. He sent his servants to those who had been invited to the banquet to tell them to come, but they refused to come"* (Matthew 22:2, 3). The bridegroom can only be the king's son, the Lord Jesus Christ. John the Baptist made it clear he was not the Christ. He referred to Jesus as the bridegroom, and to himself as the friend who waits and listens for the bridegroom, and is full of joy when he hears His voice (John 3:29). Consequently, the Lord Jesus Christ is referred to as the *Bridegroom* as well as the Lamb.

The verses of importance regarding the identity of the bride are found in Paul's epistle to the Ephesians. The apostle, speaking to husbands and wives of their relationship together, wrote comparing the husband to Christ and the wife to the Church: *"For this reason a man will leave his father and mother and be united to his wife, and the two will become one flesh. This is a profound mystery – but I am talking about Christ and the church"* (Ephesians 5:31, 32). Paul's description clearly illustrates that the perfect picture of a relationship between the Lord Jesus Christ and the Church is one of a bridegroom and bride.

Paul also wrote indicating the manner in which the bride will be presented to Christ: *"A radiant church, without stain or wrinkle or any other blemish, but only holy and blameless"* (Ephesians 5:27). This condition will only exist after the judgment seat of Christ when all believers have been cleansed and their sanctification consummated. All Christians who have trusted in Jesus Christ during the dispensation of grace – that is, from the day of Pentecost to the Rapture of the Church, will make up Christ's bride. In these verses, John describes the bride of Christ in like manner as did Paul: *"... his bride has made herself ready"* (v.7) with wedding attire of, *"fine linen, bright and clean"* (v.8) that portrays *"... the righteous acts of the saints"* (v.8). The relationship of Christ and the Church is intimate, delightful, and unique. No other creature will enjoy such sweetness. You see, Christ loved the Church and gave His life for her. Take a moment and read Christ's prayer for all believers (John 17:20 – 26).

The Wedding Supper of the Lamb

The wedding of the Lamb will take place in heaven, but the *wedding supper of the Lamb* will take place on earth. This teaching is illustrated by the Lord in *The Parable of the Ten Virgins* (Matthew 25:1 – 13). The virgins are not the bride because Christ has only one bride, and that is the Church. The virgins are guests who await the return of the bridegroom. Christ will return not only to judge the earth, but also to have the wedding supper, which the ten virgins of the story are hoping to attend. Sadly, as the parable goes, five of the virgins were foolish and not prepared (genuinely saved) when the bridegroom arrived and were thus shut out of the supper (the kingdom).

19:9: *"Blessed are those who are invited to the wedding supper of the lamb!"* Those who are invited are friends or guests, and they are blessed because of their personal relationship with Christ. As mentioned earlier, John the Baptist, one of the last OT saints, indicated he was a friend of the bridegroom (John 3:29). Therefore, we can conclude that all the OT saints who have the righteousness of God through faith will be guests at this feast. In addition, there will be those who have accepted the Lord Jesus as Savior during the Tribulation Period. They are the redeemed remnant of the nation of Israel and the Gentile nations; both groups enter into the Millennial Kingdom as invited guests. Our Lord described this scene in His parable of *The Sheep and the Goats* (Matthew 25:31 – 46). The wedding supper is apparently the Millennium. This thousand-year period is a long supper!

The supper is distinguished by the use of the sacrificial name of the Lord – *Lamb*. Some commentators cite the fact that angels have never been the recipients of the blessings of the redeemed. Therefore; one might wonder if only those who have lived a human existence, have sinned, and have been redeemed by the blood of the Lamb will be in attendance. There is still much about angels that we do not know; thus, I will not discount their role and/or involvement with the redeemed during the Millennium.

19:10: Here is another transition verse, this time between the wedding of the Lamb in heaven and the revelation – i.e., the return of the Lord Jesus Christ to earth.

At this point, John appears completely overwhelmed by the angel and the visions shown him. This angel is probably the same mighty angel we saw in chapter 18; and in his weakened state, John feels compelled to worship him, but is restrained from doing so. John is an apostle of Jesus Christ – he knows better. He is commanded by the angel: *"Do not do it!"* Only God is to be worshiped.

In the book of Revelation, believers are considered fellow servants with the angels, because of our testimony of Jesus. However, pastor and best-selling author, Dr. Charles Stanley stated: "Through redemption we are lifted higher than the angels." The writer of Hebrews likewise wrote: *"Are not all angels ministering spirits sent to serve those who will inherit salvation?"* (Hebrews 1:14). The writer further stated: *"Both the one who makes men holy and those who are made holy are of the same family. So, Jesus is not ashamed to call them brothers"* (Hebrews 2:11). In his letter to the church in Corinth, the Apostle Paul wrote: *"Do you not know that we will judge angels?"* (1 Corinthians 6:3). Paul's statement likely refers to fallen angels who are imprisoned awaiting judgment, not angels that make up the heavenly host. Perhaps some of us may be given this tremendous responsibility. The role of angels in God's eternal plan is uncertain and for God to direct as He determines; our focus always remaining on Jesus.

The phrase, "the testimony of Jesus," represents the best description of the spirit of prophecy to be found in Scripture. Prophecy receives its value and meaning from its relation to Christ. From the first prophetic utterance of God (Genesis 3:15) to the last prediction of Revelation, the heart of prophecy has been directed at the Person of Jesus Christ. The study of the book of Revelation should cause our hearts to burn within us (Luke 24:32) because it is the revealing of Jesus Christ in all His glory. He is the One who forms the heart of all prophecy.

The Revelation of Jesus Christ

The Apostle Paul wrote: *"… we wait for the blessed hope – the glorious appearing of our great God and Savior, Jesus Christ"* (Titus 2:13). This is the most exciting event every believer and student of God's Word anticipates – the day when the Lord Jesus Christ will truly be glorified. At His First Coming, He allowed Himself to suffer abuse and beatings by His enemies, even to the point of allowing men to spit on Him and crucify Him. The next time the Lord will not come in humility, but in His own words, *"They will see the Son of Man coming on the clouds of the sky, with power and great glory"* (Matthew 24:30). His Second Coming will be the final display of the wrath of God upon a sinful world. All rebellion and wickedness of mankind will finally be crushed and judged at Christ's return in order that He may establish His righteous kingdom on earth. Since the revelation of Christ is such a climactic event in the Bible, we can expect to find many references to it (cf. Isaiah 63:1 – 6, Zechariah 14:3 – 5, Matthew 24:27 – 31, and Jude 14, 15).

19:11: *"I saw heaven standing open and there before me was a white horse, whose rider is called Faithful and True …."* What an awesome scene! John's vision begins with heaven standing open to allow the rider on the white horse to exit. Recall earlier that heaven was opened to allow John in to see the throne room of heaven and all its heavenly host (chapter 4). Here heaven opens again, this time to let Christ come forth. The Lord Jesus Christ is the rider of this white horse, which stands in complete contrast to Antichrist, the rider on the white horse of chapter 6 (v.2). The significance of the white horse is typical of the difference between Christ's Second Advent and His First. In His First Coming, the Lord Jesus fulfilled the words of the Prophet Zechariah (9:9) by entering Jerusalem on a lowly donkey, which denotes peace. However, the time for humility is over. The mercy that God has given unrepentant mankind by delaying its judgment will have run its course. At His Second Coming, the Lord will come in all His majesty riding a white horse, an animal of warfare, which emphasizes His awesome power and glory. In addition, Christ's eternal nature is revealed for He is called *Faithful and True*. Christ is Faithful, because He has come to execute God's judgment and eternal plan for unrepentant humanity. Christ is True, because He is the truth (cf. John 14:6). He is the only One you and I can trust. The Apostle Peter wrote: *"In the last days scoffers will come … They will say, 'Where is this coming he promised?'"* (2 Peter 3:3, 4). Here, Christ will make good on His promise. He is faithful, because He has returned to earth as Judge and Warrior-King, For John says that He has come to judge and make war, not to die again on a cross.

19:12: *"His eyes are like blazing fire ..."* is the same description John gave earlier when he first saw the glorified Christ (1:14). Just as then, these eyes speak of the judgment to come upon the earth as Christ tramples all unrighteousness. He is the righteous King as indicated by the many crowns on His head. Crowns are a symbol of authority, and this means He will come with absolute authority. When Christ comes, all power and authority will be His as the absolute and supreme Judge and King of the earth.

"He has a name written on him that no one knows but he himself." This passage would suggest that either some aspects of Christ's divine nature are incomprehensible to us, or that Christ has not yet chosen to reveal them to us. Do you really know Jesus? I would say that no one really knows the Son except the Father; but, learning to know Him is one of the things that will make heaven and eternity exceedingly special for God's people. Christ is so wonderful, that it is going to take all of eternity to really know Him.

19:13: The phrases describing Jesus, "dressed in a robe dipped in blood" and treading "the winepress of the fury of the wrath of God Almighty" (v.15), coincide with the prophecy of Isaiah (63:1 – 6) and our earlier discussion of the harvest of the wicked (14:17 – 19). The expression, "his name is the Word of God," reminds us of the opening words of the Gospel of John: *"In the beginning was the Word, and the Word was with God, and the Word was God ... The Word became flesh and made his dwelling among us. We have seen his glory, the glory of the One and only, who came from the Father, full of grace and truth"* (John 1:1, 2, 14). If we want to know God, we need only study about His Son Jesus Christ for He has declared Him (John 1:18).

19:14: *"The armies of heaven were following him, riding on white horses and dressed in fine linen, white and clean."* This is an interesting statement. Who are these armies of heaven following behind the Lord? The word "armies" refer to those who go to fight in battle, such as we saw with Michael and his angels as they fought against the dragon (Satan) and his demons (12:7). Therefore, these armies must include the multitudes of angelic legions faithful to our Lord (cf. 5:11). However, I believe that the armies of heaven encompass much more, and our clue was mentioned earlier in chapter 17 (v.14). There the final war between the beast and the Lamb was briefly fore-mentioned and those returning with Jesus were referred to as His called, chosen, and faithful followers. All three of these terms represent believers – the raptured Church that has now become the bride of Christ. Recall that the word "church" is translated from the Greek word meaning "called out" – the called out ones. Additionally, the Patriarch Enoch prophesied the following: *"See, the Lord is coming with thousands upon thousands of his holy ones to judge everyone and to convict all the ungodly ..."* (Jude 14, 15). That would certainly substantiate the words of the Apostle Paul: *"Do you not know that the saints will judge the world?"* (1 Corinthians 6:2). Once joined together at the marriage of the Lamb, it is difficult to imagine Christ ever being anywhere without His bride. That is the glorious wonder of the omnipresent nature of God. The significance here is that these armies of heaven are all dressed in fine linen, white and clean. It is believed that no member of the armies of Christ returning with Him at His glorious appearing will do battle. Not one of them will lift a finger, for the battle will be won by the spoken Word of the Lord.

Recall again from chapter 14 that we were given a fore-glimpse of the scene where the angels (here referred to as the armies of heaven) returning with Christ would be used in the great harvest of both the elect (believers) and the wicked (unbelievers) upon His return to earth (14:14 – 19). This is the final judgment of those surviving the Tribulation Period following Christ's victory over the forces of Antichrist (Matthew 13:36 – 43, 24:30 – 31).

19:15 – 16: Lastly, the rider, Jesus Christ, is described having a sharp sword that comes out of His mouth. The word "sword" is used symbolically to represent a sharp instrument of war with which He will destroy the armies of the nations of Antichrist and establish His absolute rule. Christ's sword will be His spoken Word. The Word that called the universe into creation will ultimately call the kings and armies of the world into judgment and destruction. The expression, "rule them with an iron scepter," fulfills the prophecy of Psalm 2 (vv.6 – 9) and represents absolute, unyielding government under which all men are required to conform to the righteous standards of God.

Instead of a sword on His thigh (as with most warriors going into battle) there will be His name:

KING OF KINGS AND LORD OF LORDS

Finally, the words of the Prophet Isaiah will be truly fulfilled: *"For to us a child is born, to us a Son is given, and the government will be on his shoulders. And he will be called Wonderful Counselor, Mighty God, Everlasting Father, Prince of Peace"* (Isaiah 9:6).

The Battle on the Great Day of God Almighty

19:17 – 21: *"And I saw an angel standing in the sun, who cried in a loud voice to all the birds flying in midair, 'Come, gather together for the great supper of God ....'"* These verses deal primarily with Christ as the righteous Warrior, because He is coming to do battle with the armies of Antichrist in what is often called the *battle of Armageddon*. In reality, this is more a war or campaign of multiple battles. The battle of Armageddon is a misleading expression, because Armageddon refers to the beautiful valley to the east of Mount Megiddo, and the word "battle" literally means "campaign" or "war." This conflict takes place in a single day, and the battle of Armageddon will be just one of the battles of this war. Actually, it will encompass more than just the Valley of Megiddo. As we will see, it covers much of the land of Israel which was promised in the covenant between Abraham and God. This event, when Christ destroys the armies of Antichrist, will be made up of a series of at least four campaigns. Consequently, the battle is more appropriately named the *battle on the great day of God Almighty* (16:14).

The first battle occurs immediately following the destruction of commercial Babylon. It is believed that the Lord will proceed directly to Edom (present-day Jordan) and bloody His robe in battle. He will rescue the redeemed remnant of Israel who has fled Jerusalem and persecution by Antichrist and his forces (Isaiah 63:1 – 6).

"Then I saw the beast and the kings of the earth and their armies gathered together to make war against the rider on the white horse and his army" (v.19). From Edom, Christ will go to the Valley of Megiddo for the second great battle. There the armies of the world will be gathered in opposition to Him. This conflict can literally be called the *battle of Armageddon* (16:16). In these verses, John implies that when Christ meets the armies of Antichrist in the Valley of Megiddo, it will be *all* nations of the earth united together. Christ will then destroy them with the sharp sword that comes out of His mouth, i.e., His spoken Word. All that will be left of these armies is little more than a gigantic feast for birds of prey and other scavengers and is referred to as the great supper of God (v.17). God must have included this scene at the end of His Word to remind us of how disgusting the deeds of the

flesh are to Him. Men who have lived in the flesh will have their flesh destroyed, or gorged upon as John says. The Prophet Ezekiel gave a similar description of the massacre following God's judgment and destruction of the forces of Gog in their future invasion of Israel (Ezekiel 39:17 – 22). However, Ezekiel's vision is merely a fore-shadow of the devastation the Lord Jesus Christ will inflict upon the global forces of Antichrist.

The third battle is the battle of the Valley of Jehoshaphat (Joel 3:1 – 3, 9 – 17). This valley is part of the Kidron Valley between the temple and the Mount of Olives. The name *Jehoshaphat* means, "Jehovah is Judge." In this battle, the multitudes that the prophet describes are more of the armies of the nations who will be brought into war by the lying spirits. In these verses, we also see the prophecy concerning the harvest and judgment of the wicked described earlier (14:17 – 20).

The fourth and final battle in the war of the great day of God Almighty will be the battle of Jerusalem. Antichrist and what is left of his forces will storm Jerusalem. This last conflict between Antichrist (Satan incarnate) and Jesus Christ, until after the Millennium, will find Satan making one last fiendish effort to destroy the Son of God, the promised seed of David. Antichrist will order his forces to destroy the entire city of Jerusalem, but Christ will come to her deliverance. The prophet wrote: *"On that day when all the nations of the earth are gathered against her, I will make Jerusalem an immovable rock for all the nations … I will set out to destroy all the nations that attack Jerusalem"* (Zechariah 12:3 – 9).

Satan's two pawns, Antichrist and the false prophet, will defy God right up to the very end. Nevertheless, they have the distinction of being the first two of all mankind to be cast into eternal hell, for John says: *"The two of them were thrown alive into the fiery lake of burning sulfur"* (v.20). The rest of the unrighteous remain in Hades until they are resurrected to stand in judgment before Christ at the great white throne (20:11 – 15).

Jesus Christ the Victor

This will be the most dramatic and thrilling moment in world history! After sweeping four successive battles (or concurrent; the order is irrelevant – God is omnipotent and omnipresent), Christ will set His feet on the Mount of Olives, for the prophet wrote: *"Then the Lord will go out and fight against those nations, as he fights in the day of battle. On that day his feet will stand on the Mount of Olives, east of Jerusalem, and the Mount of Olives will be split in two from east to west, forming a great valley, with half of the mountain moving north and half moving south,"* (Zechariah 14:3, 4).

When Christ conquers all before Him through judgments of earthquakes, fire, hailstorms, and the sharp sword that proceeds out of His mouth, not only will Jerusalem lay in ruin, but the entire Holy Land as well will be literally bathed in the blood of all the unrepentant, God-opposing degenerates of mankind. Not one person will escape the warrior Christ in this great battle at the end of the age. Those who opposed Him during the Tribulation Period will be slain by Him at the revelation and His glorious appearing. The "sword" that comes from the mouth of the Lord Jesus Christ is His spoken Word. This symbolism is clearly explained in both the OT and the NT (Isaiah 11:4; Ephesians 6:17; Hebrews 4:12). Unlike you and me, Christ does not have to use His hands or a weapon to strike His foe. Christ speaks, and His will is accomplished. It was His Word that created this universe, and it will be His Word that will bring an everlasting end to all wickedness and rebellion to God. It is the Word of God that will save you.

> *"As surely as I live, declares the Sovereign Lord,*
> *I take no pleasure in the death of the wicked,*
> *but rather that they turn from their ways and live.*
> *Turn! Turn from your evil ways!*
> (Ezekiel 33:11)

Review Questions

1) The rejoicing in heaven that opens this chapter is a result of the completion of _____

_____.

2) The wedding of the Lamb is a beautiful description of _____

_____.

3) This wedding of the Lamb takes place where and when? _____

_____

_____.

4) The wedding supper of the Lamb takes place where and when? _____

_____.

5) The most exciting event that every believer anticipates is _____

_____.

6) The sharp sword that comes out of the mouth of Christ is used to symbolically represent a sharp instrument of war, but in reality, it refers to _____.

7) Antichrist and his false prophet have the distinction of being the first two of all mankind to be

_____.

Up For Discussion

"And behold a white horse, and he that sat upon him was called Faithful and True."
(Revelation 19:11 KJV)

Read through the related lesson entitled, *The Judgment Seat of Christ.* The five crowns mentioned in Scripture and in the lesson may be just a few of many that will be rewarded by the Lord Jesus Christ when all believers appear before His judgment seat in heaven. Does this lesson assist you in understanding the believer's judgment; and if so, in what way?

When a person joins the Church, they are asked to support it with their prayers, their presence, their gifts, and their service. Does this lesson cause you to reevaluate your commitment to your home church? Of the four areas mentioned above, can you increase your commitment to one or more?

The Judgment Seat of Christ

The Bible speaks of three events whereby every individual will be resurrected at some future time in order to stand before Jesus Christ for judgment.

The first event or judgment is referred to by the Apostle Paul as the judgment seat of Christ. The apostle wrote to the church in Rome: *"For we will all stand before God's judgment seat. It is written: As surely as I live, says the Lord, every knee will bow before me, every tongue will confess to God. So then, each of us will give an account of himself to God"* (Romans 14:10 – 12).

This judgment is often called the bema. *Bema* is the Greek translation of judgment seat. This is the believer's (the Church) judgment. This judgment will commence just after the Rapture when all Christians, dead and living, from the day of Pentecost to the present, will be resurrected into our new glorified bodies to meet the Lord Jesus Christ in the clouds (1 Thessalonians 4:13 – 18; 1 Corinthians 15:51 – 53). We will then return with Christ to the Father's house, the place He has prepared for us (John 14:2). The question many believers have is: "Will we have to account for our sins? Will Christ bring our sins before us at judgment?"

Many Christians believe that their sins will be brought to light according to the following words from Paul: *"For we must all appear before the judgment seat of Christ, that each one may receive what is due him for the things done while in the body, whether good or bad"* (2 Corinthians 5:10). A closer look at this passage reveals that the phrase, "things done while in the body," refers to works – that is, works of service to others for the kingdom of God after being saved and becoming a member of the body of Christ. The body of Christ on earth is the Church, having Jesus as its head. Paul reinforces this analogy: *"And he is the head of the body, the church; he is the beginning and the firstborn from among the dead"* (Colossians 1:18). Therefore, what Paul is talking about here are our Christian works, not secular works or worldly sins.

Paul elaborated on this teaching using the following illustration: *"For no one can lay any foundation other than the one already laid, which is Jesus Christ. If any man builds on this foundation using gold, silver, costly stones, wood, hay, or straw, his work will be shown for what it is, because the Day will bring it to light. It will be revealed with fire, and the fire will test the quality of each man's work. If what he has built survives, he will receive his rewards. If it is burned up, he will suffer loss; he himself will be saved, but only as one escaping through the flames"* (1 Corinthians 3:11 – 15).

Our good or bad works are determined by how fruitful we were for God's kingdom here on earth; in other words, how productive we were in bringing others to the knowledge of Christ. The apostle's prayer for those in the Church was: *"… that you may live a life worthy of the Lord and may please him in every way: bearing fruit in every good work, growing in the knowledge of God"* (Colossians 1:10). Bearing fruit, in the biblical sense, is simply sharing the Gospel and bringing people to Christ! It means to bring others to the knowledge of salvation offered by the grace of God through faith in His Son Jesus Christ.

Good works can be likened to producing much fruit for the kingdom of God, whereas bad works can be likened to producing very little fruit for God's kingdom – not our sins. Either way we are all saved by our faith in Jesus Christ and will enjoy eternity with our Lord and Savior, regardless of whether we produced much or little fruit. This is not to say that some might receive a rebuke from Christ for missed opportunities to witness or minister; however, it is believed that the Lord's rebuke will be minor in His eternal plan and result only in loss of some heavenly reward or opportunity.

The Lord illustrated judgment and rewards in *The Parable of the Talents* (Matthew 25:14 – 30). In this parable the master is Christ, the three servants represent professed believers, and the talents of money represent the time, talents, and gifts that the Holy Spirit gives to all genuine believers. In the parable, two of the servants were faithful (fruitful) with what the master gave them. In other words, they used their God-given talents to advance God's kingdom on earth. However, one was unfaithful (unfruitful) because he hid his master's talent and kept it to himself. When the master returned and called his servants before him, the two faithful servants were rewarded with more and given charge over many things. However, the unfaithful servant lost what he had and was cast outside, into the darkness, where there was weeping and gnashing of teeth. The darkness, weeping, and gnashing of teeth are representative of the extreme opposite characteristics of what we know to be heaven. Consequently, the unfaithful servant, with no fruit, is cast into hell, where he will suffer eternal punishment and separation from God.

Let's compare this unfaithful servant to the five unprepared virgins of another parable of Christ – *The Parable of the Ten Virgins* (Matthew 25:1 – 13). Five of the ten virgins had no oil for their lamps when the bridegroom arrived. As a result, they were shut out of the wedding banquet (Christ's earthly kingdom). The oil is symbolic of the Holy Spirit and the lamps (light) represent the Word of God. Without the Holy Spirit working in you, you have no light. You are unprepared to bring the light of God – that is, the Word of God and the Gospel of Jesus Christ to others. This brings us to the words of James, the Lord's brother: *"For as the body without the spirit is dead, so faith without works is dead also"* (James 2:26). It is faith that produces the works. Believers serve Christ and produce fruit for the kingdom of God as a result of their love for the Savior.

Thus, there is a distinction between little works and no works. Little works are proof of your salvation, but no works means you probably were not saved in the first place. Only God knows a person's true heart.

The Lord Jesus Christ died on a Roman cross for the sins of all mankind. He paid our sin debt once and for all. When you accept Jesus Christ as your Lord and Savior and confess your sins, then those sins are forever forgiven and forgotten. The Apostle John says that the blood of Jesus purifies us from all sins (1 John 1:7). The word "purifies" is in the present tense; thus the blood of Jesus continues to purify believers from their sin, as long as they confess, repent, and continue to seek God's will and grow in their spiritual maturity. Purifies means removes – our sins are removed. Paul reminds us that there is no condemnation for those who are in Christ Jesus, because through Christ Jesus the law of the Spirit of life sets believers free from the law of sin and death (Romans 8:1). This should give all Christians comfort and confidence on that glorious day when we come into the presence of our Lord and Savior Jesus Christ.

Consider for a moment the following: If all our earthly sins were paraded before us at judgment, how would that make us feel? Would that bring us joy or sorrow? On the other hand, if our worldly sins were brought to light at judgment (I do not want to be dogmatic), I believe that in our new, selfless, glorified state, our sins would only serve to magnify God's grace as He stamped each with a great big "PARDONED."

Shame and disgrace are emotions that are not characteristic of heaven and its inhabitants. The Prophet Isaiah wrote regarding the future kingdom of God: *"The Sovereign Lord will wipe away the tears from all the faces; he will remove the disgrace of his people from all the earth"* (Isaiah 25:8; cf. Revelation 21:4). My brethren, we are able to start over!

Let me reiterate, our worldly sins are washed clean by the blood of the Lamb – past, present, and future, and they will likely not be part of the believer's judgment. The Prophet Micah says that the sins of the righteous are hurled into the depths of the sea (Micah 7:19). According to the psalmist, our sins are removed from us as far as the east is from the west (Psalm 103:12).

In early times, the city of Corinth was famous for its festival of athletic events similar to our Olympic Games. At the end of the contests the athletes would appear before a large decorated platform called a bema. Here, the emperor sat on the judgment seat and handed out rewards to the victorious athletes for their years of dedicated training, perseverance, and endurance in the heat of competition.

Likewise, the judgment seat of Christ will also include rewards, as alluded to earlier in our discussion. Christ will reward crowns to all believers for their years of dedication to God's Word, perseverance in the face of trials, and endurance through the heat of a corrupt and fallen world. The NT speaks of five different crowns:

1) Victor's crown for faithful service (1 Corinthians 9:25; Revelation 3:11).
2) Crown of life for perseverance under trial (James 1:12; Revelation 2:10).
3) Crown of glory for overseeing the church – the elder's crown (1 Peter 5:4).
4) Crown of rejoicing for winning souls for Christ (1 Thessalonians 2:19, 20).
5) Crown of righteousness for those who long for Christ's appearing (2 Timothy 4:8).

So, what will we do with these crowns? The Apostle John gives us the answer to that question. We will do just as the twenty-four elders in heaven – fall down and cast our crowns before the throne of God and of the Lamb and sing eternal praises to our Creator, Lord, and God (Revelation 4:10, 11).

The second judgment event is the judgment of *The Sheep and the Goats* (Matthew 25:31 – 46). This judgment occurs when Christ returns to earth at the end of the Tribulation Period. This is also referred to by some commentators as the *judgment of the nations*, whereby the surviving remnant of the Gentile nations will be judged to determine who enters the Millennial Kingdom to eternal life as sheep, and who are turned away to eternal punishment as goats. At that time the OT saints, along with the slain Tribulation saints will be resurrected and also allowed entrance into Christ's earthly Millennial Kingdom. The first two judgments make up the *first resurrection* with Jesus Christ as the firstfruit.

The third judgment event and final resurrection is that of the *great white throne* (Revelation 20:11 – 15). This judgment occurs at the end of the Millennium. Scripture refers to this as the *second resurrection*, at which time unbelievers from all ages of history will be resurrected and summoned to give an account of their lives. This judgment is one of works alone; however, we are not saved by our works, but only through faith in Jesus Christ. Consequently, none of their names will be found in the *book of life* belonging to the Lamb, and therefore, all are thrown into the lake of fire to be tormented for eternity.

In the last chapter of the book of Revelation, our Lord gives us the following words of encouragement: *"Behold, I am coming soon! My reward is with me, and I will give to everyone according to what he has done"* (Revelation 22:12). Are you ready to stand before the bema seat of Christ? Out of our love for Jesus Christ and in appreciation for His gifts of salvation and eternal life, we should serve God faithfully now, and we will be rewarded later. Being awarded any one of these crowns or given an opportunity to reign alongside Christ would be an honor beyond anything we can imagine.

Chapter 20

Please follow along in your Bible.

This chapter introduces the long awaited reign of the Lord Jesus Christ on earth – the Millennial Kingdom. In the first seven verses, John mentions the phrase, "thousand years," six times. It must be important for the apostle to have placed so much emphasis on it; thus, we will take this period of time as literal. This period of one thousand years is God's answer to the prayer the Lord Jesus taught His followers: *"Thy kingdom come, thy will be done, on earth as it is in heaven …."* (Matthew 6:10 KJV) This coming Kingdom Age will be an age of righteousness, that of true peace and perfect justice. There can be no doubt as to the scriptural evidence for this coming kingdom of Christ on earth. There are literally hundreds of passages in our Bible that predict an earthly kingdom of God, ruled by the Messiah, the Lord Jesus Christ and superseding all the kingdoms of the world. All the OT prophets spoke of this kingdom – not one of them missed it. They often held it out as a source of encouragement to the children of Israel during times of distress. Take a moment and read at your convenience what some of the prophets foretold (Psalm 2:5 – 12, Isaiah 2:1 – 5 and 65:17 – 25, Jeremiah 23:3 – 8, Ezekiel chapters 40 – 48, Daniel 2:44 – 45, Micah 4:1 – 8, and Zechariah 14:6 – 11 and 16 – 21).

Satan Bound for A Thousand Years

20:1 – 3: *"And I saw an angel coming down out of heaven, having the key to the Abyss and holding in his hand a great chain. He seized the dragon … and bound him for a thousand years …."* The entirety of Scripture testifies that the only way to establish a righteous era is for Satan to be taken out of the world. As I noted earlier, this angel coming down out of heaven having the key to the Abyss, is likely the same angel as the *star* we discussed in chapter 9 (v.1). He is given the awesome responsibility of controlling access into and out of the Abyss. This is yet another illustration of the ministry of angels in accomplishing God purpose on earth. Remember, we have already seen the four angels that control the winds (7:1), the angel in charge of the fire from the altar in heaven (8:3 – 5; 14:17), and the angel in charge of the waters (16:5).

According to John, the angel seized the dragon, i.e., Satan, and bound him with a great chain. What a remarkable feat! Think about it; either this angel is the most powerful angel we have seen thus far, or upon His return, the Lord Jesus Christ renders Satan completely defenseless against him.

Nevertheless, Satan, our greatest adversary, is apprehended and imprisoned. Equally amazing are these great chains that bind Satan. Whatever supernatural properties these chains possess, evidently they again render Satan completely inactive and powerless, and for a thousand years.

Satan's goal has always been to deceive, divide, and destroy people, thus separating them from a relationship with God. The binding of Satan will restrict him from doing the thing he does best, for God's purpose in binding him is, *"… to keep him from deceiving the nations anymore until the thousand years were ended"* (v.3). The Millennium cannot begin until Satan is removed from the earth. Subsequently, with Satan unable to tempt or influence mankind, God is going to use the Millennium as a final testing of mankind under ideal conditions. Although Satan will no longer be an influence, mankind's heart will still be human and capable of rebellion and rejection. Multitudes of both Jews and Gentiles will enter Christ's Millennial Kingdom in natural bodies, having survived the Tribulation Period. These are the ones, together with those who are born during the Millennium, who will be tested during this thousand-year period.

Think of mankind's rebellion to God as the result of three sinful factors. Satan is but one factor that manipulates humanity. The other two influences are the world and the flesh. These two represent greed and lust respectively, and are the carnal tendencies of mankind's self-indulgent nature that pulls them away from a righteous relationship with God. Despite Christ's absolute rule as King during the Millennium, both of these influences will still be present to lead natural mankind away from God and into sin.

In writing about the future kingdom of God, the Prophet Isaiah gives us some interesting insight: *"He who dies at a hundred will be thought a mere youth; he who fails to reach a hundred will be considered accursed"* (Isaiah 65:20). The word "accursed" is translated from the Greek word *anathema*, which means "to bind under a great curse." It literally means "let him be damned," a reference to delivering someone over to the wrath of God for eternal destruction (cf. Galatians 1:8, 9 NKJV). This suggests that the natural children of the Millennium will be given a hundred years to make a decision to accept Jesus Christ as Lord and enjoy fellowship with Him for eternity, or to reject Him and die. Regardless, John tells us in verse 3 that Satan will be released at the end of this period for one last time of deception.

The Believers' Resurrection

20:4: *"I saw thrones on which were seated those who had been given authority to judge…."* This is another statement where there is disagreement amongst commentators. Who are the ones seated on these thrones? There are two responses to this question to be found in Scripture that we should consider. First, and foremost, are the words of the Lord Jesus Christ to His disciples: *"I tell you the truth, at the renewal of all things, when the Son of Man sits on his glorious throne, you who have followed me will also sit on twelve thrones, judging the twelve tribes of Israel"* (Matthew 19:28). This same discourse is also recorded in the Gospel of Luke (Luke 22:28 – 30). The statement is very specific. Apparently, Christ will give all judgment authority for the nation of Israel over to the twelve apostles as they reign alongside Christ during the Millennium.

The second response would be the Church Age saints, now called the bride of Christ. Since our next Scripture reference comes from the Apostle Paul, the apostle to the Gentiles, Christ apparently will, in like manner as above, give all judgment authority for the Gentile nations over to the saints, as they too reign alongside Christ. In writing to the early church, the apostle explained: *"Do you not know that the saints will judge the world?"* (1 Corinthians 6:2). In our context, it is highly probable that both responses are true and appropriate in order to guarantee a righteous government for both the Jewish and Gentile branches during Christ's millennial reign (see, end-of-chapter illustration: *The Government of the Messianic Kingdom*).

The next sentence starts with the phrase, "and I saw," indicating a different group from those in the first sentence. *"And I saw the souls of those who have been beheaded because of their testimony for Jesus and because of the word of God."* This passage is an obvious reference to the slain Tribulation saints because John further states that they had not worshiped the beast or his image and had not received his mark on their body.

20:5: The expression, "the rest of the dead," is a reference to unbelievers of all ages throughout earth's history. In His parable of *The Rich Man and Lazarus* (Luke 16:19 – 31), the Lord Jesus illustrated that after death the spirits of the wicked go to hell (Hades), a place of torment (see: *Hades Illustration*, end of chapter 9) to await their judgment. These unbelievers will make up the second or final resurrection that occurs at the end of the Millennium. We will see shortly that these unbelievers will not be resurrected to life, but to death, a state of separation from God referred to as the *second death* (v.6).

The word "death" is translated from the Greek word *thanatos*, which has the basic meaning of separation. The first death is the separation of the soul (spirit) from the body. When a Christian dies, their body returns to the earth while their soul goes to heaven to be with the Lord (2 Corinthians 5:8). The two will be reunited in resurrection at the Rapture when the believer's redemption is made complete in the presence of Christ. The second death, reserved for nonbelievers, is unfortunately the separation of the soul (spirit) from God – and it is eternal!

20:6: *"Blessed and holy are those who have part in the first resurrection …."* The first resurrection is made up of believers throughout all of history. The Greek word for "resurrection" is *anastasis* which means "a standing up again, a resurrection from death." Listed below in order of their occurrence, are four groups that are included in the first resurrection with Jesus Christ as the Firstfruit:

1) Church Age saints: The first group making up the believers' resurrection is the Church. The Church is made up of all believers who have accepted Jesus Christ as Savior and Lord beginning on the day of Pentecost up through the present. As we stated earlier in chapter 4, these believers will be resurrected at the Rapture. This occurs prior to the Tribulation Period when all Christians, dead and living, are caught up to meet the Lord in the clouds and taken to heaven (1 Thessalonians 4:13 – 18). The Church becomes the bride of Christ and will reside in the New Jerusalem where she will reign alongside Christ from that exalted place.

2) The two witnesses: Recall from chapter 11 that these two supernatural witnesses will prophesy during the first half of the Tribulation Period, but are killed at the mid-point by Antichrist. After three and a half days they are resurrected and raptured up to heaven to be with the Lord.

3) Old Testament saints: The Prophet Daniel suggests that deliverance is promised to these patriarchs at the close of the Great Tribulation (Daniel 12:1, 2). We saw in chapter 19 that these OT saints will be in attendance at the wedding supper of the Lamb, which makes up the

Millennium. These saints, with David as their prince, will reign from the earthly Jerusalem alongside Christ. This is the kingdom that God promised to David (Ezekiel 34:22 – 24 and 37:20 – 28; Psalm 89:34 – 37).

4) The martyred Tribulation saints: In chapter 6 (vv.9 – 11) we saw that these saints are waiting for their resurrection, but were told to wait a little longer until the number of their fellow servants and brothers who were to be killed was complete. This refers again to the end of the Tribulation Period. When Christ returns in glory, these slain Tribulation saints will be resurrected, and together with the OT saints, *"… will be priests of God and of Christ and will reign with Him for a thousand years"* (v.6).

All who are resurrected in the first or believers' resurrection will be resurrected holy; in other words, incorruptible and immortal (1 Corinthians 15:53 KJV), meaning incapable of sin. As a result of their faith and the blessings of a loving and merciful God, these believers will hold positions of honor in the government of the Messianic Kingdom. Additionally, the book of Revelation clarifies that no Christian should ever fear death. Recall that our Lord and Savior Jesus Christ holds the keys to death and Hades (1:18), and therefore, the second death, i.e., the lake of fire (20:14) has no power over them.

Over whom will these saints reign? In our related lesson, *The Judgment Seat of Christ*, prior to this chapter, we discussed three judgment events, the second being illustrated in the parable of *The Sheep and the Goats* (Matthew 25:31 – 46). This event, also referred to as the *judgment of the nations*, occurs at the end of the Tribulation Period when Christ returns to earth as Judge and Warrior-King. At that time, Christ will judge the surviving remnant of the nation of Israel and the Gentile nations to determine who will enter into His Millennial Kingdom and who will not. With Satan out of the world and the curse lifted, so also will disease, famine, violence, and murder be absent during the Millennium, resulting in a population explosion the likes of which we have never seen. These are the children of the Millennium. The prophet tells us: *"Never again will there be in it an infant who lives but a few days, or an old man who does not live out his years …."* (Isaiah 65:20).

The Renewal of the Earth by Fire

Three destructions of the earth are described in the Bible, one past and two yet to come. The first destruction came when the Flood covered the earth in the days of Noah (Genesis 6 – 8). In the prophet's description of the Millennium, Isaiah mentions the second destruction of the earth as occurring before the kingdom is established: *"Behold, I will create new heavens and a new earth …"* (Isaiah 65:17 – 25). This means God will create a new atmospheric heaven around the earth and reestablish a far better planet. A thorough look at Isaiah's prophecy suggests that since death appears in his message, Isaiah was obviously not talking about the Eternal Age, but the Millennium. It is believed that this same period of time is referred to by the Apostle Peter (cf. 2 Peter 3:10 – 13). In his epistle, the apostle foretold that the day of the Lord would usher in a time of cataclysmic change on the earth. This will commence with the destruction of the old earth and the renewal of its surface (as described earlier at the conclusion of chapter 16) on which Christ will establish His kingdom of righteousness. The third destruction and renewal of the earth is described in the opening verse of chapter 21.

Scripture also speaks of three heavens:

1) The "third heaven" is the throne room of God (cf. 2 Corinthians 12:2).
2) The stellar heaven is that which contains the great galaxies (cf. Ephesians 4:10; Hebrews 4:14).
3) The atmospheric heaven is that which surrounds the earth (cf. Hebrews 4:14). It is the atmospheric heaven, along with the earth, that are polluted and corrupted by Satan; and therefore, will require being created new, as Isaiah suggests.

Satan's Release after the Millennium

20:7 – 9: *"When the thousand years are over, Satan will be released from his prison and will go out to deceive the nations in the four corners of the earth …."* Here is the last rebellion of Satan and mankind against God. At the beginning of the Millennium Satan was bound in the Abyss by a great angel. Subsequently, mankind would not be tempted by Satan for a thousand years. After being released from his thousand-year imprisonment, Satan will immediately go out to do what he has done for centuries, deceive the nations. According to the prophecy of Isaiah (65:17 – 25), if a person reaches a hundred years old and has not accepted Jesus Christ as Lord, then he/she will be accursed – that is, they will die.

The question begs to be asked, "Whom will Satan deceive?" John tells us that those who gather for battle against the Lord are as many as the sands on the seashore (v.8). This reinforces our belief in a great population explosion that will occur during the Millennium. Even though Satan is imprisoned during this time, the human heart remains unchanged and open to worldly allures. Apparently, there will be a great many born during the last century who will turn their backs on God and be deceived into following Satan upon his release. Perhaps God, in his omniscience, saved Satan from the first judgment so that He might also give to the last generation, those born during the last hundred years of the Millennium, the free will to make their own choice – Jesus Christ or self-reliance. Sadly for them, this is the end of mankind's rebellion and disobedience to God. All that remains is the final judgment.

Imagine the scene: Hordes of armies from all around the world, referred to here as *Gog* and *Magog* (OT symbolism taken from Ezekiel for the enemy of God's people), led by Satan, gather around Jerusalem to challenge the Lord Jesus Christ once more. At one moment, Satan stands amid the multitudes of his global military forces and war machines all pointed at Jerusalem, and the next, he is standing there alone, surrounded by nothing but smoldering ashes. All that is left for Satan is to bow down on both knees and confess, "Jesus is Lord!" The Apostle Paul echoes the words of the Prophet Isaiah: *"… Before me every knee will bow; by me every tongue will swear."* (Isaiah 45:23; cf. Philippians 2:10, 11).

20:10: *"And the devil, who deceived them, was thrown into the lake of burning sulfur …."* The enemy of God and His children is once and for all brought to eternal justice. Satan suffers the same fate as that of the beast and the false prophet. Eternal hell is described as a lake of burning sulfur. The Lord Jesus is the One who gave the most solemn description of hell: *"But the subjects of the kingdom will be thrown outside, into the darkness, where there will be weeping and gnashing of teeth"* (Matthew 8:12). In His parable of *The Sheep and the Goats*, Jesus gave a final warning to those who would oppress and persecute His people: *"Then he will say to those on his left, 'Depart from me, you who are cursed, into the eternal fire prepared for the devil and his angels'"* (Matthew 25:41). Hell is darkness, hell is fire, and hell is a literal place. The Word of God tells us here: *"They will be tormented day and night for ever and ever."*

The Great White Throne

20:11: *"Then I saw a great white throne and him who was seated on it ...."* This ultimate judgment of the great white throne is for unbelievers only – the lost from all ages of history. This judgment occurs at the conclusion of the Millennium, for the passage begins with the phrase, "then I saw." This is the final resurrection, as the lost are raised to stand before the Lord in judgment of their works for salvation. However, at this judgment no one will be saved, because Scripture makes it clear that a person cannot be saved solely by their works. The late pastor and radio commentator, J. Vernon McGee, explained: "When you stand in the white light of the righteous presence of God, your little works will seem so puny that they won't amount to anything at all." The one seated on the throne is the Lord Jesus Christ, for the apostle wrote: *"Moreover, the Father judges no one, but has entrusted all judgment to the Son,"* (John 5:22). The fact that earth and sky fled from his presence illustrates the holiness of this throne and represents a prelude to the third and final destruction of the heavens and the earth that were again polluted as a result of Satan's final insurrection.

20:12: The expression, "dead, great and small," refers to the fact that these individuals are dead and lost in their sins because of their rejection of the Lord Jesus Christ. They never turned to God for salvation. The books that are opened are the records of their deeds – these are the books of works. This multitude wanted to be judged by their works. However, no one is saved by works, but only through faith in Jesus Christ as Lord and Savior. Subsequently, none of their names are found in the *book of life.*

20:13: *"The sea gave up the dead that were in it, and death and Hades gave up the dead that were in them ...."* The sea will give up all those who were drowned or buried at sea, never having accepted Jesus Christ. *Death* represents the grave where the body lies, and *Hades* the place of torment where the souls/spirits of the unsaved have gone. These verses teach us that there will be a physical resurrection reuniting the bodies of the dead with their souls/spirits. They will be resurrected in order to stand before Jesus at the great white throne. Twice in our NT, the Apostle Paul quotes the words of the Prophet Isaiah (Romans 14:11 and Philippians 2:10, 11), and it is appropriate that I mention them here once more: *"... that at the name of Jesus every knee should bow, in heaven and on earth and under the earth, and every tongue confess that Jesus Christ is Lord, to the glory of God the Father."*

20:14 – 15: *"Then death and Hades were thrown into the lake of fire ...."* Death, the great enemy of man, is finally eliminated. Paul writes: *"The last enemy to be destroyed is death ... Where, O death is your victory? Where, O death is your sting?"* (1 Corinthians 15:26, 55). Hades, the prison of lost souls, is thrown into the lake of fire as well. Finally, the lost no longer exist in Hades, but are also cast into the lake of fire – eternal hell.

As we have already seen (3:5 and 13:8), the book of life contains the names of all humanity. Unfortunately for many, their names will be blotted out because they rejected God and refused to accept His gift of salvation and eternal life through the sacrificial death and resurrection of His Son Jesus Christ. If a man will not accept the life of God, then he must accept the only alternative – to abide eternally with Satan in the lake of fire. God did not create mankind to suffer an eternity in hell, but there is no other place for those who have chosen to reject His grace in favor of self-gratification. Pastor and best-selling author, Dr. Charles Stanley, stated: "God is a God of grace! You have to absolutely run over God to go to hell." The second death means absolute and eternal separation from God.

When we accept Jesus Christ as our Lord and Savior, our name is forever sealed in the Lamb's book of life, where it is impossible to be removed or blotted out. Scripture emphasizes one consistent principle and that is there are only two kinds of people: The righteous and the unrighteous – that is, the believer and the nonbeliever, and resulting in the saved and the unsaved. Our Lord teaches: *"He that is not with me is against me; and he who does not gather with me scatters"* (Matthew 12:30).

Is your name written and sealed in the Lamb's book of life?

Review Questions

1) The only way to establish a righteous era is _____.

2) In the absence of Satan (and temptation), God is going to use the Millennium as _____
   _____.

3) The first resurrection occurs in four phases and is made up of _____.

4) When Satan is released after the thousand years, he immediately proceeds to do what?_____
   _____.

5) Satan's final fate is _____.

6) The judgment of the great white throne is for _____.

7) The Lamb's book of life lists only the names of those who have _____
   _____.

Up For Discussion

*"For unto us a child is born, unto us a son is given: and the government will be upon
His shoulders: and his name shall be called Wonderful, Counseller, The mighty
God, The everlasting Father, The Prince of Peace."* (Isaiah 9:6 KJV)

The Apostle Paul wrote: *"Everyone must submit himself to the governing authorities, for there is no authority except that which God has established. The authorities that exist have been established by God"* (Romans 13:1). Therefore, as with all preceding governments, so also the government of the Messianic Kingdom will have its chain of authority as well.

Review the illustration entitled, *The Government of the Messianic Kingdom*. Start at the top with Jesus Christ as King and the Church as His Bride and follow it downward to those judging, reigning, and residing on earth. Discuss each block and read the Bible references associated with each group. Keep in mind that our King and Lord Jesus Christ is God, and as such is omnipresent.

Review the illustration entitled, *The Third Heaven*. Read from left to right on your own or discuss as a class the various events of the timeline. Notice that some of the blocks relate back to our Hades illustration from chapter 9.

Read on your own or as a class FAQ: *Satan's Final Assault*.

As class time permits, review and discuss the illustration entitled, *Time Intervals in the Latter Days Timeline*.

THE GOVERNMENT OF THE MESSIANIC KINGDOM

"For unto us a child is born, unto us a son is given: and the government will be upon his shoulders" (Isaiah 9:6)

JESUS CHRIST– The King
The CHURCH– His Bride

Gentile Nations		Jewish Nation
Church Saints 1 Corinthians 6:2 Revelation 20:4a	To Judge the Nations	**The Twelve Apostles** Matthew 19:28 Luke 22:28-30
The slain Tribulation Saints Revelation 20:4b-6	To Reign over the Nations	**David/OT Saints** Jeremiah 30:9 Ezekiel 34:23-24 Ezekiel 37:24-25
Kings Psalm 72:10-11 Isaiah 60:11 Revelation 21:24-26		**Princes** Isaiah 32:1; Ezekiel 45:8
		Judges & Counselors Isaiah 1:26
Gentile Nations Matthew 25:31-46		**Israel** The Redeemed Remnant

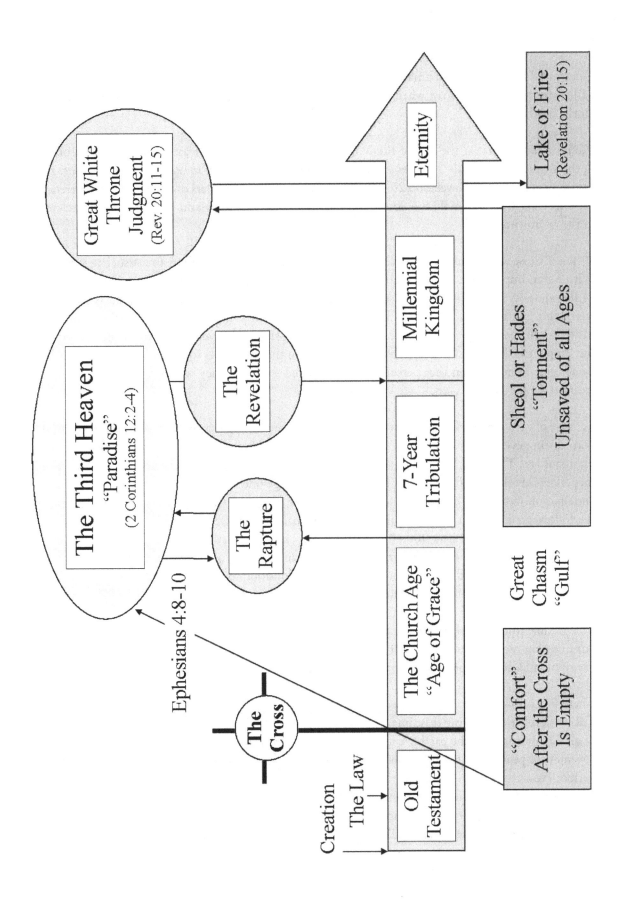

157

FAQ: Satan's Final Assault

Question: How could Satan amass such an enormous army from all corners of the earth during the Millennium to oppose Christ when he is bound in the Abyss and Christ Himself reigns as King over all the earth?

We just learned that at the end of the Millennium, when Satan is released from his imprisonment in the Abyss, that he will *"... deceive the nations in the four corners of the earth – Gog and Magog – to gather them for battle"* (Revelation 20:7, 8). The expression, "four corners of the earth," is a reference to the entire earth – the North, the South, the East, and the West. Gog and Magog is an OT reference to the enemies of Israel.

Who are those that Satan will deceive, and how will he have time enough to amass such a great army? With Satan imprisoned, as we said, he would be unable to tempt mankind; thus, God will use the Millennium as a testing of natural mankind under ideal conditions. Though Satan is bound and restrained, the hearts of all natural beings will still be human and capable of rebellion during the Millennium. We also predicted a great population explosion. However, we learned from the words of the Prophet Isaiah (65:20) that if anyone born during this time fails to receive Jesus Christ as Lord by age one hundred then that person will be accursed – that is, they will physically die and spend eternity separated from God.

Because of carnal man's fallen nature and God-given freewill, apparently there will be many children born during every generation of the Millennium that will choose self-reliance over following God's righteous law. They may likely form an underground movement, i.e., an alternative *Way*, which Christ may likewise tolerate – for a time. Though they die at age one hundred, they may naively look with anticipation to Satan's release, his victory over Christ, and thus their resurrection to serve him. As the followers of this cult grow in numbers, influence, and resources with each passing century, it is not difficult to imagine after 900 plus years of peace, that the earth would be comprised of literally millions born during the last century who would reach the end of the Millennium at various ages (but not yet one hundred) in complete rebellion and opposition to God in favor of self-reliance. These are the ones who will follow Satan in his final rebellion against God.

The gradual amassing of resources (armaments) over the course of the Millennium might help with our question of time. Jesus may well allow this in order to make one final point for eternity – He is omnipotent! Christ is the Creator, Satan and mankind are merely His creations.

There is a presumed period of time between the Rapture of the Church and the beginning of the Tribulation Period. During this time, the world will be in a state of chaos following the disappearance of all Christians from the earth. Antichrist will come onto the scene as a great diplomat and sign a covenant of peace with the nation of Israel, thus triggering the beginning of the 7-year Tribulation Period. However, the length of this time interval is uncertain. There is also a period of time between the end of the Tribulation Period and the beginning of the Millennium. According to the Prophet Daniel, there is a seventy-five day interval between the return of Christ and the beginning of the blessed kingdom (see the following illustration: *Time Intervals in the Latter Days Timeline*).

Considering the above, there may likely be a time interval as well between the end of the Millennium and the beginning of the Eternal Age. During this time, Satan will be released to deceive the nations and do battle with Christ one last time. As the Lord Jesus Christ stands atop the temple stairs looking out over the plains surrounding Jerusalem, these rebellious youth of the Millennium with their military might, led by Satan, will gather in opposition to the King of kings. Finally, just as the Lord God Almighty spoke to Moses from the burning bush, so too will the Lord Jesus Christ proclaim, "I AM WHO I AM" (Exodus 3:14).

Afterwards, Satan, the great deceiver of mankind, will be left standing alone surrounded by nothing but smoldering ashes. All that is left is for him to bow down on both knees and confess, "Jesus is Lord!"

How long all of this takes to accomplish, again is uncertain; however, in God's perfect plan, it will seem quite insignificant.

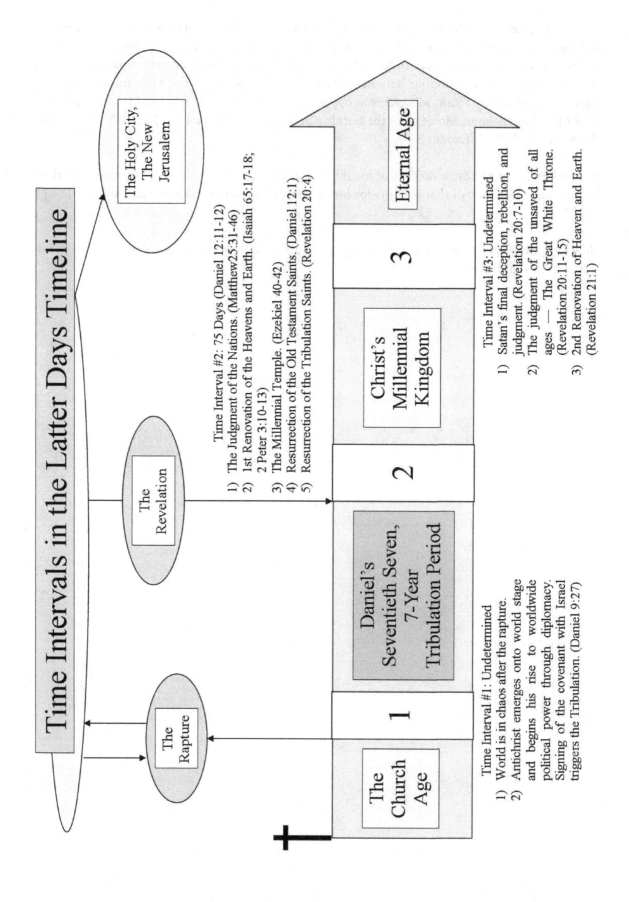

Time Intervals in the Latter Days Timeline

The Holy City, The New Jerusalem

The Revelation

The Rapture

The Church Age

1

Daniel's Seventieth Seven, 7-Year Tribulation Period

2

Christ's Millennial Kingdom

3

Eternal Age

Time Interval #1: Undetermined
1) World is in chaos after the rapture.
2) Antichrist emerges onto world stage and begins his rise to worldwide political power through diplomacy. Signing of the covenant with Israel triggers the Tribulation. (Daniel 9:27)

Time Interval #2: 75 Days (Daniel 12:11-12)
1) The Judgment of the Nations. (Matthew 25:31-46)
2) 1st Renovation of the Heavens and Earth. (Isaiah 65:17-18; 2 Peter 3:10-13)
3) The Millennial Temple. (Ezekiel 40-42)
4) Resurrection of the Old Testament Saints. (Daniel 12:1)
5) Resurrection of the Tribulation Saints. (Revelation 20:4)

Time Interval #3: Undetermined
1) Satan's final deception, rebellion, and judgment. (Revelation 20:7-10)
2) The judgment of the unsaved of all ages — The Great White Throne. (Revelation 20:11-15)
3) 2nd Renovation of Heaven and Earth. (Revelation 21:1)

Chapter 21

Please follow along in your Bible.

In the previous chapter, we saw the ultimate judgment and fate of all the unrighteous, nonbelievers of all ages of history. In contrast, chapter 21 gives us an amazing glimpse of eternity for the believer in Christ beginning with a new heaven, a new earth, a New Jerusalem, and a new age. No two chapters of Scripture provide a more profound side-by-side contrast of the eternal destiny for the lost and the saved. This chapter begins our discussion of the believer's eternity, which follows the Millennium. In these two remaining chapters, John also reveals the wondrous details of the Holy City, the New Jerusalem – the eternal home of the Church, the bride of the Lamb, Jesus Christ.

The Eternal Age

21:1: *"Then I saw a new heaven and a new earth, for the first heaven and the first earth had passed away …."* The expression, "then I saw," is repeated here again by John, indicating that the events of this chapter follow in sequence those of the previous chapter. It also serves to remind us that John is eyewitness to all the revelation, including these final scenes that usher in eternity.

In this opening verse, John reveals Scripture's third and final destruction and renewal of the heaven and the earth. In chapter 20, we discussed the last insurrection and final overthrow of Satan, resulting again in the heavens and the earth being polluted by his wicked rebellion and evil influence. Consequently, God will again destroy and renew the earth. God will include the atmospheric heaven to guarantee that all traces of evil have been cleansed completely and permanently. Finally, the words of the Lord Jesus, *"Heaven and earth will pass away, but my words will never pass away,"* (Matthew 24:35) will be fulfilled with this prophecy.

It is God's plan for the faithful, redeemed remnant of the Jewish and Gentile nations to inhabit the earth forever in fulfillment of His promises. For this reason, He will create a new heaven and a new earth, better than anything this universe has ever known – including the Garden of Eden. In this opening verse, we also see the first of many changes that will apparently be made: *"… there was no longer any sea."* The absence of oceans will naturally change earth's climate and atmosphere as we know it. In addition, without the sea, the population on earth can multiply itself many times over because of the increase in land surface. More importantly, this reference may also imply unhindered movement around the globe among the nations in order to facilitate travel to and from the earthly Jerusalem to worship and commune with Christ.

21:2: *"I saw the Holy City, the new Jerusalem coming down out of heaven from God …."* This is the eternal home of the Church, the bride of Christ, prepared by the Lord as He promised His disciples: *"I am going there to prepare a place for you. And if I go and prepare a place for you, I will come back and take you to be with me that you also may be where I am"* (John 14:2, 3). The New Jerusalem, that John sees descending down from heaven, should not be identified with the old Jerusalem, which is the earthly Jerusalem. The New Jerusalem reveals God's ultimate purpose for the Church which, according to the writer of Hebrews, is, *"in bringing many sons to glory"* (Hebrews 2:10). I cannot think of a more beautiful description than what John gives us here: *"… prepared as a bride beautifully dressed for her husband."* The marriage between Christ and the Church took place in heaven before the Millennium, and the Millennium was a long honeymoon. The marriage relationship is the most beautiful, delightful, and intimate of all the relationships instituted by God, and it is the oldest sacrament established for mankind. As Christians, we are going to celebrate throughout eternity that we are with Jesus Christ, and that we have been joined in a wonderful marriage relationship to our Lord and Savior.

21:3: *"And I heard in a loud voice from the throne saying, 'Now the dwelling of God is with men, and he will live with them ….'"* The loud voice from the throne, as with each time before, is the voice of the Lord Jesus Christ. The apostle wrote: *"The Word became flesh and made his dwelling among us"* (John 1:14). Jesus, God manifest in the flesh, was crucified on a cross, raised on the third day with a glorified body, and ascended into heaven to sit at the right hand of God the Father. All who have placed their faith and trust in Jesus Christ will also rise and be given glorified bodies. Believers today will abide with the Father and the Son for eternity. Deity will no longer dwell in the third heaven, some far off place in space or another dimension where we cannot see them. As we will see in the next chapter, the throne of God and of the Lamb will be in the city – that is, in the New Jerusalem.

21:4: *"He will wipe every tear from their eyes …."* The wiping away of all tears means the normal reaction to present-day life, sadness and loneliness, will be eliminated. This would also suggest that God in His great mercy will erase all memory of the unsaved from the minds of His children (Psalm 34:16). Additionally, John says, *"There will be no more death or mourning or crying or pain."* Since sin produces all of these, a sinless eternity will not allow these miseries. Imagine for a moment – no more hospitals, clinics, nursing homes or cemeteries – for the Lord tells us, *"… the old order of things has passed away."*

21:5: The One seated on the throne is the King, Jesus Christ, and here He says, *"I am making everything new!"* In this life, none of us have been completely satisfied with ourselves. We have all experienced frustration and failures. We have all, at times, made bad or unhealthy decisions resulting in negative consequences both in our lives and in the lives of those we love. What Christ is saying here is that we will have the glorious prospect of all things made new. We can start over, and there will never be an end to our growth. Recall the words of the prophet: *"Of the increase of his government and peace there will be no end"* (Isaiah 9:7).

21:6: *"It is done. I am the Alpha and the Omega, the Beginning and the End."* This, "I am," statement is messianic and identifies the speaker as the Lord Jesus Christ, just as it did back in chapter 1. It echoes the message from the throne we heard earlier which proclaimed the completion of God's wrath (16:17) – all these things have now come to pass.

"To him who is thirsty I will give to drink without cost from the spring of the water of life" is a statement from Christ which fulfills the promises He gave throughout the Gospels. In His sermon on the mount, the Lord said, *"Blessed are those who hunger and thirst for righteousness, for they will be filled"* (Matthew 5:6). The Lord also proclaimed to the people of His day: *"If anyone is thirsty, let him come to me and drink. Whoever believes in me, as the Scripture has said, streams of living water will flow from within him"* (John 7:37, 38). To the Samaritan woman at the well, Jesus explained, *"Whoever drinks the water I give him will never thirst. Indeed the water I give him will become in him a spring of water welling up to eternal life"* (John 4:14). Throughout eternity, the people of God will thirst for His presence and His ways, and all will be satisfied.

21:7: The expression, "he who overcomes," simply means all believers are overcomers of a fallen and corrupt world because of their faith in the Savior, Jesus Christ. Consequently, believers will inherit God's new creation because it was promised to God's children. The Apostle Paul explains: *"The Spirit himself testifies with our spirit that we are God's children. Now if we are children, then we are heirs – heirs of God and co-heirs with Christ, if indeed we share in his sufferings in order that we may also share in his glory"* (Romans 8:16, 17). The second promise given here, *"I will be his God and he will be my son,"* describes a special relationship God has with His children, and one that is incomprehensible to most of us today. In his first epistle, the apostle wrote: *"Dear friends, now we are children of God, and what we will be has not yet been made known. But we know that when he appears, we shall be like him, for we shall see him as he is"* (1 John 3:2).

21:8: Verses 7 and 8 together confirm the consistent message throughout Scripture that God sees only two kinds of people, believers (righteous) and unbelievers (godless). Either they are overcomers who have their share with God eternally or unbelievers who have their share in the fiery lake of burning sulfur. Notice the creation of the new heaven and earth did not affect the status of the lake of fire and those condemned to it. The lake of fire, i.e., the second death, also goes into eternity; and it represents absolute and eternal separation from God. I cannot think of anything more fearful or frightening.

The New Jerusalem

21:9 – 10: The magnificent glory of the New Jerusalem descending out of heaven from God is beyond all comprehension. It is pictured beautifully in the remainder of this chapter, and the next, as the ultimate preparation of God for His people. Inviting John to a high mountain, the angel shows him, *"… the bride, the wife of the Lamb,"* (v.9) described as *"… the Holy City, Jerusalem"* (v.10). The New Jerusalem that John sees descending from heaven is the eternal home of the Church, the bride of Christ. The Holy Spirit is going to describe to John the city the Lord Jesus promised to His disciples. The New Jerusalem is indeed the Father's house, of which there are many rooms being prepared for the people of God (cf. John 14:2). The earthly Jerusalem does not pass away, but it takes second place in eternity. The late pastor and radio commentator, J. Vernon McGee, stated: "Righteousness *reigns* in Jerusalem; it will *dwell* in the New Jerusalem."

The redeemed of the Church received glorified bodies like Christ. The wedding of the Lamb took place in heaven and the honeymoon, the wedding supper of the Lamb, was the Millennium on earth. The rest of the redeemed from earth also rejoiced in the blessings of the Millennial Kingdom under the righteous rule of the Messiah, Jesus Christ. Now, the Millennium is over, and the Lord Jesus tells John: "I am making everything new!" (v.5). A new universe suggests new methods and approaches to life. New laws will regulate God's new universe. Let's look at the possibilities as we also include elements from chapter 22.

No longer will there be a curse – that is, temptation, sin, disease and testing of man's heart in the new creation. This alone makes a radical difference. We have already seen that Christ will wipe away every tear from the eyes of His people and that no longer will there be death, mourning, crying, or pain because the old order of things has passed away (v.4).

Three times John describes the New Jerusalem as coming down out of heaven from God (3:12; 21:2, 10). The emphasis must therefore hold great significance. Although it is stated three times that the city comes down out of heaven, there is no mention or suggestion that it comes down to earth. These passages of Scripture leave the city suspended above the earth. The logical conclusion is that the New Jerusalem will become the new center of God's universe, and the New Earth and all other activity will revolve around it. In chapter 22, John tells us: *"The throne of God and of the Lamb will be in the city, and his servants will serve him"* (22:3). God will be there, it will be His dwelling, and His universe is God-centered. The New Jerusalem is therefore worthy to merit such an important position for eternity.

21:11: The New Jerusalem, *"shone with the glory of God and its brilliance was like that of a precious jewel, clear as crystal."* The word "shone" speaks of light. Skipping ahead, John says: *"The city does not need the sun or the moon to shine on it, for the glory of God gives it light, and the Lamb is its lamp"* (v.23). Again, in chapter 22, John tells us: *"They will not need the light of a lamp or the light of the sun, for the Lord God will give them light"* (22:5). Scripture teaches that God is light, and in Him there is no darkness (1 John 1:5). Apparently, the sun and moon will no longer be needed in the Eternal Age. In the New Jerusalem, there will be no created light, simply because Christ Himself, who is the Light of the world (John 8:12), will be there. God is making it abundantly clear that the Holy City, the New Jerusalem is a light giver. It does not reflect light as does the moon, nor does it generate light like the sun. It originates light and is the source of light. God will provide sufficient light for His new universe by His very presence.

If the New Jerusalem is indeed the new center of God's universe, then the law of gravity, as we know it, will be radically altered. There will likely be travel between the New Jerusalem and the New Earth. Consider for a moment; following His resurrection, Jesus walked with His disciples for forty days in His glorified body and then ascended into heaven. So too will the bride of Christ (residing in the New Jerusalem), in glorified bodies, along with the people of God's Eternal Age (residing on the New Earth), in glorified bodies, travel back and forth between the New Jerusalem and the New Earth. When confronted by the Sadducees regarding the resurrection, the Lord Jesus replied: *"When the dead rise, they will neither marry nor be given in marriage: they will be like the angels in heaven"* (Mark 12:25). Angels are able to travel back and forth between heaven and earth at ease as directed by God.

John writes: *"The nations will walk by its light, and the kings of the earth will bring their splendor into it. On no day will its gate ever be shut, for there will be no night there. The glory and honor of the nations will be brought into it"* (21:24 – 26). Not only will Israel come up to worship, but all the Gentile nations and kings of the earth as well. It is believed that those who make up the Church (the bride of Christ) will be the priests at that time. The Apostle Peter referred to the Church as a *priesthood* of believers – he wrote: *"... you also, like living stones, are being built into a spiritual house to be a holy priesthood ...."* (1 Peter 2:5). Moreover, there will be no night (cf. 22:5). Night would imply darkness, and we have already stated the biblical fact that God is light and in Him there is no darkness (1 John 1:5). Evidently, our new glorified bodies will have no need of rest. I cannot wait for that!

To emphasize the glory of God, the New Jerusalem is pictured as a crystal clear, precious jewel, referred to as jasper. This rare, transparent stone is likened in appearance to a diamond. Further on, John tells us: *"The great street of the city was of pure gold"* (v.21). The imagery is astounding; the New Jerusalem is a diamond in a gold setting – a wedding ring, which symbolizes the wedding of the Church to Christ.

21:12 – 13: The gates of the Holy City: The Holy City, the New Jerusalem had twelve gates, and on the gates were inscribed the names of the twelve tribes of Israel. There were three gates on each side. This immediately reminds us of the order in which the children of Israel camped around the tabernacle in the wilderness (Numbers 2:1 – 31). The tribe of Levi was the priesthood and served in the tabernacle. The New Jerusalem, in a sense, is representative of a temple or tabernacle since God is present dwelling with man. The bride of Christ, like the Levites of the OT, makes up the priesthood who serve Him. The New Jerusalem will be a tabernacle to Israel and to all the nations of the New Earth.

The nation of Israel on earth, along with the Gentile nations of the world, now one people united in God, will come into the Holy City to worship throughout eternity. They will not dwell in the city anymore than they dwelt in the tabernacle of old. The bride of Christ now occupies the closest place to God in eternity.

There are twelve angels, one at each gate, representing the relationship and role of angels even in the Eternal Age.

21:14: The foundations of the Holy City: The city is built on twelve foundations, and inscribed on them were the names of the twelve apostles of Christ. According to the Apostle Paul, who many consider to be the twelfth apostle, the Church is, *"built on the foundation of the apostles and prophets, with Christ Jesus himself, as the chief cornerstone"* (Ephesians 2:20). To these apostles were committed all the writings of the Church. These men preached the first sermons, established the first churches, and were among the first martyrs. The Lord Jesus Christ is the chief cornerstone, and His Church is built upon the foundation the apostles laid.

21:15 – 16: The size and shape of the Holy City: The size of the New Jerusalem is tremendous: 12,000 stadia (1,380 miles) in length, and as wide and high as it is long. The Lord Jesus, Carpenter of Nazareth, is the One who built this city. When you consider all His hands have made, i.e., beautiful mountain ranges, lush forests, enormous oceans, and vast galaxies, there is no wonder this city also bears the trademark of its Creator. Commentators do not agree as to whether the city will be a cube, pyramid, or sphere in its shape. Based on our discussion thus far, and suggesting that the New Jerusalem will be the new center of God's universe, I lean toward the latter, that of a sphere, the common shape of all celestial bodies. Although the shape is described in terms of a cube, the emanating light – that is, the glory of the Lord shining forth in all directions will give the appearance of a brilliant sphere.

The Lord originally created the law of gravity to hold us onto the earth; otherwise we would fly out into space. Today, we walk on the outside of the earth, but let me suggest that we will walk on the inside of the New Jerusalem. Its great size will afford sufficient space for inhabitation of the saints of all ages. If you were to enclose a cube measuring 1,380 miles on each side into a crystal clear sphere, you would come up with the diameter of the New Jerusalem to be about 2,390 miles, somewhat larger than our moon, which is about 2,160 miles in comparison.

21:17 – 18: The wall of the Holy City: Throughout history, the wall of a city was for protection. A walled city ensured safety and peace. The name Jerusalem originally came from the Hebrew word *Shalem*, which is derived from the same root as the word *shalom*, meaning "peace." Thus, the common interpretation of the word Jerusalem is *city of peace*. The wall of the New Jerusalem symbolizes absolute and eternal peace. However, despite its great thickness of 144 cubits (216 feet), it is beauty, not protection that is the intention of its design. The wall was made of clear jasper, which gives the appearance of a diamond. Together with the city of gold, pure as glass, as a setting, the two represent the beautiful symbol of a wedding ring – the pure and holy gift that Christ bestows to His bride, the Church.

21:19 – 20: The stones in the foundation of the Holy City: The twelve foundations of the city not only have the names of the twelve apostles, but are also decorated with every kind of precious stone. These stones express in human terms the magnificence of the New Jerusalem. These stones, with their varied hues and tints, form a beautiful array of rainbow colors. Let us look at each:

1) Jasper: It is commonly defined as an opaque variety of quartz, but here it is clear. Clear jasper is extremely rare and, as mentioned above, gives the appearance of a diamond. This clear, crystal-like jasper serves as a reflector of light and color.
2) Sapphire: Its color is blue. This stone is mentioned as the pavement under the feet of God and clear as the sky itself (Exodus 24:10).
3) Chalcedony: Its color is greenish, possibly the green silicate of copper from the mines of Chalcedon in Asia Minor.
4) Emerald: Its color is green, brilliant, and transparent.
5) Sardonyx: Its color is red and white in alternating parallel layers.
6) Carnelian: Its color is fiery red. It is one of the gems found most frequently in Palestinian excavations.
7) Chrysolite: Its color is golden yellow. It is valued for its hardness and transparency.
8) Beryl: Its color is green, closer to pale blue or sea green.
9) Topaz: Its color is greenish yellow. These are said to have come from the islands of the Red Sea.
10) Chrysoprase: Its color is golden green, a green apple variety occurring in slabs large enough to make counter tops.
11) Jacinth: Its color is violet, the color of the hyacinth.
12) Amethyst: Its color is purple, a clear purple variety of quartz crystal. Although abundantly found in Egypt, the finest amethyst comes from India and Ceylon.

The foundations of the New Jerusalem are constructed of the flashing brilliance of rich and costly gems. I suspect it will be a most breathtaking sight. The New Jerusalem is a city of light and a city of color. God is light, and He is there. The light shining from within through the jasper stone, acting like a prism, will produce every color of the rainbow, and probably even some you and I cannot even begin to imagine. A rainbow, as we know it, will likely seem faint in comparison to the beauty emanating from our future, heavenly home.

21:21: The city gates and the street of gold of the Holy City: *"The twelve gates were twelve pearls, each gate made of a single pearl ...."* Pearls have always been prized for their beauty, rarity, warmth of color and symmetry. This reminds us of *The Parable of the Pearl* (Matthew 13:45, 46). In this parable, the merchant who bought the pearl was the Lord Jesus Christ, and the pearl was His bride. The Lord paid a great price to purchase His bride. We are told here that each gate will be made of a single pearl, obviously large enough for people to pass through. John further writes, *"on no day will its gate ever be shut"* (v.25). They will stand open for eternity, as a beautiful reminder to God's people on earth to come and worship and enjoy complete and uninterrupted access to the throne of God the Father and the Son.

Next, John describes the great street of the city as being of pure gold and transparent as glass. John has already portrayed the Holy City as crystal clear (v.11) and made of pure, clear gold (v.18). All of these descriptions imply transparency throughout. This is why I believe what we are looking at is the inside of a sphere. The fact the street is transparent gold means that light will shine out. Not even the street will hinder the light.

21:22: *"I did not see a temple in the city, because the Lord God Almighty and the Lamb are its temple."* In the earthly tabernacle, the golden lampstand was symbolic of Christ, but in the New Jerusalem, Christ is the golden lampstand. Although the city may be thought of as a temple, the actual presence of God dwelling amongst His people eliminates the need for a temple. The nations of the New Earth, including Israel, will come to the New Jerusalem just as the high priest of the OT did when entering the Holy of Holies, to worship in the very presence of God Himself.

21:23: *"The city does not need the sun or the moon to shine on it, for the glory of God gives it light, and the Lamb is its lamp."* From the very beginning of creation, it was God's desire to commune and fellowship with mankind. However, once sin entered into the old creation, God withdrew His physical presence. Thereafter, He used His created lights – the sun, moon, and stars – to illuminate His universe. Today, in a spiritual sense, the Lord Jesus Christ is the Light of the world (John 8:12). In the Eternal Age, the Lord God Almighty and the Lamb, Jesus Christ, will be both physical and spiritual lights. The New Jerusalem will be independent of the sun and moon for light and life, for the One who is light will be there and His glory will be unhindered. It is more likely that the sun and moon will be dependent on the New Jerusalem for its power to transmit light.

21:24 – 26: *"The nations will walk by its light, and the kings of the earth will bring their splendor into it ...."* This does not mean that the nations will live there, but that the New Jerusalem will give light unto the earth. The word "nations" literally means "the people." In the Eternal Age, all the redeemed of the earth will merge into the one people of God, no longer divided by race or ethnicity. The word "splendor" simply refers to their praise and worship; thus, all the people of the New Earth will travel back and forth in glorious worship of God the Father and the Son, Jesus Christ.

All who dwell in the New Jerusalem and on the New Earth are not only redeemed from sin, but have lost all attraction to it. God's people come through the gates that are never closed. In John's day, just as in ours, a walled city or fenced in property has gates for the purpose of protection and keeping an intruder out. However, there is no longer an enemy outside; and so the procession through these gates will be continuous. Lastly, there will be no night. God is the source of all light, and as mentioned earlier, in him there is no darkness. God's people will no longer have need for rest in His eternal order.

21:27: Scripture does not give us the location of the lake of fire, only that those committed there will be tormented day and night for ever and ever (20:10). One thing is for certain; it is somewhere outside the gates of the New Jerusalem. There will still remain a great gulf between the saved and the unsaved. In this last verse, John relates God's last warning to all people who are shameful or deceitful. Those who reject His Son will not be admitted into His Holy City. We have already confirmed that their place will be in the fiery lake of burning sulfur (v.8).

The greatest joy imaginable in the hearts of the redeemed will be that of abiding in the presence of our Lord and Savior Jesus Christ for eternity. *"That you also may be where I am"* (John 14:3) is what the Lord Jesus told His disciples. Heaven is to be with Christ. Revelation is all about Jesus Christ – He is the centerpiece of God's universe.

The wonderful blessings that God has in store for His people, as seen in this and the next chapter, should inspire every individual to accept Jesus Christ as their Lord and Savior and thus ensure that their names are recorded in the Lamb's book of life.

Review Questions

1) Why does God destroy and renew the heaven and earth? _____

    _____.

2) The Holy City, the New Jerusalem, is the eternal home of _____

3) The Alpha and the Omega, the Beginning and the End, identifies the speaker as _____

    _____.

4) The New Jerusalem becomes the new _____.

5) The twelve gates of the Holy City are twelve pearls, and written on them are _____

    _____.

6) The Holy City is built on twelve foundations, decorated with every kind of precious stone, and on the foundations is written _____.

7) With its walls of clear crystal, and the city and street of pure gold, the New Jerusalem is a beautiful symbol of a _____, the gift that Christ bestows to His bride, the church.

Up For Discussion

"And I heard a great voice out of heaven saying, Behold, the tabernacle of God is with men, and he will dwell with them, and they shall be his people, and God himself shall be with them, and be their God."
(Revelation 21:3 KJV)

Review the illustration entitled, *The New Jerusalem*. As we discussed, the New Jerusalem will be a city of light and of color. Take a moment and imagine the sight, as the redeemed of the New Earth look up at the New Jerusalem. With the light of the glory of God within shining through the crystal stones, acting like a prism, the sight will be eternally breathtaking! What are your thoughts and feelings?

Consider for a moment that among the foundations of the New Jerusalem, the Apostle John saw his own name. Keep in mind John survived his stay on the Isle of Patmos. Writings of the early church fathers indicate that he returned to Ephesus after his exile. Now, try to imagine how the remainder of John's life and ministry was impacted by all he saw in the Revelation. As the apostle recalled over and over again in his memory the vision of that wall and its foundations – can you imagine how he was both overcome and humbled that God honored him so?

In further discussion, review the illustration entitled, *Millennium to Eternity*. Do the illustrations help reinforce your overall understanding of the message?

The Holy City, the New Jerusalem
The Eternal Home of the Church, the Bride of Christ

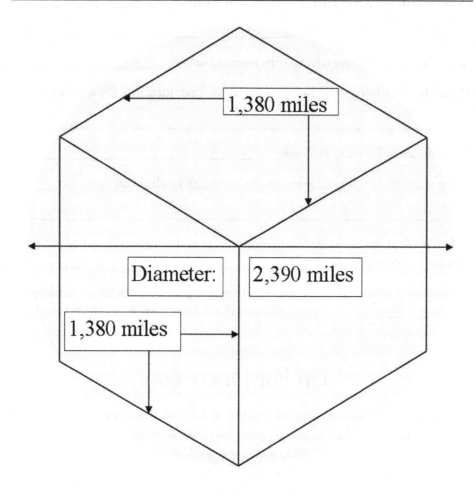

1,380 miles

Diameter: 2,390 miles

1,380 miles

Our Lord Jesus Christ is its Creator:
"In my Father's house are many rooms; if it were not so, I would have told you. I am going there to prepare a place for you. And if I go and prepare a place for you, I will come back and take you to be with me that you also may be where I am" (John 14:2, 3).

"The throne of God and of the Lamb will be in the city" (Rev. 22:3).

Thus, the glory of the Lord will shine forth in all directions giving the appearance of a brilliant sphere.

The diameter is about 2,390 miles, somewhat larger than our moon, which is about 2,160 miles.

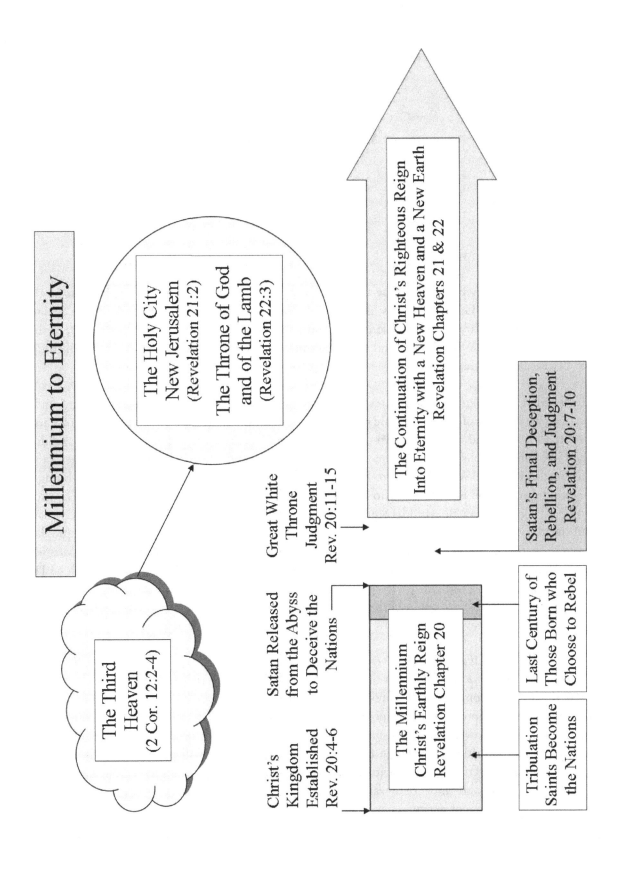

Millennium to Eternity

The Third Heaven (2 Cor. 12:2-4)

The Holy City New Jerusalem (Revelation 21:2)

The Throne of God and of the Lamb (Revelation 22:3)

The Continuation of Christ's Righteous Reign Into Eternity with a New Heaven and a New Earth Revelation Chapters 21 & 22

Satan's Final Deception, Rebellion, and Judgment Revelation 20:7-10

Great White Throne Judgment Rev. 20:11-15

Christ's Kingdom Established Rev. 20:4-6

Satan Released from the Abyss to Deceive the Nations

The Millennium Christ's Earthly Reign Revelation Chapter 20

Last Century of Those Born who Choose to Rebel

Tribulation Saints Become the Nations

Chapter 22

Please follow along in your Bible.

This chapter not only brings us to the end of the greatest of all books on prophecy, but also to the end of the Word of God. God gives us His final words here; therefore, these words hold greater significance. In this life, many questions remain unanswered and problems unresolved; but, in this final chapter of God's Word, mankind enters eternity in fellowship again with God, and all things will be revealed and made new (21:5).

The Word of God – our Holy Scriptures – opens and closes with basically the same type of setting. In the first two chapters of Genesis, we are given God's description of creation and the paradise on earth prepared for mankind. These last two chapters of John's Revelation describe the heavenly paradise that God will reestablish for His people – those from all ages of history who have placed their faith and trust in Him and were obedient to His ways. Remember that God is sovereign. He has brought mankind through the ages according to His master plan, and He has always been in absolute control. God paid a great price. He sent His Son to die on a cross because He loves us so much. The victory and the glory belong to God and He is satisfied. Over twenty-seven hundred years ago, the prophet wrote these touching words: *"After the suffering of his soul, he will see the light of life and be satisfied; by his knowledge my righteous servant will justify many and he will bear their iniquities"* (Isaiah 53:11).

The opening five verses give us additional details of the eternal heavenly home of the Church (the bride of Christ) we have come to know as the Holy City, the New Jerusalem.

22:1: *Then the angel showed me the river of the water of life, as clear as crystal, flowing from the throne of God and of the lamb ...."* The river of the water of life is a description reminiscent of the river of water flowing out from under the threshold of the temple in the prophet's vision of the Millennial Temple (Ezekiel, chapter 47). We cannot live without water in this life, and apparently, in our eternal life, we will thirst as well. However, our thirst for this water will not necessarily be life-sustaining, but rather life-nourishing. As a living fountain, this endless supply will proceed directly from the throne of God and of the Lamb indicating that God the Father and the Lord Jesus Christ will be the source of this sweet and wholesome water. Notice again that the description of the water is as clear as crystal – the essence of purity.

22:2: *"On each side of the river stood the tree of life, bearing twelve crops of fruit yielding its fruit every month ...."* Way back in the beginning, in the Garden of Eden, we learned that after Adam and Eve had sinned, God forbade Adam from reaching out his hand and taking from the tree of life to eat and thereby, live forever (Genesis 3:22). At last, eternity reveals that man will finally be allowed to eat of the tree of life, thus testifying to our blessed future state. In the New Jerusalem, these trees on each side of the river will continually bring forth crops of fruit each month; therefore, we will be able to eat and drink without fear or consequence in our new heavenly home.

John reveals an interesting truth: *"... the leaves of the tree are for the healing of the nations."* This passage does not indicate that anyone will be sick. Instead, the analogy concerns the nations of the world who have fought throughout earth's history. The nations, now one people of God, will be healed in their relationships and live in perfect harmony for eternity. The Prophet Ezekiel gave a similar description from his vision of the river flowing from the throne of the Millennial Temple; he wrote: *"Fruit trees of all kinds will grow on both banks of the river. Their leaves will not wither, nor will their fruit fail. Every month they will bear, because the water from the sanctuary flows to them. Their fruit will serve for food and their leaves for healing"* (Ezekiel 47:12). In a spiritual sense, the tree of life could symbolically represent the New Earth and the leaves symbolic of the nations of the earth. The tree with its leaves is nourished by the water of the river from God – God dwelling with man. Therefore, the tree and its leaves (the New Earth and its nations) will exist together as one in perfect unity for eternity, never again to fall away and perish from the face of the earth.

22:3: *"No longer will there be any curse ...."* This is because God's new creation will never be marred by sin, such as that which came into the world as a result of Adam and Eve's disobedience. Temptation and sin will be removed forever. The very presence of God and the Lamb, Jesus Christ, will be adequate to prevent it. Man's unlimited potential will be realized for the first time. God will again commune with man just as He did with Adam and Eve before the Fall.

The throne of God and of the Lamb, the Lord Jesus Christ, will be in the New Jerusalem. In my research, I have found that some commentators note the absence of any reference to the Holy Spirit in the New Jerusalem and the Eternal Age. These writers agree that in the first creation, the Holy Spirit came to renew and renovate the earth (Genesis 1:2), and that today the Holy Spirit acts to renew the hearts and lives of sinners. However, in the new creation, when God again dwells amongst His people, these same writers suggest that there will be no need for the work of the Holy Spirit, and that the silence of Scripture at this point is appropriate. I agree with their assessment regarding the work of the Holy Spirit in past ages, as well as today; however, I strongly disagree with their suggestion that the Holy Spirit does not continue into eternity. My conviction rests in my faith in the Trinity. I am convinced that the Holy Spirit will continue as always to dwell in the hearts of God's people even into eternity. The Spirit is the cement that bonds us into a perfect and intimate relationship with the Father and with the Son. For that reason, the Trinity, including the Holy Spirit, always was, remains today, and will continue on into eternity as we have always known it – God in three Persons.

The expression, "his servants will serve him," simply means that the New Jerusalem and the New Earth will not be a place of unoccupied idleness, but a place of ceaseless activity. God's people will all perform some service throughout eternity, including governmental and priestly duties (20:4 – 6; 21:24 – 26). Furthermore, since there will be no night in the Eternal Age (21:25), there will evidently be no need for rest. God's people will at last achieve their full God-given potential on the New Earth.

22:4: *"They will see his face ..."* is the most wonderful and the most glorious revelation of this final chapter of Scripture. According to Scripture, no natural human being could see God's face and live (Exodus 33:20 – 23; John 1:18). However, in the New Jerusalem, God's people will see His face without harm because they will be glorified and holy in all their being. This was the ultimate desire expressed by Moses and David in the OT and Philip in the NT. It is the believer's highest objective for living. We will know the Lord God to the fullest extent possible. The Apostle Paul likewise wrote: *"Now we see but a poor reflection as in a mirror; then we shall see face to face"* (1 Corinthians 13:12). The fact that His name will be on their foreheads illustrates again that all believers are the blood-bought children of God, and stands in stark contrast to the mark of the beast that will identify those who chose to worship Antichrist in rebellion to God. This fulfills the promise our Lord Jesus made earlier to the Church (3:12).

22:5: *"There will be no more night. They will not need the light of a lamp or the light of the sun, for the Lord God will give them light ...."* John reiterates what we have already discussed (21:11, 23); God the Father and the Son, who are light, will illuminate eternity from the New Jerusalem by their very presence. The phrase, "they will reign for ever and ever," speaks again of the Church. In the same manner as the Church will rule alongside Christ during the Millennium, it will also reign alongside Christ for eternity. The Church, the bride of Christ, will hold the closest position to Christ forever and ever.

22:6: The angel is sent by the Lord Jesus Christ to tell John that these words are trustworthy and true. This means the Lord is putting His seal of approval upon this book. The Lord's endorsement is final, and thus mankind is not to spiritualize or reduce it to meaningless symbols. The Lord Jesus Christ is talking about realities yet to come.

22:7: The words of the Lord Jesus are quoted here: *"Behold, I am coming soon! ..."* The Lord expresses these words three times in this final chapter of John's Revelation. The Lord is not saying this to refer to some appointed time soon to come. The phrase, "coming soon," refers to the time period described in this book; and at that time, the events of the Revelation come to pass in a short period of not more than seven years. The reference here is the end of the Tribulation Period, and the encouragement is the Lord saying it will not be a long period. In fact, the Lord Jesus told His disciples: *"If those days had not been cut short, no one would survive, but for the sake of the elect, those days will be shortened"* (Matthew 24:22).

The Lord continues, *"Blessed is he who keeps the words of the prophecy in this book."* Jesus repeats the blessing we read in the beginning of this book (1:3). The book of Revelation is not only meant to be read, but also to be acted upon. What does the study of the Revelation of Jesus Christ motivate you to do? Is it to be a better witness, to spend more time studying Scripture, or to become a Bible study teacher? Pastor and best-selling author, Dr. Charles Stanley, describes the work of the Church, that of all believers, as evangelism and states: "You cannot invest your life in anything better than sharing and bringing the Gospel of Jesus Christ to someone who does not know." Therefore, our first and greatest responsibility is to offer the message of grace – that is, the message that God loves everyone and is willing to save them through faith in His Son Jesus Christ. And our efforts should begin at home with those closest and dearest to us.

22:8 – 9: Here John, an apostle of Jesus Christ, reiterates that he heard and saw these things. He is the firsthand eyewitness to all the scenes and visions of the Revelation. Strangely however, John again bows before the angel, and as before, he is forbidden to do so. The consistent message in the Word of God is that we worship God only. Satan's primary objective is to entice us to bow to anything or anyone other than God; but, just as before, the angel commands John: *"Do not do it!"* (cf. 19:10) It is interesting to note here the humility of this angel. Although angels were created above man (Psalm 8:5), this angel identifies himself as a fellow servant with John and the other prophets. He is merely a messenger. The Lord Jesus Christ is the centerpiece of the book of Revelation.

22:10 – 11: The angel then tells John, *"Do not seal up the words of the prophecy of this book, because the time is near …."* Daniel was told to seal up the words of his prophecy because of the long interval of time before its fulfillment. The angelic messenger told the aged prophet: *"But you, Daniel close up and seal the words of the scroll until the time of the end. Many will go here and there to increase knowledge"* (Daniel 12:4). In contrast, John lived over sixty-five years after the time of Christ's resurrection and ascension, the era which began the dispensation of grace – the Church Age. The prophecy given to John was even then in the process of being fulfilled, and for almost two thousand years, the Church has been evolving through the time periods of the seven churches (chapters 2 and 3).

"Let him who does wrong continue to do wrong; let him who is vile continue to be vile …." This statement is yet another reference to the sinful condition of the lost. It is permanent and eternal, and suggests that the condition of the lost gets progressively worse. On the other hand, the verse further states that the righteous continue to grow in their righteousness and holiness. What a wonderful prospect for the people of God to know they have all eternity to grow in knowledge.

22:12 – 16: These five verses are again the quoted words of the Lord Jesus Christ beginning with: *"Behold, I am coming soon! My reward is with me, and I will give to everyone according to what he has done."* The Lord personally promises that He is coming again, and no believer can doubt or deny His promise. Christ will personally reward each believer individually. Those who make up the Church will be rewarded after the Rapture, at the judgment seat of Christ (2 Corinthians 5:10). Those who receive Jesus Christ as Lord and Savior during the Tribulation Period, including the remnant of the nation of Israel, will receive their reward at the time of Christ's return to establish His earthly kingdom just prior to the Millennium (Matthew 25:31 – 46). There is no wonder the Apostle Paul could write so passionately about the resurrection (Take a moment and read Philippians 3:10 – 14). On the basis of His reward, all believers will reign alongside Christ for eternity.

Here at the conclusion, just as in the beginning of the book of Revelation, the Lord Jesus Christ asserts His deity with the following messianic titles: *"I am the Alpha and the Omega, the First and the Last, the Beginning and the End."*

Christ continues His proclamation: *"Blessed are those who wash their robes, that they may have the right to the tree of life and may go through the gates into the city."* Only those who have washed their robes in the blood of the Lamb – that is, the righteousness of Christ through faith, have a right to the tree of life and entry into the Holy City. Paul wrote concerning the fulfillment of all things brought under Christ (Take a moment and read Ephesians 1:7 – 10).

Regarding the wicked, Christ reiterates one last time: *"Outside are the dogs, those who practice magic arts, the sexually immoral, the murderers, the idolaters, and everyone who loves and practices falsehoods."* In Disney movies, cats are oftentimes portrayed as the villain; but in Scripture, dogs get the bad rap. Dogs were scavengers in the ancient world and were considered unclean and impure. The term "dogs" was also another word for Gentiles (Matthew 15:22 – 28), and Paul used the same word for Judaizers (Philippians 3:2). Here, it simply refers to those who are eternally lost because of their wickedness and rebellion to God and confined to the lake of fire.

The Lord continues. *"I, Jesus, have sent my angel to give you this testimony for the churches."* Jesus is the name of our Savior; the name He received when He took on humanity. The expression, "testimony for the churches," is the eternal Gospel. Jesus Christ is alive today and is seated in heaven at the right hand of God the Father. He promises that when we accept Him as Lord and Savior, our eternity will be spent with Him and centered on Him.

The Lord concludes His proclamation with the following messianic titles: *"I am the Root and the Offspring of David, and the bright Morning Star."* The Root and Offspring of David identifies Jesus as a descendant of the royal line of David and the fulfillment of the covenant God made with David: *"When your days are over and you rest with your fathers, I will raise up your offspring to succeed you, who will come from your own body, and I will establish his kingdom"* (2 Samuel 7:12).

Jesus is the bright Morning Star to all of God's people. The bright morning star always appears at the darkest time of the night, and its appearance indicates the sun will be coming up shortly. The OT ends with these words from the prophet: *"But to you who fear My name the Sun of Righteousness shall arise with healing in His wings; and you shall go out and grow fat like stall-fed calves"* (Malachi 4:2 NKJV). This is the OT hope for the nation of Israel. And to the rest of the saints, Jesus Christ is the bright Morning Star who will come at the very last moment of earth's darkest age to usher in everlasting righteousness and healing to all the nations.

22:17: *"The Spirit and the bride say, 'Come!' …."* The Spirit is the Holy Spirit that is in the world today convicting, wooing, and converting the hearts of sinners. The bride is the Church. Together they issue a dual invitation – an invitation to Christ to return and an invitation to sinners to come to Christ before He returns. As mentioned earlier, the mission of the church is to evangelize; believers are to sow the seeds of the Gospel of Jesus Christ. The Holy Spirit will water those seeds and do the rest. The words of our Lord Jesus Christ tell us: *"If anyone is thirsty, let him come to me and drink. Whoever believes in me, as the Scripture has said, streams of living water will flow from within him"* (John 7:37, 38). The water of life is found in the words of Christ, and His invitation goes out still today.

22:18 – 19: Here is one of the most fearful warnings from the Lord against tampering with the Word of God. It is a dreadful thing to disbelieve or worse, to deny God, and it is unbelief that causes someone to twist the Scriptures to fit their own personal agenda. Pastor and best-selling author, Dr. Charles Stanley, has often stated: "The Bible is not a pick and choose book, but a trust and obey book." Although this is not a reference to Bible-believing students of God's Word who mistakenly translate a passage and inadvertently minimize it, it does serve as a soul-stirring challenge to all of us, and especially those of us who have taken on the responsibility to write and teach on the Word of God.

22:20: Here are Jesus' final words: *"Yes, I am coming soon."* As mentioned earlier, this refers to the period in time during which the events of the Revelation begin to come to pass.

"Amen. Come, Lord Jesus," ought to be the daily prayer of every true and faithful believer. I close my prayers each morning with these very words.

22:21: *"The grace of the Lord Jesus be with God's people. Amen."* John's final words reflect God's ultimate blessing. The OT ends with a curse upon the nation of Israel if she does not repent, but the NT ends with a benediction of grace upon all of God's people. Grace is offered to all who repent and put their faith in Jesus Christ; it is God's method for saving sinners. This entitles all of God's people free entry into the Holy City, the New Jerusalem, access to the living water and the tree of life, and the eternal blessings of a loving God.

The Apostle John lived to be a very old man. In her book, *The Beloved Disciple*, best-selling author, Beth Moore, wrote: "His passionate heart continued to beat wildly for the Savior he loved so much … Only disciples who are convinced they are beloved will in turn love beyond themselves." In closing, let us read together some of the words obviously written upon this disciple's heart from that last earthly night spent with Jesus:

"My command is this: Love each other as I have loved you. Greater love has no one than this that he lay down his life for his friends. You are my friends if you do what I command. I no longer call you servants, because a servant does not know his master's business. Instead, I have called you friends, for everything that I learned from my Father I have made known to you. You did not choose me, but I chose you and appointed you to go and bear fruit – fruit that will last. Then the Father will give you whatever you ask in my name. This is my command: Love each other" (John 15:12 – 17).

Review Questions

1) The crystal clear river of the waters of life flow from _____.

2) On each bank of the river stood _____.

3) The throne of God and of the Lamb is no longer in heaven, but is now in _____ _____.

4) What two things are mentioned as being absent for eternity? _____ _____.

5) Christ's "coming soon" refers to _____.

6) The angel forbids John from bowing before him because the Word of God tells us to _____ _____.

7) The testimony for the churches is _____.

Up For Discussion

"Blessed is he that keepeth the sayings of the prophecy of this book."
(Revelation 22:7 KJV)

The Lord Jesus repeats the blessing we read back at the beginning in chapter 1. The book of Revelation is not only meant to be read, but also to be acted upon. What does this study of John's Revelation of Jesus Christ motivate you to do?

Has it encouraged you to become a better witness in the world?

Has it motivated you to spend more time reading and studying the Scriptures?

Will you volunteer to facilitate a Bible study or even consider becoming a regular teacher of God's Word in your church?

As stated earlier, pastor and best-selling author, Dr. Charles Stanley, describes the work of all believers today as evangelism and states: "You cannot invest your life in anything better than sharing and bringing the Gospel of Jesus Christ to someone who does not know." Our first and greatest responsibility is to share the message of grace, and that God loves you and is willing to save you through faith in His precious Son, the Lord Jesus Christ.

Amen. Come, Lord Jesus.

CHART OF EVENTS

THE FIRST HALF OF THE TRIBULATION PERIOD

THE SEAL JUDGMENTS – Revelation 6

1) The rider on the white horse: Antichrist and his kingdom.
2) The rider on the red horse: War that follows.
3) The rider on the black horse: Famine that follows war.
4) The rider on the pale horse: Name is Death and represents plague and pestilence. Hades follows and 1/4 of the earth's population dies.
5) Vision of the souls under the altar: The Old Testament saints and the martyred Tribulation saints awaiting God's final judgment.
6) The Wrath of the Lamb: Great earthquake, sun turns black, moon turns blood red, and stars (meteorites) fall to earth.
7) Silence in Heaven: This introduces the seven trumpet judgments.

Revelation 7: 144,000 Jewish servants are sealed, and the vision of the great multitude standing before the throne of the Lamb.

THE TRUMPET JUDGMENTS – Revelation 8 and 9

1) Hail and fire rain down, and 1/3 of the earth burns up.
2) Something like a huge mountain falls into the sea, and 1/3 of the sea turns to blood, 1/3 of the living creatures die, and 1/3 of the ships are destroyed.
3) A blazing star (meteor or comet) named Wormwood falls from the sky and pollutes 1/3 of the earth's water supply.
4) The light from the sun, the moon, and the stars is diminished by 1/3.
5) The first woe: Demonic locust creatures are released from the Abyss to torment the unsaved for five months.
6) The second woe: Four evil angels are released along with their demonic army and 1/3 of mankind is killed.
7) Rejoicing in heaven: This brings us to the mid-point of the Tribulation Period and introduces the seven bowl judgments.

Revelation 11: The temple in Jerusalem is rebuilt, and Old Testament worship is reinstated. The two supernatural witnesses prophesy for 1,260 days.

CHART OF EVENTS

MID-POINT OF THE TRIBULATION PERIOD

Revelation 11: The two supernatural witnesses are killed by the beast (Antichrist). After three and a half days they are resurrected and ascend to heaven in a cloud.

Revelation 12: The Woman (nation of Israel) flees into the desert to escape persecution from Antichrist for 1,260 days. God will again care for them as He did during Israel's desert wanderings following the Exodus.

Revelation 12: There is war in heaven, and the dragon (Satan) is hurled to earth. Satan's banishment and confinement to earth during the second half of the Tribulation Period is the third woe of the book of Revelation.

Revelation 13: After the beast (Antichrist) receives a fatal wound, Satan will possess him to produce a counterfeit resurrection. Antichrist becomes Satan incarnate.

Revelation 13 and Daniel 9:27: Antichrist breaks his covenant with Israel, then along with the second beast (the false prophet) desecrates the temple by setting up an idol image of the beast (Antichrist). People are forced to worship the idol image of the beast and to receive his mark – 666.

Revelation 17 – Destruction of Religious Babylon: A system of false religion that operates during the first half of the Tribulation Period emphasizing idolatry and sexual immorality. Termed "the Great Prostitute," this worldwide religious system will likely be headquartered in present-day Rome and headed up by the second beast, the false prophet. This false church takes over after Christ removes the true Church from earth in the Rapture. Antichrist will allow this false system of religion to operate during the first half of the Tribulation Period while he gathers power. At the mid-point of the Tribulation Period, Antichrist, along with the ten kings, destroys this false church, sets himself up as world dictator (and god), and relocates his idol worship to the temple in Jerusalem.

CHART OF EVENTS

THE SECOND HALF OF THE TRIBULATION PERIOD

THE BOWL JUDGMENTS – Revelation 16

1) Ugly and painful sores break out on the people who worship the beast and take his mark. This parallels the 6th plague of Egypt in Exodus.
2) The remainder of the sea turns to blood, and every living thing in it dies.
3) The rivers and springs (the only remaining sources of water) turn to blood. The 2nd and 3rd bowl judgments parallel the 1st plague of Egypt where the Nile River was turned to blood. The passage does not state such; however, this means more human death on an even greater scale because people simply cannot live without water!
4) The sun scorches people with fire. They refuse to repent and glorify God. Remember, there is no water to quench them.
5) The kingdom and headquarters of the beast is plunged into darkness. This is similar to the darkness of Egypt during the 9th plague. The people still refuse to repent.
6) The Euphrates River is dried up to make way for the kings of the East, and the three evil (deceiving) demonic spirits that looked like frogs. These verses refer to the Oriental nations of the world, and Satan's ability to deceive them into uniting with him in his upcoming battle against Christ.
7) A horrendous earthquake shakes the whole earth, and 100-pound hailstones fall upon men.

Revelation 18: Babylon the Great is destroyed. The governmental and commercial headquarters and kingdom of Antichrist (most likely the rebuilt city of Babylon in present-day Iraq) is destroyed in one day as a result of the seventh bowl judgment from God.

Revelation 19: The Revelation and glorious appearing of our Lord Jesus Christ as King of Kings and Lord of Lords, and the battle on the great day of God Almighty (Armageddon). The Lord Jesus Christ returns to earth and defeats the armies of Antichrist, and all who stand in opposition to Him with the sharp sword from out of His mouth – His spoken Word.

The beast (Antichrist) and his false prophet are thrown into the lake of fire.

CHART OF EVENTS

THE MILLENNIAL KINGDOM

THE WEDDING SUPPER OF THE LAMB – Revelation 19:9

This is God's answer to the prayer He taught us: *"Thy kingdom come. Thy will be done in earth, as it is in heaven ..."* (Matthew 6:10 KJV).

Revelation 20: The Millennium begins with the binding and imprisonment of Satan in the Abyss where he will no longer be able to deceive mankind. This is God's final testing of man under ideal conditions. The prophet describes the Millennial Kingdom in Isaiah 65:17 – 25, beginning with the creation of new heavens and a new earth.

The Wedding Supper of the Lamb
Christ's Millennial Kingdom on Earth

Those invited to attend and enter into Christ's earthly kingdom:

1) The martyred Tribulation saints: Revelation 20:4b – 6.
2) The Old Testament saints: Daniel 12:1, 2, Psalm 50:1 – 5.
3) The redeemed remnant of Israel: Jeremiah 23:3, Romans 11:5.
4) The redeemed remnant of the Gentile nations: Matthew 25:31 – 46.

The Millennium ends with the release of Satan, his last deception of mankind and rebellion against Christ, and his final defeat by being thrown into the lake of burning sulfur along with Antichrist and the false prophet.

The Great White Throne: The final judgment of the unsaved from all ages of history. They will be resurrected to stand before Christ in judgment for their works. However, we are not saved by our works, but through faith in Jesus Christ as Savior; consequently, their names are not found in the Lamb's Book of Life, and they are also thrown into the lake of fire.

THE ETERNAL AGE

Eternity begins with a new heaven and a new earth. The throne of God and of the Lamb is in the Holy City, the New Jerusalem. God's dwelling is once again with men.

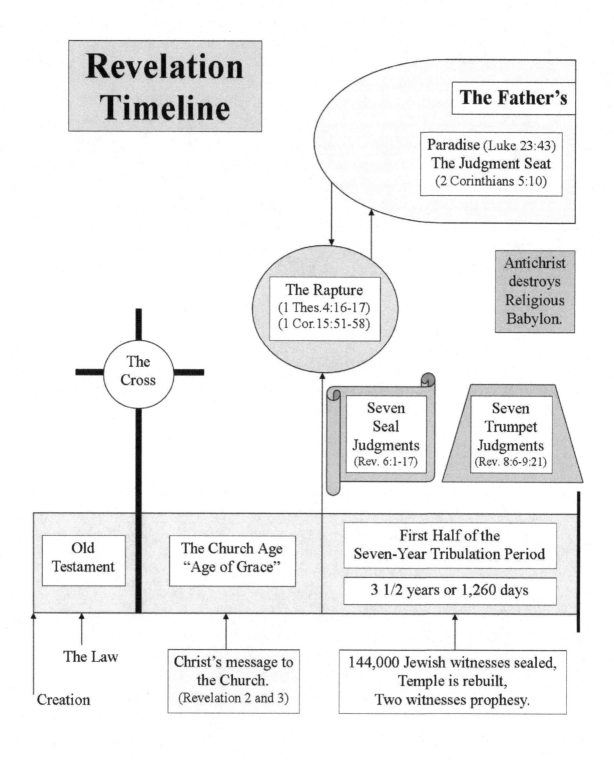

Revelation Timeline

The Father's

Paradise (Luke 23:43)
The Judgment Seat
(2 Corinthians 5:10)

Antichrist
destroys
Religious
Babylon.

The Rapture
(1 Thes.4:16-17)
(1 Cor.15:51-58)

The
Cross

Seven
Seal
Judgments
(Rev. 6:1-17)

Seven
Trumpet
Judgments
(Rev. 8:6-9:21)

Old
Testament

The Church Age
"Age of Grace"

First Half of the
Seven-Year Tribulation Period

3 1/2 years or 1,260 days

The Law

Creation

Christ's message to
the Church.
(Revelation 2 and 3)

144,000 Jewish witnesses sealed,
Temple is rebuilt,
Two witnesses prophesy.

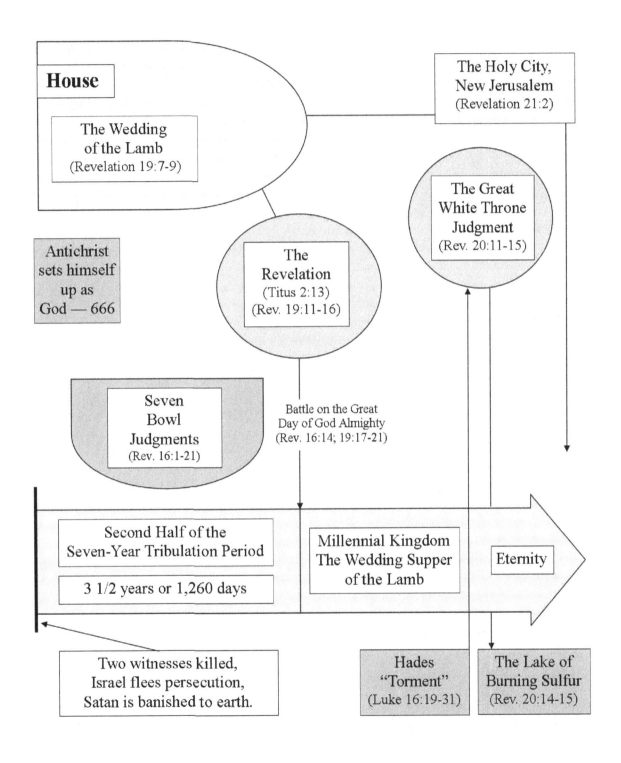

House

The Wedding
of the Lamb
(Revelation 19:7-9)

The Holy City,
New Jerusalem
(Revelation 21:2)

The Great
White Throne
Judgment
(Rev. 20:11-15)

Antichrist
sets himself
up as
God — 666

The
Revelation
(Titus 2:13)
(Rev. 19:11-16)

Seven
Bowl
Judgments
(Rev. 16:1-21)

Battle on the Great
Day of God Almighty
(Rev. 16:14; 19:17-21)

Second Half of the
Seven-Year Tribulation Period

3 1/2 years or 1,260 days

Millennial Kingdom
The Wedding Supper
of the Lamb

Eternity

Two witnesses killed,
Israel flees persecution,
Satan is banished to earth.

Hades
"Torment"
(Luke 16:19-31)

The Lake of
Burning Sulfur
(Rev. 20:14-15)

Answers to Chapter Review Questions

Chapter 1

1) Appearing; to uncover or unveil.
2) Perfection or completeness.
3) The person of Jesus Christ and His return in power and great glory as Judge of all the earth.
4) The seven churches.
5) The spiritual leaders or pastors of those seven churches.
6) He fell at His feet as though dead.
7) I am the First and the Last, I am the Living One, I am alive for ever and ever, and I hold the keys of death and Hades.

Chapters 2 and 3

1) The Church is the body of all believers who have put their faith and trust in Jesus Christ as their Lord and Savior. The church is the body of Christ and Jesus is its head.
2) To worship God, to pray, and to edify fellow believers.
3) To evangelize the world.
4) The Lord Jesus Christ.
5) The churches at Smyrna and Philadelphia.
6) The church at Laodicea.
7) Put their faith, trust, and hope in Jesus Christ.

Chapter 4

1) The Church in heaven with Christ.
2) The Tribulation Period.
3) The rapture before the Tribulation Period and the revelation at the end of the Tribulation Period.
4) Our High Priest, Jesus Christ.
5) The Church in heaven.
6) Seraphim (angels).
7) The Lord Jesus Christ on His throne.

Chapter 5

1) The Lord Jesus Christ.
2) Book of Judgement.
3) A power or authority.
4) Knowledge and wisdom.
5) The music and praise in heaven.
6) The prayers of the saints.
7) They are power, wealth, wisdom, strength, honor, glory, and blessing.

Chapter 6

1) The 7-year covenant confirmed between Israel and Antichrist.
2) The end-times Antichrist and his kingdom.
3) War.
4) Famine.
5) One-fourth of the world's population dies.
6) The righteousness of Christ through faith.
7) The wrath of the Lamb.

Chapter 7

1) Tribulation saints.
2) God's judgment or wrath.
3) Their worship of idols.
4) Protect them from the judgments to come upon the earth.
5) The Holy Spirit.
6) People from all over the world who receive Christ as a result of the ministry of the 144,000 servants – Tribulation saints.
7) The blood of the Lamb.

Chapter 8

1) The Lord Jesus Christ.
2) The prayers of the saints under the altar in heaven.
3) The answer to those prayers in the form of the next set of judgments – the trumpets.
4) It burns up one-third of all the earth's vegetation.
5) It turns one-third of the sea to blood, kills one-third of the living creatures in the sea, and destroys one-third of the ships.
6) The contamination of one-third of the earth's fresh water supply.
7) It diminished the light from the sun, the moon, and the stars by one-third.

Chapter 9

1) A good angel from heaven entrusted with the keys.
2) Hell or Hades; the present abode of all wicked/unsaved spirits.
3) Torment people for five months.

4) Abaddon, or in the Greek, Apollyon.
5) They are evil or fallen angels.
6) Babylon.
7) They killed one-third of mankind.

Chapter 10

1) The Angel of the Lord.
2) The Son of God in all His deity.
3) Service.
4) The voice of God.
5) The salvation of all mankind, Jew and Gentile, through Jesus Christ.
6) Mentally feeding on the Word of God and receiving it with faith.
7) It is sweet to those who hear and accept it, but it is bitter to those who reject it.

Chapter 11

1) The covenant confirmed with Antichrist.
2) The Court of the Gentiles.
3) An individual who brings God's light (truth) to the world.
4) The work of the Holy Spirit through that individual.
5) Prophesying, witnessing, and testifying to the gospel of Jesus Christ.
6) Resurrected and raptured up to heaven in a cloud.
7) Introduces the next set of judgments.

Chapter 12

1) The nation of Israel.
2) The twelve tribes of Israel.
3) The devil – Satan.
4) Christ's rule during the Millennium.
5) To escape persecution from Antichrist.
6) Satan's expulsion from heaven and his confinement to earth during the second half of the Tribulation Period.
7) God will deliver her to safety.

Chapter 13

1) The end-times Antichrist and his kingdom.
2) The nations of the earth.
3) First, one blasphemes by thinking of themselves as equal to God, and secondly, by slandering and taking God's name in vain.
4) Antichrist is one who is against Christ, and Antichrist is one who imitates Christ.
5) Satan enters the dead body of Antichrist resulting in Antichrist becoming the incarnation of Satan.
6) The first beast – Antichrist.
7) Worship Antichrist by demanding everyone to take this mark in order to buy or sell.

Chapter 14

1) The seal of the living God.
2) The eternal gospel of Jesus Christ to all the inhabitants of the earth, and to fear God and give Him glory.
3) Religious Babylon.
4) Worships the beast and receives his mark.
5) The Lord Jesus Christ.
6) Elect or believers – Tribulation saints.
7) Wicked or unbelievers – those who have rejected Christ and followed Antichrist.

Chapter 15

1) A symbol of revelation.
2) The Word of God.
3) The persecution endured by the saints during the Tribulation Period.
4) God's deliverance, salvation, and faithfulness.
5) Jesus Christ as our Redeemer.
6) God is dealing with the nation of Israel.
7) Complete.

Chapter 16

1) Worshiped the beast and took his mark.
2) The death of all living creatures in the sea.
3) Antichrist had shed the blood of His saints and prophets.
4) The sun scorched people with fire.
5) Antichrist and his kingdom.
6) Euphrates River; the Lord Jesus Christ.
7) A severe earthquake that collapses all the cities around the world, and huge hundred- pound hailstones fell upon men.

Chapter 17

1) Idolatry and immorality.
2) The rapture of the true church.
3) Have never trusted Jesus Christ as Savior.
4) Control the masses as he gains power.
5) At the mid-point of the Tribulation Period.
6) Antichrist and the ten kings, as God purposed.
7) To establish Antichrist as the sole object of worship.

Chapter 18

1) On the rebuilt site of ancient Babylon.
2) To flee before judgment falls.
3) Her pride and arrogance.

4) Revenue and corrupt profits gained through commerce.
5) One day.
6) The seventh bowl judgment.
7) The Great Tribulation.

Chapter 19

1) God's judgments upon the earth.
2) The final and complete union of Jesus Christ and the Church.
3) The wedding takes place in heaven and just after the judgment seat of Christ when all believers have been cleansed and their sanctification is consummated.
4) The wedding supper takes place on earth in Christ's kingdom during His millennial reign.
5) The glorious appearing and second coming of our Lord and Savior Jesus Christ to earth.
6) His Spoken Word.
7) Thrown into the lake of burning sulfur – the eternal hell.

Chapter 20

1) For Satan to be taken out of the world.
2) A final testing of mankind under ideal conditions.
3) Believers throughout all generations.
4) He proceeds to deceive the nations.
5) Being thrown into the lake of burning sulfur.
6) Unbelievers from all ages of history.
7) Put their faith and trust in Jesus Christ as Lord and Savior.

Chapter 21

1) To completely cleanse them of the pollution caused by Satan and his final rebellion against God.
2) The Church – the bride of Christ.
3) The Lord Jesus Christ.
4) Center of God's universe.
5) The names of the twelve tribes of Israel.
6) The names of the twelve apostles.
7) Wedding ring

Chapter 22

1) The throne of God and of the Lamb.
2) The tree of life.
3) The Holy City, the New Jerusalem.
4) No longer will there be any curse or night.
5) The short period of only seven years after the events of the Revelation begins.
6) Worship God only.
7) The eternal gospel of Jesus Christ.

Bibliography
(Recommended for further study)

Barry, Mark. *Map of Ancient Israel and Judah*. Australia: Australian Fellowship of Evangelical Students. 2009. Used by permission.

Cahn, Jonathan. *The Harbinger II*. Lake Mary, Florida: Frontline/Charisma/Charisma House Book Group, 2020.

Clower, Ronald A. *Captivity to Eternity, DANIEL, God's Faithful Servant*. Bloomington, Indiana: WestBow Press. A Division of Thomas Nelson & Zondervan, 2015.

Clower, Ronald A. The Apostles, Their Post-Resurrection Lives and Ministries. Peachtree City, CenterpieceMinistries.com, 2020.

Clower, Ronald A. *The Millennium*. Peachtree City, Georgia: CenterpieceMinistries.com, 2020.

Hagee, John. *In Defense of Israel*. Lake Mary, Florida: Charisma Media/Charisma House Book Group, 2007.

https://www.atlasobscura.com/articles/babylon-iraq-saddam-hussein

https://en.wikipedia.org/wiki/Constantine_the_Great_and_Christianity

https://en.wikipedia.org/wiki/Jerusalem

Jeffrey, Grant R. *Heaven, The Mystery of Angels*. Canada: Harmony Printing Limited, 1996.

LaHaye, Tim. *Revelation Unveiled*. Grand Rapids: Zondervan Publishing House, 1999.

LaHaye, Tim, and Jerry B. Jenkins. *Are We Living in the End Times?* Wheaton, Illinois: Tyndale House Publishers, Inc. 1999.

LaHaye, Tim, and Jerry B. Jenkins. *Kingdom Come*. Carol Stream, Illinois: Tyndale House Publishers, Inc. 2007.

LaHaye, Tim. *Prophecy Study Bible*. United States of America: AMG Publishers, 2000.

Lindsey, Hal. *Planet Earth, The Final Chapter*. Beverly Hills: Western Front Ltd, 1998.

Lucado, Max. *When Christ Comes*. Nashville: Word Publishing, 1999.

McBirnie, Ph.D., William Steuart. *The Search for the Twelve Apostles*. Wheaton: Living Books, Tyndale House Publishers, Inc. 1973.

McFarland, Dan. *Bible Reading Calendar*. Sharpsburg, Georgia: 2004.

McGee, J. Vernon. *Thru The Bible*. Nashville: Thomas Nelson Publishers, 1983.

Moore, Beth. *The Beloved Disciple*. Nashville: Broadman and Holman Publishers, 2003.

Pfeiffer, Charles F., Vos, Howard F., Rea, John, Editors. *Wycliffe Bible Dictionary*.

Peabody, Mass.: Hendrickson Publishers, Inc., 2000.

Radmacher, Earl (General Editor); Allen, Ron (Old Testament Editor); House, H. Wayne (New Testament Editor). *Nelson's Bible Commentary*. Nashville: Thomas Nelson Publisher, 2004.

Stanley, Dr. Charles F. *The Revelation*. Atlanta, Georgia: In Touch Ministries, 1994.

Strauss, Lehman. *The Book of Revelation*. Neptune, N.J.: Loizeaux Brothers, 1964.

Strong, James, LL.D., S.T.D. *Strong's Expanded Exhaustive Concordance of the Bible*. Nashville, Tennessee: Thomas Nelson Publishers, 2001.

Swindoll, Charles R. et all. *The Road to Armageddon*. Nashville: Word Publishing, 1999.

The Lost Books of the Bible. The Gospel of Nicodemus. Translated from the original tongues.

New York: Gramercy Books, 1979.

Van Impe, Jack. *Revelation Revealed*. Dallas: Word Publishing, 1996.